ASSESSING THE TEACHING OF WRITING

ASSESSING THE TEACHING OF WRITING

Twenty-First Century Trends and Technologies

Edited by
AMY E. DAYTON

UTAH STATE UNIVERSITY PRESS
Logan

© 2015 by the University Press of Colorado

Published by Utah State University Press
An imprint of University Press of Colorado
5589 Arapahoe Avenue, Suite 206C
Boulder, Colorado 80303

 The University Press of Colorado is a proud member of
The Association of American University Presses.

The University Press of Colorado is a cooperative publishing enterprise supported, in part, by Adams State University, Colorado State University, Fort Lewis College, Metropolitan State University of Denver, Regis University, University of Colorado, University of Northern Colorado, Utah State University, and Western State Colorado University.

The paper used in this publication meets the minimum requirements of the American National Standard for Information Sciences—Permanence of Paper for Printed Library Materials. ANSI Z39.48–1992

ISBN: 978-0-87421-954-8 (paperback)
ISBN: 978-0-87421-966-1 (ebook)

Library of Congress Cataloging-in-Publication Data
Assessing the teaching of writing : twenty-first century trends and technologies / edited by Amy E. Dayton.
    pages cm
  ISBN 978-0-87421-954-8 (pbk.) — ISBN 978-0-87421-966-1 (ebook)
1. English language—Rhetoric—Study and teaching—United States—Evaluation. 2. Report writing—Study and teaching—Evaluation. 3. English Teachers—Rating of—United States. 4. College teachers—Rating of—United States. I. Dayton, Amy E.
  PE1405.U6A77 2015
  808'.042071173—dc23
                          2014011494

Cover illustration © VLADGRIN/Shutterstock.

CONTENTS

FOREWORD

Edward M. White

There is always a well-known solution to every human problem—neat, plausible, and wrong.
     —H. L. Mencken, *Prejudices: Second Series* (1920, 158)

This important book comes twenty years after the first book on its subject, Christine Hult's (1994) edited collection, *Evaluating Teachers of Writing.* During this period, evaluating the performance of teachers has been a hot button topic for educational reformers of every stripe and background—with the notable absence of writing teachers. The well-known problem, though not a consistently or convincingly documented one, is that American students at all levels are not learning what they should be learning; the well-known solution, to follow Mencken's aphorism at the head of this page, is to evaluate teachers in simple-minded ways, place the blame on them and their unions, and replace bad teachers (particularly tenured teachers) with good ones (without tenure). Just where these better teachers are to come from, eager to take notably low-paying jobs without the protections of unions or tenure, has never been made clear. While most of the reformers' attention has been on public schools, which they would like to replace with charter or religious schools, university teaching has suffered from the same concerted attack. Writing teachers at universities have been on the front lines of this struggle for several reasons: most writing teachers in American universities are teaching assistants, relatively inexperienced and powerless graduate students, and the very nature of writing instruction is not suited to pleasing all students, who, in turn, are not likely to rate the teacher highly who asks them to revise work they feel is plenty good enough in their first draft.

Working within these unpromising conditions, university writing researchers tend to focus on the ways all teachers can improve student performance by giving better assignments, responding to the work of student writers in more productive ways, and developing theory-based writing curricula; researchers have also sought ways of developing college writing programs that can foster the development of both students and teachers. Sometimes, the demands for teacher assessment are met from a defensive crouch, as a distraction from the more profound problems of teaching students from a wide variety of backgrounds and levels of preparation for college study. At the large, public universities and two-year colleges where most American students begin advanced study, the economic problems of many students are a primary concern, since they have been a strong negative influence from early childhood. It is no accident that scores on the SAT correlate more with parental income than with any academic measure. When some of the best teachers are working to help poorly prepared students succeed, it is patently absurd to judge the effectiveness of their teaching by the success of their students, particularly in comparison to those students from privileged homes.

Nonetheless, the demand for assessment of writing teachers is not wholly based on political agendas or a profound distrust of public schools. Enough research has shown that truly expert teaching can help students succeed where less expert teaching fails. Some teachers are clearly better at the job than others, and it is reasonable to inquire into ways of identifying and rewarding these outstanding professionals and then place them in positions to influence the teaching of others. It is also clear that if professionals do not undertake this task, it will be—as it has been—undertaken by those who do not understand the enormous complexity of teaching itself and the even greater complexity of teaching writing. The essays in this collection demonstrate constructive ways of assessing teacher performance, with attention to the immense number of variables involved. We need state-of-the-art research in this area— so much has changed since the Hult collection was published, in the nation as well as in the field of rhetoric and composition.

The wide range of essays in this collection demonstrates how much has improved in teacher evaluation over the last two decades. The writers and editor draw from various disciplines, as composition studies itself has done; they are sophisticated in their understanding and use of data; and they are wise to the complexity of their subject. Every reader of this substantial book will experience the goal of the collection: to foster new ways of thinking about teacher evaluation.

EDWARD M. WHITE
August 2014

References

Hult, Christine, ed. 1994. *Evaluating Teachers of Writing*. Urbana, IL: NCTE.

Mecken, H. L. 1920. *Prejudices: Second Series*. New York: A. A. Knopf.

ACKNOWLEDGMENTS

The idea for this book evolved out of a series of conversations with my friend and colleague Karen Gardiner—specifically, our shared concern about the tendency of both teachers and administrators to focus exclusively on student ratings, and particularly on the negative ones, in assessing teaching effectiveness. I am grateful to Karen for her many contributions to the book, especially in developing the initial concept and reviewing and responding to proposals and chapters. This project would not have taken shape without her.

I am also grateful to the anonymous reviewers, who read earlier drafts of the book and offered thoughtful suggestions on how to put the chapters in conversation with one another. Their astute comments pushed both me and my contributors to keep our readers in mind as we revised the work. This collection has also benefitted from the advice of several friends and colleagues who offered practical advice throughout the process—particularly Amy Kimme Hea, Gwen Gray Schwartz, and Nancy Sommers. Michael Spooner at Utah State University was an invaluable resource in shaping the concept and scope of the book and helping to prepare it for publication. Alex Cook, Jerry Nelms, Nathalie Singh-Corcoran, and Ed White provided insightful readings of chapters 1 and 3. Allen Harrell assisted with research, and Nathanael Booth and Andy Currie helped assemble the manuscript. Rebecca Cape served as copyeditor extraordinaire. And the University of Alabama provided me with a one-semester sabbatical, during which I made final revisions to the manuscript.

On a personal note, I am grateful to my family—especially my parents, Margaret and William Dayton—and to my dear friends in Tuscaloosa, Alabama, who helped me create a supportive village in which to raise a child while doing the work I love.

ASSESSING THE TEACHING OF WRITING

SECTION I

Frameworks and Methods for Assessing Teaching

1

ASSESSING TEACHING
A Changing Landscape

Amy E. Dayton

Assessing the teaching of writing is a process fraught with conflict. Despite a significant body of research pointing to the importance of multiple assessment measures and careful interpretation of the data, the evaluation of postsecondary teaching still relies heavily on a single measure of performance—the student ratings score—and interpretation of this score is often done in a hasty, haphazard fashion. Aside from student ratings, other data on teaching effectiveness tend to be collected in piecemeal fashion, without sufficient space for reflection and dialogue. When it comes to assessment, practical realities—including a lack of time, administrative resources, or knowledge about best practices—frequently trump our intentions to do a comprehensive job of evaluating classroom performance. Without clear guidelines for collecting and interpreting data, the outcome can be influenced by individual biases about what counts as evidence of good teaching. This collection offers new perspectives on that question of "what counts," pointing to ways that we can more effectively gather data about teaching and offering practical guidance for interpreting it. It also suggests ways we can improve our practice, mentor new teachers, foster dialogue about best practices, and make those practices more visible.

This book is for teachers who want to improve their practice, administrators and program directors who hire and train instructors, and faculty and staff in writing programs, centers for teaching and learning, and other instructional support units on college campuses. Although its primary audience is composition specialists, the collection offers practical suggestions and perspectives that apply to many contexts for postsecondary teaching. The tools presented in these chapters—mid-semester focus groups, student evaluations of instruction, classroom observations,

DOI: 10.7330/9780874219661.c001

teaching portfolios, and so on—are used across the disciplines, in many instructional settings. While some chapters focus on specific methods, others provide new frameworks for thinking about assessment. In her chapter on writing center(ed) assessment, for instance, Nichole Bennett describes a philosophy that could work for both writing programs and other sites for teacher training across campuses. This approach involves bringing teachers and tutors into the broader conversation about the program's missions and goals, and asking them to reflect on assessment data. By making assessment a broad, program-wide conversation, we invite stakeholders at every level to participate in setting goals and outcomes and gauging how well those outcomes have been met. The authors of chapters 6 and 7 argue for an ethos of transparency, suggesting a need to set clear standards for how materials might be read, to give teachers a sense of agency in deciding how to represent their work, and to share evidence of teaching quality with broader audiences while contextualizing the data for outside readers. These more inclusive, transparent models allow us to engage both internal and external audiences in more productive dialogue.

This collection arrives at a time when the public dialogue and political context for postsecondary teaching are particularly fraught. Challenges include a decline in state funding, public anxiety over the rising cost of college, concern about the value of a degree in today's lagging economy, and, to some extent, hostility toward college professors. An example of this hostility is found in Richard Arum and Josipa Roksa's recent book, *Academically Adrift*, which criticizes faculty for being more interested in their research and the advancement of their disciplines than in their students' progress or the well-being of their institutions—a trend that, in the authors' view, has contributed to an epidemic of "limited learning" on college campuses[1] (Arum and Roksa 2011, 10–11). (See Richard Haswell [2012] for a critique of their findings and methodology). At the state level, this picture of the self-interested, disengaged faculty member permeates our political rhetoric. The *Chronicle of Higher Education* reports that recent state election cycles have been dominated by efforts to curb faculty rights, including measures to limit salaries and collective bargaining rights, attacks on tenure and sabbaticals, and proposals to require college faculty to teach a minimum number of credit hours (Kelderman 2011). In a 2010 *Wall Street Journal* piece, "Putting a Price on Professors," Simon and Banchero (2010) point to some other developments. Texas state law now requires that public universities publicize departmental budgets, instructors' curriculum vitae, student ratings, and course syllabi, making all of this data accessible "within three clicks" of the university's home page. At Texas A&M, university officials have gone even further, putting a controversial system in place to offer cash bonuses to faculty who earn the highest student ratings, and creating a public "profit and loss" statement on each faculty member that "[weighs] their annual salary against students taught, tuition generated, and research grants obtained" (Simon and Banchero 2010; see also Hamermesh 2010, Huckabee 2009, June 2010, and Mangan 2000).

This push to make college faculty more accountable—and to quantify their contributions—comes, ironically, at a time when tenured, sabbatical-eligible faculty members are dwindling in numbers, being replaced by part-time and non-tenure track teachers whose situations are often tenuous at best. A *New York Times* article reports that "only a quarter of the academic work force is tenured, or on track for tenure, down from more than a third in 1995" (Lewin 2013). The challenge facing many university writing programs, then, is not the task of fostering commitment to teaching among research-obsessed, tenured faculty members, but rather supporting teachers who are new to the profession—like graduate teaching assistants—or who are working without job security, a full-time income, or adequate professional resources (such as office space or support for professional development). Because first-year composition (FYC) is one of the few courses required for most students at public universities, and because personalized, process-based instruction requires low student-to-faculty ratios, university writing programs find themselves at the front lines of these labor issues in higher education.

Despite the challenging times, composition studies, as a field, has capitalized on the accountability movement and current zeal for assessment by taking a proactive stance, seeking meaningful ways to gather data about teaching and participate in large-scale evaluations of student learning. In the aftermath of the No Child Left Behind Act, the Spellings Commission on Higher Education, and initiatives such as the ones put in place in Texas, we recognize that developing thoughtful, context-sensitive assessments is the best insurance against having hasty, reductionist evaluations imposed upon our programs.[2] Many writing programs have either fully adopted the WPA Outcomes Statement on First-Year Composition (Council of Writing Program Administrators 2000), or have modified the statement to create local outcomes. Other programs are participating in large-scale, national assessments and making use of the data for local purposes. As Paine and his colleagues explain in chapter 11, the Council of Writing Program Administrators has teamed up with the consortium for the National Survey of Student

Engagement (NSSE) to create a writing component within that national assessment. In chapter 12, Deborah Goodburn and Amy Minter point to the ways that the trend toward "big data" can provide methods for analyzing trends and understanding patterns on our campuses and in our programs (they also acknowledge the need to use data mining in a responsible manner). These large-scale assessment projects have raised the visibility of our professional associations. More importantly, they have helped ensure that efforts to standardize outcomes or measure students' experiences with writing are informed by a solid understanding of composing processes and best practices for teaching.

While the national context for higher education has changed in recent years, the assessment landscape is also shifting. One way to gauge some of those changes is by considering the essays in this volume in relation to Christine Hult's 1994 text, *Evaluating Teachers of Writing*. On one hand, many of the central concerns of Hult's volume—the impact of the teaching-as-scholarship movement, the need to develop equitable practices to assess adjunct and graduate student teachers, and the overreliance on student surveys—are still important issues. On the other hand, the methods we use to assess teaching have evolved in ways that make them quite different from their predecessors. Take, for example, the practice of gathering mid-semester feedback from students. While Peter Elbow (1994), in the Hult volume, presents this method as an informal exchange between the students and the teacher, in chapter 5 of this volume Gerald Nelms explains how the small-group instructional diagnosis (SGID) method has formalized and systematized this practice, yielding more data and more reliable results. My point here is not that formal methods should always be privileged over informal, organic ones, but that with a range of methods at our disposal teachers have more choices about the kinds of feedback they would like to obtain.

Similarly, emerging technologies create new options for sharing our results. Electronic portfolios, teachers' homepages, professor rating websites, and other digital spaces now function not just to display data but also to foster conversation about their meaning. The dialogic nature of Web 2.0 technologies can make our assessments more open and transparent—but they also bring challenges for teachers who may not want to be visible in the way that technology allows (or compels) us to be. In chapters 7 and 10, Chris Anson and Amy Kimme Hea present contrasting perspectives on the tension between teachers' visibility and vulnerability online. While Anson urges writing programs and teachers to consider making assessment data more visible (by posting student opinion surveys online, for instance), Kimme Hea suggests ways that teachers can monitor and manage their online presence, noting that today's teachers are being "written by the web" in ways we could not have predicted before the arrival of Web 2.0.

KEY TERMS

For readers who are new to the assessment landscape, the following section gives a brief overview of the key concepts that appear throughout this book. This section will also complicate these common terms, and will show how we might blur the boundaries between them in order to consider anew the potential, and the peril, of the approaches we choose.

Assessment

The term *assessment*, with its origins in the Latin phrase "to sit beside," suggests the possibilities inherent in formative, cooperative methods for training and mentoring writing instructors. Traditionally, composition scholarship, rooted in a humanist, progressive tradition that values the potential of the individual, has privileged that cooperative work of "sitting beside" our developing teachers over the sometimes necessary, but less pleasant, task of ranking, sorting, and judging them.

In recent years, writing assessment research has reached a kind of crossroads, with opposing visions of the work that we ought to be doing. On one hand, most scholars are deeply invested in empirical methods, drawing from the methodologies of our colleagues in educational measurement (Huot 2007; O'Neill, Moore, and Huot 2009; Wolcott and Legg 1998). These traditional approaches provide us with the means for gauging validity and reliability, as well as reading statistical results. On the other hand, an emerging body of work calls on composition scholars to take a more critical stance, and to interrogate the ideologies implicit in standardized assessments. Patricia Lynne (2004), for instance, rejects psychometric approaches entirely, advocating a rhetorically-based approach that eschews positivist assumptions, while Inoue and Poe (2012) urge us to consider "how unequal or unfair outcomes may be structured into our assessment technologies and the interpretations that we make from their outcomes" (6). That concern about the positivist assumptions and ideologies embedded in assessment work is not unique to scholars in the humanities, but is also the focus of an evolving conversation among scholars in the social sciences, including the field of educational measurement. In her influential essay, "Can There Be Validity without Reliability?" Pamela Moss (1994) argues that we cannot make reliability judgments solely from statistical analyses of numerical data. Rather, they require an interpretive or "hermeneutic" approach involving "holistic, integrative" thinking "that [seeks] to understand the whole in light of its parts, that [privileges] readers who are most knowledgeable about the context in which the assessment occurs, and that [grounds] those interpretations not only in the . . . evidence available, but also in a rational debate among the community of interpreters" (7). In other words, assessment is, at least in part, a rhetorical practice, regardless of the disciplinary home of the person conducting the evaluation. When we assess, therefore, we must ask: Who are the stakeholders? Whom and what are we assessing? For what purposes? Who will be the ultimate audience? (Huot 2002; O'Neill, Moore, and Huot 2009). For this reason, most of the essays in this volume strike a balance between empirical and interpretive modes, without privileging one approach over the other.

Formative vs. Summative Assessment

Assessment scholars traditionally distinguish between formative and summative evaluation. Formative evaluation is "ongoing," designed to encourage improvement, while summative evaluation is "more fixed and 'retroactive,' bearing the connotation of finality in its sense of accountability" (Wolcott and Legg 1998, 4). Formative assessment is a tool to help teachers; it involves an element of self-evaluation that is best used in situations where instructors have the opportunity to reflect on the feedback, set goals for improvement, and implement the results in their classroom. Summative assessment, on the other hand, is done for external audiences, for the purpose of sorting, ranking, and making decisions about teachers—for example, when giving awards or making decisions about staffing, merit raises, contract renewals, and promotions.

In practice, the categories of formative and summative assessment are not clearly distinct from one another, nor should they be. Chris Anson argues in chapter 7 that summative evaluation should include some evidence of formative, or reflective, thinking about teaching. Moreover, when programs do not have the time and resources to offer both formative and summative evaluation (through multiple course observations, for instance), they tend not to make distinctions between them. It may be more productive, then, to use the term *instructive assessment*, as Brian Huot (2002) suggests. Instructive assessment shifts the focus to the teacher's growth and continuous improvement, even when making summative judgments. This stance reflects the growing consensus in educational circles "[recognizing] the importance of holding all educational practices, including assessment, to rigorous standards that include the enhancement of teaching and learning" (18). This may be especially true for university writing programs. Considering the marginalized status of many of our teachers, it is critical that our assessments facilitate their continued improvement and professional development—and lead to some discussion about the resources our teachers need to be successful and the ways that programs and WPAs can provide better support.

Validity and Reliability

Almost all scholarly discussion of assessment begins with a review of the concepts of validity and reliability. In common parlance, validity—more specifically, *construct validity*—is thought of as the "truth" of an assessment, or the degree to which a test or tool measures what it purports to measure. When we say that a test or tool is "valid," we mean exactly that—it measures what it purports to measure. In assessment language, however, we tend not to make validity judgments about the tools themselves; rather, *validity* refers to the data produced by our instruments. That is, "tests [and other assessments] are not in and of themselves valid or invalid but rather the *results* are considered to be valid or invalid according to their intended use" (O'Neill, Moore and Huot 2009, 47, emphasis original). Determinations about validity include thoughtful interpretation of the data and careful construction of "a sound argument to support the interpretation and use of test scores from both theoretical and scholarly evidence" (O'Neill, Moore, and Huot 2009, 47). That evidence may include: the context of the evaluation, the process of administering it, the influence of external variables, and the consequences of the assessment (46–47). Thus, the emerging view of validity is that it is not "some pronouncement of approval but rather . . . an ongoing process of critical reflection" (Huot 2002, 51).[3] Another trend in our view of validity is the realization that we must attend to the ethical dimensions of the tools we have chosen, and that those aspects factor into our validity judgments. In chapter 3, I discuss the move toward *consequential validity*, the notion that our validity judgments must consider the results, whether intentional or unintentional, of how data (such as student opinion survey results) are interpreted.

In contrast, reliability refers to the *consistency* of results achieved over time from repeated use of the same instrument. For standardized assessment, reliability is generally thought of as a quantitative determination: for example, on large-scale writing tests, reliability is determined by the scores assigned by trained readers. Yet, as Moss (1994) notes, for smaller-scale or non-standardized assessments (such as classroom observations or teaching portfolios), reliability is more difficult to establish through quantitative means—when it comes to qualitative evidence about teaching, reliability may be determined by an informed community using a process of thoughtful deliberation of shared norms (7).[4] For small-scale assessments (with the exception of student ratings), reliability can be seen as a set of values that includes "accuracy, dependability, stability, and consistency" (O'Neill, Moore, and Huot 2009, 52).

OVERVIEW OF THE BOOK

The book is divided into two sections. Each chapter in the first section focuses on a different method or tool for evaluation: heuristics for evaluating teaching, student evaluations, classroom observations, mid-semester focus group feedback, and teacher portfolios. In chapter 2, Meredith DeCosta and Duane Roen draw from Ernest Boyer's teaching-as-scholarship model to suggest a framework that attempts to capture the complexity and intellectual rigor that good teaching requires. Their chapter offers a set of heuristics that functions as both a theoretical guide and a generative tool for helping us to evaluate teaching and identify areas where more development may be needed. The other chapters in section I complicate and refine our understanding of well-established assessment methods, such as teaching portfolios, course observations, and student evaluations of instruction. Brian Jackson, for instance, suggests in chapter 4 that the course observation offers an opportunity for WPAs to practice macro-level teaching and see how programmatic goals and outcomes are understood at the classroom level. And chapters 5 and 6 suggest that by formalizing other methods, or implementing them via new technologies, we can transform them into tools that offer more data, or more opportunities for sharing data with various audiences.

The chapters in section II look beyond specific methods to unique contexts and emerging trends. As in the previous section, technology is an important component: emerging technologies (like e-portfolios) create new potential for assessment, but they also raise new challenges (chapters 7 and 10). Chapters 8 and 12 suggest ways that WPAs and other administrators can build a "shared language" for assessment among teachers, students, tutors, administrators, and other stakeholders, as well as make use of both "big" and "small" data. They offer guidance for teachers and programs on managing their online presence, both by monitoring feedback on external sites and, where appropriate, by taking charge of their own data and making it accessible to the public (chapters 7 and 10). Sharing our results, Chris Anson suggests in chapter 7, allows writing teachers and programs to provide a rhetorical context in order to help the audience understand what student ratings or syllabi/course materials mean and how they are used. This section also offers pragmatic guidance. Cindy Moore, for instance, notes in chapter 9 that one of the biggest obstacles to good assessment is a lack of time and resources, and she offers suggestions for overcoming these challenges. Chapters 11 and 12 explore the trend toward large-scale assessment, suggesting ways that writing programs can use big data to better understand the dynamics of local programs.

ASSESSMENT AS RHETORICAL PRACTICE

Individually, the essays in this book address particular methods and models for assessment. Collectively, they present an argument for new ways of thinking about evaluating teaching. They respond to the public call to make teaching data more transparent and available for public discussion, and they suggest ways of contextualizing our assessments and using them to arrive at more nuanced understandings of what good teaching is. In making the case for new modes and models, they mimic the process of evaluation itself. When assessing their work, teachers and programs create narratives that illustrate what they have set out to do and show how they are working toward those goals and achieving results. Evaluating teaching, then, involves looking at a collection of evidence and analyzing and interpreting the argument it presents. When viewed in this light, the task of analyzing evidence, evaluating pedagogical approaches in their particular rhetorical context, and fostering a dialogue about best practices should present an appealing challenge for a group of scholars and teachers who are steeped in the scholarly tradition of critical interpretation, analysis, and thoughtful debate.

Notes

1. The actual findings of their study were far more modest than the broad claim the book suggests: their study found that college students made "modest gains" from the first semester of their freshman year to the second semester of their sophomore year.
2. See Brian Huot's (2007) "Consistently Inconsistent: Business and the Spellings Commission Report on Higher Education."
3. For a more thorough discussion of emerging views of validity and its types, see Messick (1989).

4.   Moss (1994) notes that the danger of previous conceptions of validity and reliability—which insist upon quantification—is that they might lead us not to engage in good teaching and assessment practices merely because they are small scale, qualitative, and/or nonmeasurable (6).

References

Arum, Richard, and Josipa Roksa. 2011. *Academically Adrift: Limited Learning on College Campuses.* Chicago: University of Chicago Press.

Council of Writing Program Administrators. 2000. "WPA Outcomes Statement for First Year Composition." http://wpacouncil.org/positions/outcomes.html.

Elbow, Peter. 1994. "Making Better Use of Student Evaluations of Teachers." In *Evaluating Teachers of Writing,* ed. Christine Hult. Urbana, IL: NCTE.

Hamermesh, Daniel. 2010. "What's Your Econ 101 Professor Worth?" *The New York Times,* October 26.

Haswell, Richard. 2012. "Methodologically Adrift: Review of Arum and Roksa, *Academically Adrift.*" *College Composition and Communication* 63 (3): 487–91.

Huckabee, Charles. 2009. "Professors Question Texas A&M's Plan to Award Bonuses on Basis of Student Evaluations." *The Chronicle of Higher Education,* January 11.

Hult, Christine, ed. 1994. *Evaluating Teachers of Writing.* Urbana, IL: NCTE.

Huot, Brian. 2002. *(Re)Articulating Writing Assessment for Teaching and Learning.* Logan: Utah State University Press.

Huot, Brian. 2007. "Consistently Inconsistent: Business and the Spellings Commission Report on Higher Education." *College English* 69 (5): 512–25.

Inoue, Asao, and Mya Poe. 2012. *Race and Writing Assessment.* New York: Lang.

June, Audrey Williams. 2010. "Texas A&M to Revise Controversial Faculty Rewards Based on Student Evaluations." *The Chronicle of Higher Education,* October 12.

Kelderman, Eric. 2011. "State Lawmakers Seek More Say over Colleges." *The Chronicle of Higher Education,* February 27.

Lewin, Tamar. 2013. "More College Adjuncts See Strength in Union Numbers." *The New York Times,* December 3.

Lynne, Patricia. 2004. *Coming to Terms: A Theory of Writing Assessment.* Logan: Utah State University Press.

Mangan, Katherine. 2000. "Bonus Pay Based on Student Evaluations Evokes Skepticism at Texas A&M." *The Chronicle of Higher Education,* January 20.

Messick, Samuel. 1989. "Validity." In R. L. Linn, *Educational Measurement,* 3rd ed. Old Tappan, NJ: Macmillan.

Minter, Deborah, and Amy Goodburn. 2002. *Composition, Pedagogy, and the Scholarship of Teaching.* Portsmouth, NH: Boynton/Cook.

Moss, Pamela. 1994. "Can There Be Validity without Reliability?" *Educational Researcher* 23 (2): 5–12. http://dx.doi.org/10.3102/0013189X023002005.

O'Neill, Peggy, Cindy Moore, and Brian Huot. 2009. *A Guide to College Writing Assessment.* Logan: Utah State University Press.

Simon, Stephanie, and Stephanie Banchero. 2010. "Putting a Price on Professors." *Wall Street Journal,* October 22.

Wolcott, Willa, and Sue M. Legg. 1998. *An Overview of Writing Assessment: Theory, Research, and Practice.* National Council of Teachers of English.

2
ASSESSING THE TEACHING OF WRITING
A Scholarly Approach

Meredith DeCosta and Duane Roen

In *What the Best College Teachers Do*, Ken Bain (2004) argues that effective teachers "develop their abilities through constant self-evaluation, reflection, and the willingness to change" (172). As they do so, they place student learning front and center. To assess teachers' effectiveness, writing program administrators (WPAs) must draw on appropriate methods for evaluating the teaching of writing, including both formative evaluations (designed to enhance performance) and summative evaluations (designed to judge performance) (Hult 1994). This means that when we assess the teaching of writing, we need to be mindful of the ultimate task: to help teachers develop their abilities in a way that supports student learning. As Jane E. Hindman (2000) observes, "Closing the gap between what our theory contends is important in the classroom and what our assessment practices actually support must involve constructing reliable teacher evaluation methods that validly measure the kind of teaching that our profession values" (16). To guide teacher evaluation, we offer a heuristic that can be used to assess and document effective teaching. We also recommend the use of teaching portfolios to demonstrate the complex, scholarly activity of teaching writing.

Despite our efforts to fairly and effectively evaluate the teaching of writing, in an era of data-driven decision making in the United States, college and university administrators are under additional pressure to measure the effectiveness of teachers and advertise the success of their programs. WPAs, in particular, are faced with many challenges as they respond to calls for accountability within and beyond the program while also recognizing the important day-to-day work of writing teachers. WPAs are tasked with examining teachers' ratings, course completion

DOI: 10.7330/9780874219661.c002

rates, and the efficiency and effectiveness of course load and class size, among other duties. They must also ensure that the work of administrators and writing teachers is seen as a challenging, scholarly activity.

If colleges and universities wish to encourage teachers of writing to engage in scholarly activity, that activity needs to result in tangible rewards, such as salary increases, awards and recognition, tenure and promotion, and/or opportunities to teach highly sought-after courses. Tenure-track and contingent faculty, and even teaching assistants, should earn rewards for activities labeled as "scholarly." As we will explain in detail later, one form of scholarship—scholarly teaching—is based on highly regarded pedagogical and curricular resources in the field. For example, if a teacher uses the "WPA Outcomes Statement for First-Year Composition" developed by the Council of Writing Program Administrators (2000) to inform his or her teaching, that is a scholarly move. Of course, we understand that different kinds of institutions value different configurations of scholarly activity. Some put a premium on the scholarship of discovery through research; some value the full range of scholarship—discovery, application, integration, teaching and learning, and engagement. What is important, though, is that academic units acknowledge the existence of a variety of scholarly activities and discuss the kinds of scholarship they value, explaining how those values can enhance faculty work.

Within the teaching of writing, a broad spectrum of work can advance the "production, clarification, connection, reinterpretation, or application" of knowledge (Council of Writing Program Administrators 1998). These forms of inquiry result in the invention of materials or activities that can be evaluated by others. The Modern Language Association's "Making Faculty Work Visible" recognizes a wide variety of intellectual work and offers examples of "projects and enterprises of knowledge and learning" that might be considered in composition studies, including:

- Developing new questions, problems, information, interpretations, designs, products, and frameworks of understanding, etc., through inquiry;
- Connecting knowledge to other knowledge;
- Applying knowledge to practical problems in significant or innovative ways; and
- Making specialized knowledge broadly accessible and usable. (Modern Language Association 1996, 15–17)

In this chapter, we draw on the insights of Ernest Boyer and those of Charles Glassick, Mary Huber, and Gene Maeroff to offer a framework for re-envisioning the work of writing teachers and WPAs. By treating teaching as a scholarly activity, we are better able to (re)assert the importance of writing programs in both our schools and our communities and position ourselves to be advocates for the work that occurs in writing programs. As Linda Adler-Kassner and Susanmarie Harrington suggest, "we do need to find a way to talk with external stakeholders about how we and they understand learning processes, find common ground among these ideas, and work together to develop shared projects that investigate whether and how students are developing and not—in ways that we consider significant" (Adler-Kassner and Harrington 2010, 91). By using a framework such as the one offered in this chapter to assess writing instruction, we can effectively demonstrate to individuals within and outside our programs that teaching writing is an important scholarly activity.

CATEGORIES OF SCHOLARSHIP

We begin our discussion of teaching-as-scholarship by exploring the kinds of intellectual activity that the teaching of writing involves. The work of Ernest Boyer (1990), in *Scholarship Reconsidered: Priorities of the Professoriate* and "The Scholarship of Engagement," offers a convincing case for revisiting the definition of "scholarship" to include five kinds of work: discovery, application, integration, teaching and learning, and engagement.

Discovery

The scholarship of discovery is roughly equivalent to traditional views of research—producing new knowledge. Boyer (1990) notes that discovery is "the commitment to knowledge for its own sake, to freedom of inquiry and to following, in a disciplined fashion, an investigation wherever it may lead" (17). Discovery, then, involves introducing/identifying new knowledge or revising disciplinary theories and approaches. This form of scholarship most frequently occurs through research. In writing scholarship, discovery can take a number of forms. For example, it can include expanding an existing approach to the teaching of writing or offering a new heuristic to assess writers. Each of the chapters in this book, for example, offers some new insight into assessing the teaching of writing and may well be considered an example of discovery.

Discovery in the field of composition can take place through formal research grants offered by organizations such as CCCC (Conference on College Composition and Communication) and WPA—which fund proposals that advance their missions—as well as through programmatic and teacher research. These latter two do not necessarily need to be used to formally evaluate a program or the effectiveness of a teacher. Rather, they can serve as a means of discovery, helping writing programs develop a stronger sense of students' levels of preparedness for a course, the writing topics that pique students' interest, students' engagement in a course, and their proclivity to transfer writing knowledge or skills between and among their courses. Teachers can draw on these insights to enhance their pedagogical strategies and curricula, and WPAs can use these discoveries to understand the population the program serves and improve success rates in writing courses.

Application

This type of scholarship draws on expertise to define problems and determine how to best address them. Application asks the question, "How can knowledge be responsibly applied to consequential problems?" (Boyer 1990, 21). By responding to this question, we can help equip faculty with a range of tools to effectively assess the teaching of writing. If faculty members express concerns about using technological tools to assess student writers, for instance, we can offer knowledge and expertise through workshops to support them. Of course, we can also assess the effectiveness of such workshops by reading faculty members' teaching portfolios, in which they make their instruction visible.

Integration

The scholarship of integration is concerned with "making connections across the disciplines, placing the specialties in larger context, illuminating data in a revealing way, often educating nonspecialists, too" (Boyer 1990, 18). Knowledge that may seem disconnected comes together with integration. This form of scholarship encourages us to contemplate how assessing the teaching of writing can be interdisciplinary and transdisciplinary. Integration can occur among and across research, teaching, and service. When scholars of writing draw on diverse fields such as education, linguistics, and feminist theory to produce new knowledge, they are engaging in the scholarship of integration. Similarly, when we assess the teaching of writing, we may draw on our own expertise in various disciplines.

Those with diverse preparation and experiences may draw on the insights and understanding from their respective fields and apply that knowledge to assess the teaching of writing. For instance, teachers and

WPAs can use their knowledge of other disciplines to help students learn the citation style needed in their chosen fields of study or to encourage students to write in genres that can be used in their future work. Teachers and WPAs can make connections with other fields of study in the classroom through relevant reading selections, topics, and techniques. WPAs can step outside of their writing programs and speak with instructors and administrators in other disciplines to better understand the genres and purposes of writing in a range of fields. They can then integrate this knowledge into what and how we teach and, ultimately, into assessing the teaching of writing.

Teaching and Learning

According to Boyer, this category makes teaching available to other scholars, and thus makes it the object of other scholars' scrutiny and critique. As noted by Lee Shulman (2000), former president of the Carnegie Foundation for the Advancement of Teaching, the scholarship of teaching and learning goes beyond effective teaching. Effective teaching results in enhanced student learning, as described in the WPA Outcomes Statement, which details expected student outcomes in five areas. The document distills the discipline's current best theoretical and pedagogical practices while also remaining true to the contextual nature of writing. The statement seeks to help make student learning, effective teaching, and the assessment of teaching visible to and measurable by others and by disciplinary standards (Council of Writing Program Administrators 2000).

The scholarship of teaching and learning "is well grounded in the sources and resources appropriate to the field" (Shulman 2000, 49). Thus, scholarly teaching is both theoretically and pedagogically sound, grounded in the ongoing conversations of the discipline. For example, as we drafted this chapter, the field was beginning to consider the teaching implications of "Framework for Success in Postsecondary Writing," a document collaboratively crafted by the Council of Writing Program Administrators (2010), the National Council of Teachers of English, and the National Writing Project.

The scholarship of teaching and learning, then, is "that which occurs when our work as teachers becomes public, peer-reviewed and critiqued, and exchanged with other members of our professional communities so they, in turn, can build on our work. These are the qualities of all scholarship" (Shulman 2000, 49). In this case, we do what various scholars have done for this edited collection—write about how to teach writing and especially how to assess the teaching of writing. Other scholars can review and critique this volume to comment on its strengths and weaknesses, as well as its applicability to a wide range of contexts.

Engagement

Boyer (1996) offers a final category in a later article, "The Scholarship of Engagement," where he argues that scholars and institutions should become involved in communities outside of academia in order to make a difference in the world. Engagement is important because "America's colleges and universities are now suffering from a decline in public confidence and a nagging feeling that they are no longer at the vital center of the nation's work" (Shulman 2000, 18). A reciprocal, collaborative relationship between institutions and their local publics is needed to connect and reconnect universities with the communities they have arguably become isolated from.

When we assess the teaching of writing, we must be aware of the approaches and organizational arrangements that can most effectively encourage writing teachers to engage with the community. In recognition of this need for writing teachers to be engaged in their communities and supported for doing so, the Conference on College Composition and Communication (2009) adopted the "CCCC Position Statement on Faculty Work in Community-Based Settings" because "public engagement will deepen and enrich the writing life on a campus while contributing to the cultural and economic strength of a region." This position statement encourages colleges and universities to develop criteria for assessing and valuing not only the products of such work but also the less tangible outcomes, such as the degree of reciprocity between the school and the community group and the long-term sustainability of the project.

We argue that writing teachers need to be engaged in their communities in many ways, such as by offering writing workshops. This can mean bringing the community into the classroom or seeking opportunities to integrate writing into the community. WPAs, along with their teachers, must engage local communities and map the means through which the program, faculty, staff, and students collaborate with the local community and work to restore public confidence.

CRITERIA FOR EVALUATING SCHOLARLY ACTIVITY

In the 1990s, as faculty and administrators began discussing Boyer's ideas—as well as the ideas of other educators such as Lee Shulman—a common question emerged: "What are the criteria for evaluating the five kinds of scholarship?" Subsequently, Charles Glassick, Mary Huber, and Gene Maeroff addressed that question when they published *Scholarship Assessed: Evaluation of the Professoriate*. After conducting extensive research on the ways that faculty work is evaluated, Glassick, Huber, and Maeroff (1997) concluded that there are six important criteria for evaluating any kind of scholarly activity: (1) clear goals, (2) adequate preparation, (3) appropriate methods, (4) significant results, (5) effective presentation, and (6) reflective critique. It is helpful to examine each criterion more closely and apply each to writing instruction and its assessment:

Clear Goals

Glassick, Huber, and Maeroff (1997) ask three questions in order to determine whether the scholar has established clear goals: "Does the scholar state the basic purposes of his or her work clearly? Does the scholar define objectives that are realistic and achievable? Does the scholar identify important questions in the field?" (25). By recasting those questions, faculty can use them to consider goals: What are the basic purposes of teaching writing? What are realistic and achievable outcomes? What are the most important questions that we can ask about our work?

When we consider the teaching of writing, we can foster conversations about the goals for instruction. As previously noted, the WPA Outcomes Statement describes a number of general areas in which students need to develop repertoires of writerly tools. Although the outcomes statement focuses on learning in FYC courses, it also suggests learning that can occur in more advanced courses and across the curriculum. The document, which is used in many institutions across the United States and around the world, reflects research and practice in the field, and it acknowledges that students need to be prepared to write not only in the academic arena but also in the professional, civic, and personal arenas.

When we evaluate the teaching of writing, clear goals are important for two reasons. First, we need to know that teachers have developed clear teaching goals and that student learning is their priority. When we tailor learning goals to the needs of our programs and the students in them, we can and should consult the widest range of stakeholders—e.g., students, professional organizations, colleagues, community leaders, and potential employers—because they all have a vested interest and can benefit when our students develop appropriate knowledge and skills.

We must also have goals for the assessment of teaching itself—that is, why are we assessing the teaching of writing? Here too we should be primarily concerned with student learning. If students are learning less than we hope, then our assessment should lead to more learning. If students are learning as much or more than we had hoped, then our assessment can reveal that happy news. As Robert Diamond suggests, "Starting with a consideration of how to facilitate effective learning will establish rapport among everyone involved" (1998, 11).

Adequate Preparation

Glassick, Huber, and Maeroff (1997) suggest the following questions to assess the scholar's preparation: "Does the scholar show an understanding of existing scholarship in the field? Does the scholar bring the necessary skills to his or her work? Does the scholar bring together the resources necessary to move the project forward?" (27). Again, we can modify these questions to apply them to writing instruction: What do we know about effective teaching? What knowledge and skills can we develop to teach more effectively? What resources can we use?

To prepare for assessing the teaching of writing, we can benefit from Lee Shulman's (2000) view of scholarly approaches in general—we should be aware of the relevant scholarly resources in the field. For our purposes here, such resources include the large body of published work on teaching and learning in writing classrooms. Although a bibliography is beyond the scope of this chapter, we can point to published work such as that found in CompPile (2004–2012), which includes annotated bibliographies. Rebecca Moore Howard has also compiled numerous bibliographies on teaching and learning writing (2014). Helpful print bibliographies include Reynolds, Herzberg, and Bizzell's (2003) *The Bedford Bibliography for Teachers of Writing*, which is also available online. Similarly, Glau and Duttagupta (2010) have published *The Bedford Bibliography for Teachers of Basic Writing*.

Beyond our field, we can look to guidance from scholars who have spent their careers writing and speaking about assessing teaching and learning. For example, Huba and Freed (1999) provide teachers in any field with tools for learner-centered assessment. A widely used and valuable resource is Angelo and Cross's (1993) *Classroom Assessment Techniques*, which offers fifty strategies for assessing teaching and learning throughout a course. Raoul Arreola (2000) offers a detailed set of approaches and strategies for evaluating faculty in any field.

Appropriate Methods

For this criterion, Glassick, Huber, and Maeroff (1997) ask straight-forward questions: "Does the scholar use methods appropriate to the goals? Does the scholar apply effectively the methods selected? Does the scholar modify procedures in response to changing circumstances?" (28). We adapt these questions to teaching writing: What teaching methods can we use to maximize learning? How can we apply the methods that we have chosen? How can we modify our teaching methods as the needs of students change?

One of the principles of assessing teaching effectively is that there should be multiple measures of teaching. Too often academic units rely on one method—most often a review of students' end-of-semester course evaluations—to determine teaching effectiveness. Although the perspectives of students are important, they must be complemented by teachers' self-evaluations and colleagues' evaluations. Assessment also needs to occur throughout a semester by using strategies such as those offered by Thomas Angelo and Patricia Cross in *Classroom Assessment Techniques.* Angelo and Cross (1993) outline scores of easy-to-use tools for measuring student learning throughout a course. Some of the most commonly used tools include a background knowledge probe, a misconception/preconception check, a one-minute paper, a "muddiest point" response, one-sentence summaries, and concept maps. Of course, some of these activities are also well known writing-to-learn strategies.

Significant Results

Here Glassick, Huber, and Maeroff (1997) pose practical questions that assess the results of the scholar's work: "Does the scholar achieve the goals? Does the scholar's work add consequentially to the field? Does the scholar's work open additional areas for further exploration?" (29). We offer these revisions: How successful are we at teaching writing? How is our teaching of writing adding value to education? How does our teaching encourage students to write more effectively?

The results of teaching are significant only if student learning occurs. Of course, that learning must reflect the goals described earlier. Incidental learning is also desirable, but planned learning is the benchmark. In order to measure our result's significance, we need to determine the extent to which students have developed the repertoires described in the WPA Outcomes Statement.

Effective Presentation

For this criterion, Glassick, Huber, and Maeroff (1997) examine the effectiveness of the scholar's work by asking the following questions: "Does the scholar use a suitable style and effective organization to present his or her work? Does the scholar use appropriate forums for communicating work to its intended audiences? Does the scholar present his or her message with clarity and integrity?" (32). Again we modify these questions: How do our teaching styles and organization affect our students? What forums should we use to communicate with students and others? To what extent is our communicating with students marked by clarity and integrity? If faculty effectively present their teaching methods, they can make the intellectual work of teaching writing more visible to those who evaluate them for annual reviews, tenure, and promotion.

Reflective Critique

For this last criterion, Glassick, Huber, and Maeroff (1997) suggest the following questions: "Does the scholar critically evaluate his or her own work? Does the scholar bring an appropriate breadth of evidence to his or her critique? Does the scholar use evaluation to improve the quality of future work? (34). We again direct such questions to the teaching of writing: How can we critically evaluate our teaching? What evidence do we need to critique our work? How can we use our evaluations of past teaching to enhance the quality of future teaching?

As John Dewey (1933) notes in *How We Think*, teachers who do not reflect on their teaching often follow routines without critically examining the effectiveness of those routines. The routine becomes so ingrained that teachers are sometimes not aware of other, more effective methods. Reflection, says Dewey, "emancipates us from merely impulsive and routine activity . . . enables us to direct our actions with foresight and to plan according to the ends in view of purposes of which we are aware. It enables us to know what we are about when we act" (17).

Similarly, Donald Schön (1987, 1995) notes that reflecting on our teaching practices leads to fresh insights into our activities. Because some of our teaching practices are internalized, it can be challenging to become explicitly aware of them. To raise tacit knowledge to the level of consciousness, Osterman and Kottkamp (1993) argue—as do we—that working with peers can be helpful: "Because of the deeply ingrained nature of our behavioral patterns, it is sometimes difficult to develop critical perspective on our own behavior. For that reason alone, analysis occurring in a collaborative and cooperative environment is likely to lead to greater learning" (25).

COMBINING CATEGORIES AND CRITERIA

If we combine Boyer's five categories of scholarship with Glassick, Huber, and Maeroff's (1997) six criteria for evaluating scholarship, we can construct a table to pose some additional heuristic questions about the five kinds of scholarly activity. By responding to these questions, we can more clearly see the diverse purposes of scholarly activity, including the scholarship of teaching and learning. We first present a table with all five categories of scholarly activity to establish the broader context for scholarship in rhetoric and composition. Duane has found this table invaluable when he writes tenure and promotion reviews for faculty at other colleges and universities because it clearly illustrates the scope of professors' scholarly achievements.

MAKING THE WORK OF WRITING PROGRAMS MORE VISIBLE

In combination, *Scholarship Reconsidered* and *Scholarship Assessed* offer teachers and WPAs a powerful lens through which to analyze the teaching of writing. It is important now to ask how teachers and WPAs might use these heuristic questions to guide the assessment and documentation of effective teaching. One way to do this is through the teaching portfolio.

Peter Seldin (2004), among others, offers practical guidance for crafting portfolios that make teaching visible to those who evaluate our instruction. Making teaching visible is crucial because those who don't inhabit our classrooms and online instructional spaces on a daily basis often can't visualize all that teachers do to enhance students' learning. Among those who offer strategies for constructing teaching portfolios that reflect scholarly approaches are Russell Edgerton, Patricia Hutchings, and Kathleen Quinlan. In *The Teaching Portfolio: Capturing the Scholarship of Teaching*, they present and describe effective teaching portfolios, noting their many advantages:

- Portfolios capture the complexities of teaching.
- Portfolios place responsibility for evaluating teaching in the hands of faculty.
- Portfolios can prompt more reflective practice.
- Portfolios can foster a culture of teaching and a new discourse about it. (Edgerton, Hutchings, and Quinlan 1991, 4–6)

Table 2.1 Combining *Scholarship Reconsidered* and *Scholarship Assessed*

Six Criteria for Assessing Scholarship Glassick, Huber, Maeroff (1997)	Five Categories of Academic Scholarship Boyer (1990; 1996)				
	Discovery	*Application*	*Integration*	*Teaching and Learning*	*Engagement*
Clear Goals	What are the goals of our research?	What are the goals of applying knowledge from our field?	When we establish goals for our work, how can we draw on scholarship from other fields?	What are our goals in teaching writing?	What are our goals for engagement with communities outside the university?
Adequate Preparation	How can we prepare ourselves to conduct meaningful research?	How can we prepare ourselves to apply research findings to real-world problems?	What can we learn from other fields to enhance work in our field?	How can we prepare ourselves to teach most effectively?	How can we effectively prepare ourselves to work with community groups outside the university?
Appropriate Methods	What research methods most effectively answer our questions?	In a particular situation, what methods are most effective in applying knowledge from our field to solve real-world problems?	What methods from other fields can we combine with methods in our field?	What are the most effective methods we can apply to teaching writing in any given situation?	What methods are most effective for working with communities outside the university?
Significant Results	When we apply knowledge in our field, what difference does it make in the world?	What difference does it make if we use methods adopted from other fields?	What difference does writing instruction make in the lives of students?	What difference can we make in communities outside the university?	When we apply knowledge in our field, what difference does it make in the world?
Effective Presentation	How can we most effectively apply the results of our research to real-world problems?	How can we effectively use presentation methods that are common in other fields?	How can we make teaching and learning more visible to students, colleagues, policy makers, and the public?	How can we make our work with community groups more visible, both within and beyond the university?	How can we most effectively apply the results of our research to real-world problems?
Reflective Critique	Does our research advance the field of rhetoric and composition?	By applying knowledge from our field, how successfully do we solve real-world problems?	When we adopt and adapt methods from other fields, how successful are we?	How effectively do we teach writing? How can we teach writing more effectively in the future?	How effective are we in working with community groups? How can we work more effectively with community groups in the future?

An effective portfolio usually includes a teaching philosophy in which the teacher says, "Here's what I do in my courses, and here's why I use these practices." Instructors can also make their work visible by including annotated syllabi and lesson plans, students' papers with the teacher's comments on them, synthesized and contextualized course evaluations, supervisors' class-visit reports, etc. In digital teaching portfolios, teachers can also include audio recordings of conferences with students, video recordings of class meetings, and links to online class materials.

As teachers of writing construct their teaching portfolios, they can use this table as a guide or record to ensure that they are engaging in the teaching of writing in a thorough and comprehensive manner. For example, if an instructor feels she adequately prepares lessons in the classroom and participates in discussions on the teaching of writing with colleagues in other disciplines, she then may turn to Boyer's (1996) category of "engagement" to consider how she might better prepare to engage and collaborate with communities outside of the university. Teachers can consider these categories, engage in a self-assessment of their work, and then tabulate and archive the work they accomplished in the classroom.

Perhaps most compellingly, WPAs can review the portfolio of a teacher in their program and draw on the questions posed in this framework to help determine the extent to which a teacher is approaching the teaching of writing in a scholarly manner. Of course, WPAs will likely focus on the questions and categories their institution values most as scholarly activity for teachers. For example, a WPA could look for evidence that the teacher has set goals for herself, not only in the research, service, and teaching arenas, but also in her work with others across disciplines and in the broader community. The WPA could then use the framework and teachers' portfolios to systematically assess and document the effectiveness of each teacher and of the program as a whole. Teaching portfolios can also offer evidence of the kinds of work that goes on in writing programs to outside agents. A clear table, such as the one inspired by Boyer (1990; 1996) and Glassick, Huber, and Maeroff (1997), offers writing teachers, WPAs, and faculty outside the discipline guiding questions to conceptualize the range and type of work that goes on within and beyond writing programs.

To further demonstrate how the table can enhance teaching and learning and the assessment of that teaching and learning, we focus here on the teaching and learning column. In particular, we show how it can be used to evaluate a teaching portfolio. Here, we indicate how

Table 2.2 Teaching and Learning

	Teaching and Learning
Clear Goals	As demonstrated in my teaching portfolio, to what extent do my teaching goals correspond to those endorsed by the program and/or professional organizations in the field— e.g., the WPA Outcomes Statement? To what extent do these goals meet the needs of students who will write in other academic, professional, civic, and personal settings?
Adequate Preparation	As demonstrated in my teaching portfolio, how effectively have I prepared myself to teach the courses assigned to me?
Appropriate Methods	As demonstrated in my teaching portfolio, how appropriate are the teaching methods I use in each of my courses? How well do these methods help students achieve the stated learning outcomes (clear goals) for each course?
Significant Results	As demonstrated in my teaching portfolio, how much learning have students experienced in each of my courses? How will that learning serve them in the academic, professional, civic, and personal writing they will do in the future?
Effective Presentation	As demonstrated in my teaching portfolio, how effectively have I engaged students with course material, with one another, and with me? How effectively have I presented my teaching practices to those who will read my portfolio?
Reflective Critique	In sum, how effective is my teaching in light of the goals for each course? Also, how I can tweak my teaching so that greater learning occurs in the future?

instructors can evaluate their own teaching portfolios, but WPAs can also use these same criteria.

By emphasizing a scholarly framework, such as the one presented here, three positive changes can result. First, it helps those in writing programs to ensure that their work is scholarly—possibly resulting in rewards such as salary increases, awards and recognition, tenure, and promotions. Second, this effort will benefit WPAs, who may be expected to lead a professional, scholarly, and regionally or nationally recognized writing program. Third, adopting a scholarly approach to the teaching of writing can increase the visibility of the program. The more recognized a program is at a university or college, in a community, or around the country, the more faculty and administrators outside of writing programs can see the importance of this kind of work. The teaching of writing, assessing the teaching of writing, and the other diverse range of activities that go on in writing programs can be brought to the forefront of what it means to do challenging, scholarly, academic work.

USING INQUIRY AND ADVOCACY TO EXPAND
THE NATURE OF *SCHOLARSHIP*

Because writing, teaching, and assessment are such complex activities, it is important to address the wide and intricate range of activities that they entail. Combining Glassick, Huber, Maeroff's (1997) criteria for assessing scholarship with Boyer's (1990; 1996) categories of academic scholarship can offer teachers and WPAs a series of important questions for documenting and assessing the teaching of writing. These heuristic questions can help teachers reflect upon their own effectiveness as scholars and teachers of writing while also supporting WPAs as they analyze the depth and breadth of writing teachers' commitment to the many activities that take place in writing programs.

In addition, Boyer's (1990; 1996) and Glassick, Huber, and Maeroff's (1997) frameworks also offer a means through which to encourage scholarly activity among tenure-track and contingent faculty, as well as teaching assistants in writing programs. By using a table with guiding questions, such as the one we have offered, WPAs and writing teachers may be encouraged to become even more active in a range of scholarly activities or, at minimum, to see that the important work they do is indeed scholarly. By broadening and opening the framework for what is considered "scholarly," we can be greater advocates for our field. Those who assess teachers of writing can draw on an expanded notion of scholarship to advocate for the importance of writing instruction—and its assessment—to those inside and outside the discipline. Through their encouragement, WPAs can help cultivate the view among, within, and beyond the writing program that it is important to acknowledge that the work we do is scholarly and must be documented. As university, college, department, and program administrators begin to use data to assess what goes on at their school, the stakes become even higher for WPAs to demonstrate the kinds (and the quality) of work that goes on in their writing programs. If we do not advocate for the importance of our work and emphasize that the work we do is scholarly, then we risk minimizing its importance in the university and beyond.

It is important to acknowledge that the framework we offer for situating the assessment of writing instruction as scholarly activity presents a number of challenges for WPAs. One such example of this tension is the movement toward faculty, adjunct instructor, and administrator accountability (see chapter 1). The push for accountability requires WPAs to balance formative assessment and summative evaluations that definitively show that teachers are basing their instruction on learning outcomes and, in turn, that students are achieving these outcomes.

This balance can, in part, be handled by collecting formative work and presenting it as part of summative program evaluations. WPAs can also negotiate this balance by communicating to chairs, deans, and provosts how formative and summative evaluations are interwoven. Summative assessments can offer insight into the day-to-day instructional work that goes on in a writing program, while formative assessment allows writing teachers and WPAs to evaluate the effectiveness of the program and the impact of this day-to-day work on the larger programmatic body. Summative and formative evaluation can work together to offer insight into the writing program, and WPAs can advance this call among other administrators by situating this evaluative work as scholarly.

Further, this model requires internal and external buy-in from various stakeholders. First, tenure-track and contingent faculty members, as well as teaching assistants, need to believe that the work they do is important and that the work within a writing program is integral to the success of the university. It is the role of the WPA to communicate this message by offering real rewards. Such rewards may include salary increases, awards, tenure, promotions, recognition, and opportunities to teach select courses. WPAs can make it clear to their teachers that teaching writing is a scholarly endeavor and involves a wide variety of scholarly activities. WPAs must also carry this message outside the program in order to make this work visible to parties not directly involved in the program and to those legislators who make policy decisions that affect the funding and accreditation of the program.

Just as there are many categories and means to assess scholarship, there are also many ways to assess the teaching of writing. As Boyer (1990; 1996) and Glassick, Huber, and Maeroff (1997) have noted, inquiry is key to effective scholarship and, we argue, to the effective assessment of writing instruction. As scholars of writing, we must insist that we raise important questions and seek new knowledge in our field. We should engage in discovering and revising theories and approaches to our discipline. But, it is equally important to ask whether we are helping to give writing teachers the tools to set goals, prepare curricula, achieve desired results with student writers, implement pedagogically sound practices in the classroom, and reflectively critique their practice. We should encourage inquiry into our own and others' approaches to the teaching of writing.

Even more, as we assess teachers of writing, we should share our scholarly work—in its many forms—with faculty leaders, administrators, and tenure and promotion committees. Because this educational era prizes measurement and data, it is important that we demonstrate the value of our work and advocate for the numerous and varied types of scholarship that writing programs bring to institutions. Examining, exploring, and investigating our discipline and the work of its various stakeholders, as well as advocating and promoting our efforts, are integral steps to taking a scholarly approach to teaching and assessment.

References

Adler-Kassner, Linda, and Susanmarie Harrington. 2010. "Responsibility and Composition's Future in the Twenty-First Century: Reframing 'Accountability.'" *College Composition and Communication* 62 (1): 73–99.

Angelo, Thomas A., and K. Patricia Cross. 1993. *Classroom Assessment Techniques: A Handbook for College Teachers*, 2nd ed. San Francisco: Jossey-Bass.

Arreola, Raoul A. 2000. *Developing a Comprehensive Faculty Evaluation System: A Handbook for College Faculty and Administrators on Designing and Operating a Comprehensive Faculty Evaluation System*, 2nd ed. Boston: Anker.

Bain, Ken. 2004. *What the Best College Teachers Do*. Cambridge, MA: Harvard University Press.

Boyer, Ernest. 1990. *Scholarship Reconsidered: Priorities of the Professoriate*. Princeton, NJ: Carnegie Foundation for the Advancement of Teaching.

Boyer, Ernest. 1996. "The Scholarship of Engagement." *Bulletin – American Academy of Arts and Sciences*. 49 (7): 18–33. http://dx.doi.org/10.2307/3824459.

CompPile. 2004–2012. http://comppile.org/.

Conference on College Composition and Communication. 2009. "CCCC Position Statement on Faculty Work in Community-Based Settings." http://www.ncte.org/cccc/resources/positions/communitybasedsettings.

Council of Writing Program Administrators. 1998. "Evaluating the Intellectual Work of Writing Administration." http://www.wpacouncil.org/positions/intellectualwork.html.

Council of Writing Program Administrators. 2000. "WPA Outcomes Statement for First-Year Composition." http://www.wpacouncil.org/positions/outcomes.html.

Council of Writing Program Administrators. 2010. "Framework for Success in Postsecondary Writing." National Council of Teachers of English, National Writing Project. http://wpacouncil.org/files/framework-for-success-postsecondary-writing.pdf.

Dewey, John. 1933. *How We Think*. Chicago: Henry Regnery.

Diamond, Robert. 1998. *Designing and Assessing Courses and Curricula*. San Francisco: Jossey-Bass.

Edgerton, Russell, Patricia Hutchings, and Kathleen Quinlan. 1991. *The Teaching Portfolio: Capturing the Scholarship of Teaching*. Washington, DC: American Association for Higher Education (AAHE).

Glassick, Charles, Mary Huber, and Gene Maeroff. 1997. *Scholarship Assessed: Evaluation of the Professoriate*. San Francisco: Jossey-Bass.

Glau, Gregory, and Chitralekha Duttagupta, eds. 2010. *The Bedford Bibliography for Teachers of Basic Writing*, 3rd ed. Boston: Bedford/St. Martin's.

Hindman, Jane E. 2000. "Fostering Liberatory Teaching: A Proposal for Revising Instructional Assessment Practices." *WPA: Writing Program Administration* 23 (2/3): 11–31.

Howard, Rebecca Moore. 2014. *Writing Matters*. http://www.rebeccamoorehoward.com/bibibliographies.

Huba, Mary E., and Jann E. Freed. 1999. *Learner-Centered Assessment on College Campuses Shifting the Focus from Teaching to Learning.* Boston: Allyn & Bacon.

Hult, Christine, ed. 1994. *Evaluating Teachers of Writing.* Urbana, IL: NCTE.

Modern Language Association. 1996. "Making Faculty Work Visible: The Report of the MLA Commission on Professional Service." http://www.mla.org/pdf/profserv96.pdf.

Osterman, Karen Figler, and Robert Kottkamp. 1993. *Reflective Practice for Educators: Improving Schooling through Professional Development.* Newbury Park, CA: Corwin.

Reynolds, Nedra, Bruce Herzberg, and Patricia Bizzell. 2003. *The Bedford Bibliography for Teachers of Writing,* 6th ed. Boston: Bedford/St. Martin's; http://bb.bedfordstmartins.com.

Schön, Donald. 1987. *Educating the Reflective Practitioner.* San Francisco: Jossey-Bass.

Schön, Donald. 1995. "Knowing-in-Action: The New Scholarship Requires a New Epistemology." *Change* 27 (6): 26–34. http://dx.doi.org/10.1080/00091383.1995.10544673.

Seldin, Peter. 2004. *The Teaching Portfolio: A Practical Guide to Improved Performance and Promotion/Tenure Decisions,* 2nd ed. Boston, MA: Anker.

Shulman, Lee. 2000. "From Minsk to Pinsk: Why a Scholarship of Teaching and Learning." *Journal of Scholarship of Teaching and Learning* 1 (1): 48–53. http://josotl.indiana.edu/article/view/1582/1581.

3
MAKING SENSE (AND MAKING USE) OF STUDENT EVALUATIONS

Amy E. Dayton

Perhaps no aspect of college teaching raises as much anxiety as the process of being evaluated by our students. Some instructors respond to this dread by refusing to read their evaluations at all, or by dismissing them as uninformed. This perception is illustrated by a comment I recently overheard on my campus: "student evaluations don't tell us anything, because students don't know enough to evaluate their instructors." Regardless of their opinion about the validity of student ratings, most instructors can relate to the sentiment expressed by the *Chronicle of Higher Education* contributor who lamented that her evaluations were filled with "zingers [that] stick . . . like burrs" (Perillo 2000). While sometimes it is those "zingers" (about our appearance, for instance, or our sartorial choices) that make evaluations unpleasant to read, sometimes it is the uncomfortable truths that they reveal about shortcomings in our course design, presentation style, or ability to connect with students. To borrow terminology from Richard Miller, the student opinion survey is a site where the "hidden transcript" of a course is exposed, revealing things we may not want to acknowledge about the dynamics of our classrooms (21). By displaying this "hidden transcript," student evaluations disrupt the power balance of our classrooms and challenge the traditional paradigm in which "teacher knows best." They also contradict popular conceptions of teaching as an art or a natural gift rather than a skill to be practiced, improved, and empirically evaluated. (For evidence of this widespread conception of teaching, consider the popular genre of "inspirational teacher" movies, such as *Dead Poets Society* or *Freedom Writers*. Also, see chapter 4 for a discussion of the notion of teaching as an art.)

The discomfort with student ratings is rooted not only in the challenge they pose to our beliefs about teaching, or the psychological discomfort they evoke, but also in the problematic ways that some

DOI: 10.7330/9780874219661.c003

institutions use them as high-stakes, single measurements. For many writing instructors, including contingent faculty and those in teaching-intensive positions, the student evaluation—particularly the quantitative score—is the most heavily weighted factor, and sometimes the only factor, in the evaluation of their performance. Thus, student evaluations of instruction (hereafter, SEIs) have an important material effect on the professional lives and career prospects of postsecondary teachers.[1] This may be especially true for teachers of composition, because those who teach lower-division courses are more likely to be untenured or adjunct faculty whose job status depends on their ratings. Despite their importance to our profession, however, composition scholars have had little, if anything, to say about student evaluations.[2] This oversight may be due, in part, to a disciplinary resistance to quantitative data—both in the form of the ratings themselves and in the primarily quantitative research that has been done about them to date. As Davida Charney (1996) has pointed out, some composition scholars, working within a postmodern paradigm, have equated empiricism with absolutism, a disregard for social justice, and a refusal to challenge the status quo. In this chapter I argue that WPAs and composition scholars alike should work toward developing a more nuanced understanding of student evaluations— particularly concerning validity, interpretation, and survey design—in order to better gauge how well we are doing, to continue demonstrating our effectiveness, and to determine how we can improve. The current context of higher education, specifically the push to collect more data on teaching effectiveness and to make the data accessible to the public, has given new urgency to this task. Rather than starting from scratch in attempting to sort through the meanings and uses of student ratings, I suggest that we look across the disciplines to the existing body of scholarship on these instruments in order to gain insight into what we do and do not know about them.

Research on SEIs dates back to at least the 1970s—the instruments have played an important role in faculty evaluation since that time. In his brief history of SEIs in higher education, John Ory (2000) notes that student governments began using the forms as early as the 1920s, but that they gained steam during the 1960s due to a student-generated push for more responsive teaching practices in American universities. While SEIs began as a student-initiated instrument, they quickly became popular with university officials, who recognized their potential for evaluating faculty. By the 1970s, institutions began to rely on these forms as a means of making personnel decisions in times of financial stress. Today, they are an established part of the higher education landscape, with nearly 100%

of postsecondary institutions collecting student feedback on teaching in one form or another (Ory 2000). They are also the focus of a large body of research from scholars in fields such as institutional measurement and educational psychology (among others). More than two thousand studies of student evaluations have been published, making research on this topic almost a subfield of its own.[3] (See chapter 10 for a historical overview of teacher evaluation practices in college composition).

Previous research can serve as a useful foundation for composition scholars and teachers as we work toward a better understanding of how to use these data in college composition. Although it is beyond the scope of this chapter to summarize this subfield in all of its complexity, here I review the key findings in order to answer this question: What do we already "know" about SEIs? I put the word "know" in quotes here to acknowledge that some readers may not readily embrace research results from studies whose methods are markedly different from those employed in the humanities—and, specifically, which are quantitative in nature, relying heavily on statistical analysis. Nevertheless, because the existing research has been persuasive in making the case for SEIs, and because these instruments have been embraced by university administrators who rely on them for information about teaching performance, I argue that we cannot afford to ignore these findings. With a perspective informed by previous research on SEIs, we can ask not just, *are SEIs valid?*, but also, *in what ways are they valid?* What are the unique considerations that we must address when using SEI instruments and interpreting SEI data in writing programs? How can we use the data more responsibly?

ARE STUDENT EVALUATIONS VALID?

In the following section, I review some of the key research findings on student evaluations, drawing from meta-analyses of groups of studies and a few noteworthy collections of essays. Two of these collections, *Evaluating Teaching in Higher Education: A Vision for the Future*, and *The Student Ratings Debate: Are They Valid? How Can We Best Use Them?*, were published as part of the Jossey-Bass series New Directions for Institutional Assessment. A final set of essays and meta-analyses comes from *American Psychologist* (the official publication of the American Psychological Association). This special issue from 1997 provides a portrait of several decades of research on student ratings, bringing together the foremost experts on the topic to review key findings and identify unresolved issues regarding the design and interpretation of SEIs.

Those who criticize the use of student ratings often argue that students do not have enough knowledge about the subject matter to evaluate their instructors' effectiveness. Michael Theall and Jennifer Franklin, who have written extensively about SEIs, acknowledge that students may not be in the best position to evaluate certain aspects of teaching, such as instructors' knowledge of the subject. But they are quite capable of reporting on factors such as "teacher behaviors, the amount of work required . . . the difficulty of the material . . . the clarity of lectures, the value of readings and assignments, the clarity of the instructor's explanations, the instructor's availability and helpfulness, and many other aspects of the teaching and learning process. No one else is qualified to report on what transpired during the term simply because no one else is present for as much of the term" (Theall and Franklin 1990, 48).

Those critics who doubt students' ability to report effectively on these (and other) aspects of teaching have often cited two early studies that appeared to show that student evaluations were inherently flawed. The first appeared in *Science* magazine (Rodin and Rodin 1972) and the other in the *Journal of Medical Education* (Naftulin, Ware, and Donnelly 1973). The Rodin and Rodin (1972) study found a negative correlation between student learning and course ratings. Among other flaws, however, the study relied on students' evaluation of their teaching assistants, who did not do the majority of the classroom teaching (Kulik 2001, 17). The second study, the infamous "Dr. Fox" experiment, has been widely cited, but is plagued by methodological flaws. In this experiment, a trained actor received high audience ratings for a lecture that was entertaining and humorous, but filled with nonsensical subject matter. The researchers used this outcome to point to a validity problem for student ratings. But, as James Kulik (2001) (and many other critics) have pointed out, the results of the Dr. Fox experiment were based on one lecture, not a semester-long course. The topic of the lecture, mathematical game theory, was entirely unfamiliar to the audience of medical educators. Kulik speculates that it may be possible to "bamboozle" an audience during one entertaining session, but it would be more difficult to do this during a semester-long course for students who have some prior knowledge of the subject (18). For these reasons, the study has been strongly criticized, and has been held up as an example of a fatally flawed experiment.

Despite these two studies (and some others) that appear to cast doubt on the merits of student evaluation, most psychometric researchers agree that, despite some flaws in these instruments, the data garnered from student evaluations do, in general, have good validity—with some exceptions, which I'll discuss below[4] (see chapter 1 for a discussion of validity and reliability). In general, students tend to give high ratings to courses in which they have successfully met the learning outcomes. This finding has been reaffirmed by a meta-analysis of forty-one prior studies that compared SEI scores to students' performance on standardized exams across multiple sections of courses taught with common outcomes and curricula (Cohen, cited in Marsh and Roche 1997). Studies have shown that students' quantitative ratings of teacher effectiveness tend to agree with other measures, including classroom observations (whether they are done by peer teachers, administrators, or external consultants) and surveys of graduating seniors and alumni.[5] Students' quantitative ratings also tend to agree with their qualitative feedback, including discursive evaluations of instructors and the comments given in research interviews (Kulik 2001, 13).

Despite the findings that student ratings have some measure of validity, questions remain regarding possible biases and limitations of student ratings, and researchers have disagreed on such issues as the extent to which ratings should be adjusted (if at all) to account for factors like class size or grading leniency. In terms of bias, some trends have been clearly demonstrated. Arreola (2007), citing Aleamoni and Hexner (1980), notes that upper division students have been found to be more generous in their ratings than first-year students, and elective courses are consistently given higher ratings than required ones (such as first-year composition) (102). Theall and Franklin (1990), in "Looking for Bias in All the Wrong Places," acknowledge that, in addition to giving lower ratings to lower division courses, students also give lower ratings to courses taken outside their major, particularly in the sciences, and to courses with large enrollment. And though there is no broad consensus on how gender affects an instructor's ratings, some studies have found that female students rate female professors more highly, and that male students likewise give higher marks to male faculty (Arreola 2007, 103). On the question of whether biases (such as gender, race, age, or other factors) affect SEI scores, Peter Seldin (2006) offers an important caution: the fact that research has not revealed broad patterns of bias in student evaluations does not mean that it doesn't exist in particular cases. In situations where there is evidence of bias, we have an ethical duty to consider this information when interpreting results (33).

SEIs have been shown to be more reliable (i.e., they yield more consistent results) in larger courses with higher numbers of students. So, in small courses like the typical college writing class, it becomes more difficult to make inferences about teaching quality. In fact, William Cashin

(1999) recommends using special caution when interpreting data from fewer than ten students, and from less than two-thirds of a class (31). On the other hand, as Marsh and Roche (1997) (and others) note, students in smaller classes do tend to rate instructors more favorably, especially on factors such as fostering "group interaction" and establishing "individual rapport" (1190). Results like this can be read in two ways. For some, they are evidence of a bias in course evaluations; for others, they accurately reflect the fact that instructors can more effectively foster group interaction and establish individual rapport in small classes. Similarly, there are questions about the effect of instructor warmth and expressiveness on SEIs—teachers with warm, expressive personalities do receive higher ratings. This trend can be interpreted as proof that SEIs are little more than a "popularity contest" for teachers. But we could also argue that enthusiastic, engaging teachers are more likely to achieve better results in the classroom—particularly in the writing classroom, where participation and active engagement are critical parts of the learning process.

A similar problem plagues the debate over grades and student ratings. The question of whether faculty can "buy" good ratings by giving higher grades has been hotly debated and frequently studied. But, according to Raul Arreola (2007), this is "not because the question is so difficult to answer—it's that faculty don't generally like the answer the literature provides" (101). In their review of questions of bias in teaching evaluations, Marsh and Roche (1997) find that support for a grading effect is weak. Although some studies show a correlation between higher grades and high SEI scores, Marsh and Roche note that "there are at least three very different interpretations" of this finding. The first is that "instructors who give higher-than-deserved grades will be rewarded with higher-than-deserved [SEIs], which constitutes a serious bias" (1191). This hypothesis assumes that grading leniency causes the SEI effect. A second hypothesis, however, views a correlation between higher grades and higher SEI ratings in a different light: as proof of student learning. In this line of thinking, students who learn more in a course are more likely to earn high grades, in which case the high SEI ratings would not be any less valid. A third explanation is that other, preexisting factors—such as student interest in the topic—can affect both their learning and their grades "so that the expected-grade effect is spurious" (1191). Many of the studies examining the grade effect are experimental, and they include deception research, in which students are given false grades, sometimes much lower than expected, and are then asked to rate their instructor. These studies are rightly viewed with suspicion in the psychometric community because of the methodological and ethical problems involved in this kind of research (one would hope that students' false grades are corrected after the experiments are complete!). Finally, some research has found that teachers who are self-reported "easy graders" actually receive lower course ratings and negative rankings on questions asking students how much they have learned—these findings, too, challenge the hypothesis that grading leniency will lead to higher student ratings (Marsh and Roche 1997, 1192). Although some researchers have concluded that grades are not a significant bias to SEI forms, others have challenged this view. Greenwald and Gillmore (1997), while acknowledging that theirs is a minority view, argue that grading leniency is a clear contaminant of student ratings.[6] Rather than arguing that we should throw out student ratings entirely, however, Greenwald and Gillmore suggest that the problem could be addressed through measures that consider instructors' grade distributions when calculating SEI results.

MAKING USE OF STUDENT RATINGS: IMPLICATIONS FOR WRITING PROGRAMS AND TEACHERS

I recently presented an overview of research on student evaluations to a group of colleagues, many of them writing teachers. When I finished, one audience member raised a hand to ask, "So, can we rely on student evaluations, or not?" The answer to this question, as it turns out, is not a simple yes or no. In chapter 1, I noted that we determine validity based not on an assessment instrument itself, but on the accuracy and consistency of the data that instrument generates. Of course, we want our student evaluations surveys to be well-designed tools (see below). But we also want to think critically about how we use the data they provide. If we look solely at one or two numerical ratings (such as the two questions that are looked at most frequently at my institution: How do you rate the teacher's overall effectiveness? How do you rate this course overall?) without considering the context of those ratings, we are probably misusing the data. We should approach our ratings form with a sense of what we value most about teaching and consider how well our forms capture those values. In short, we need to treat the readings of student evaluations as a reflective, interpretive process. The task of making sense of these forms should not be done by individuals in isolation, but it is best done when a community of teachers has discussed its standards and created some commonly held guidelines about interpreting the data. (See chapter 1 for more discussion about validity, reliability, and the hermeneutic approach to assessment). It is worth noting that, while psychometric researchers may agree in principle about the validity of SEIs, they nonetheless come to different conclusions about the various factors that may affect their validity, and what we should do to make responsible use of the data. In other words, looking at "hard numbers" does not yield universal agreement or easy resolution of the questions surrounding student evaluations.

Of course, before we begin the process of interpreting the results of our student evaluations, we should give some thought to the forms themselves, which are, quite often, not well designed or responsibly used. Marsh and Roche (1997) note that "homemade" surveys, "constructed by lecturers or committees, are rarely evaluated in relation to rigorous psychometric considerations and revised accordingly" (1188). Moreover, some forms "place too much emphasis on lecture format or traditional methods for teaching," disadvantaging those who use more active or student-centered pedagogies (Seldin 2006, 33). This problem is especially likely to affect writing teachers, who may spend very little time delivering lectures or administering tests, though the evaluation forms used for their classes may still contain questions about these nonexistent aspects of their courses. Ory and Ryan (2001) note that the questions most commonly used on student evaluation forms have been chosen because they were proven over time to produce the most reliable (i.e., *consistent*) answers, not because they correspond to empirical evidence about what constitutes the most effective teaching practices (34–35). Poorly designed forms do not give us coherent and consistent views of learning and teaching. Arreola (2007) notes that evaluation forms should be designed in consultation with psychometric experts, and then piloted to see which quvestions yield the most consistent results. They should be tailored to individual courses and tied to course outcomes, and they should be written in the language that students and teachers use in the classroom.

Despite the possible pitfalls with creating "local" student evaluation forms, writing programs can create instruments that more effectively assess teaching effectiveness by drawing from common outcomes for writing courses. The WPA Outcomes Statement for First-Year Composition (Council of Writing Program Administrators 2000), in particular, represents a carefully thought-out set of goals for writing instruction. These goals provide a useful starting point for creating writing-specific SEIs that draw on a shared sense of purpose and a common vocabulary for composition classes. In general, students are capable of evaluating whether—and what—they have learned in a specific course. But students and teachers often have different ideas about what constitutes "learning," especially in writing courses that emphasize student-centered approaches, peer collaboration, and the ability to understand and apply critical thinking skills rather than the memorization of facts and formulas. The unique challenge of evaluating writing instruction requires programs and teachers to clearly articulate our goals and outcomes in order to assess how well we have met them. Many of our WPA outcomes provide clear statements that could easily be transformed into questions on a writing-specific SEI form.

In table 3.1, I provide some examples of how learning outcomes can be translated directly into language used in student opinion surveys.[7] These instruments allow programs to tailor their forms directly to their learning outcomes. For instance, such forms can ask students how well they have learned to formulate and support a thesis. Ideal forms should have a place for explanatory comments, so students can offer a rationale behind their ratings. As O'Neill, Moore, and Huot (2009) note, these forms are especially appealing because they shift the focus toward what students have learned and away from an emphasis on "the teacher as a personality" (146).[8]

USING AND INTERPRETING STUDENT RATINGS

If student ratings have a poor reputation, most of the people who have studied them would argue that the problem lies not with the instruments themselves but with the "lack of sophistication of personnel committees who use [them]" (McKeachie 1997, 1218). The question of how student ratings are interpreted has led some scholars to focus on *consequential validity*—a term that shifts the focus to understanding how student ratings are used. As Ory and Ryan (2001) note, emerging frameworks for validity include consideration of the ideologies invested in the instruments as well as their consequences. Those consequences may be intended—such as when instructors review their student surveys and make improvements to their classes as a result, or when they are rewarded for good teaching by promotion, tenure, or merit raises. They may be unintended—such as when teachers begin to inflate their grades or attempt to "cheat" the evaluation system in order to buy higher ratings, when faculty become resist to teaching new or experimental courses due to concerns over low ratings, or when morale suffers due to the use of student evaluations to single out instructors with occasional low marks. Those unintended, negative consequences affect not

Table 3.1 WPA Learning Outcomes and Sample SEI Questions

WPA Learning Outcome	Sample SEI Question
Rhetorical Knowledge "By the end of first-year composition, students should . . ."	
focus on a purpose. respond to the needs of difference audiences.	This course helped me write for specific purposes and audiences.
Critical Thinking "By the end of first-year composition, students should . . ."	
understand writing and reading for inquiry, learning, thinking, and communicating. understand a writing assignment as a series of tasks, including finding, evaluating, analyzing, and synthesizing appropriate primary and secondary sources.	This course helped me improve my critical thinking and research skills.
Processes "By the end of first-year composition, students should . . ."	
generate flexible strategies for revising, editing, and proofreading. learn to critique their own and others' works.	This course helped me improve my strategies for revising my work and critiquing my own and others' work.
Knowledge of Conventions "By the end of first-year composition, students should . . ."	
practice appropriate means of documenting their work. control such surface features as syntax, grammar, punctuation, and spelling.	This course helped me learn how to cite my sources and correct my sentence-level errors.
Composing in Electronic Environments "By the end of first-year composition, students should . . ."	
use electronic environments for drafting, reviewing, revising, editing, and sharing texts. understand and exploit the differences in the rhetorical strategies . . . available for both print and electronic composing.	This course helped me better use technology to draft my papers.

only the individual instructors who feel punished due to low marks in a course, but they can also affect a program's overall assessment efforts as teachers and students become cynical about assessment. In urging readers to consider the consequential validity of SEIs, Ory and Ryan echo Theall and Franklin's point out that much of the resistance to student evaluations comes from the fact that they are so often misused—for instance, when universities use them as the sole measure of teaching effectiveness, or when those responsible for interpreting them do not have sufficient knowledge of statistics (Ory and Ryan 2001, 39; Theall and Franklin 1990, 46).

With an emphasis on consequential validity, then, I offer suggestions for WPAs on how to make effective—and ethical—use of student ratings data. This approach can help us avoid some of the unintended, negative consequences of SEIs, and can help us make better use of them in light of what they do offer: information about how students perceived a particular course.

- WPAs (as well as other administrators and personnel committees) should interpret SEI data in a holistic manner. Student opinion data do not have clear-cut meanings in and of themselves; rather, they suggest a range of possible interpretations. As O'Neill, Moore, and Huot (2009) put it, SEIs need to be considered in light of "each particular case and within the context of the program and institution" (145). Moreover, Wilbert McKeachie (1997) advises administrators and personnel committees to "sensibly" use SEI data for information about "broad categories, rather than attempting to interpret decimal-point differences" (1219). We must keep in mind that "good teaching" is a broad construct that takes many different forms. Therefore, good teachers may not be rated highly in all categories, such as in "enthusiasm, organization, [or] warmth" (1218).

- Writing programs should have a sense of whether they are using student evaluation data as a formative or summative tool (see chapter 1). In cases where programs are making high-stakes decisions about retention or promotion, programs should not use SEIs merely as a summative tool, but as part of a formative process that includes ongoing conversation with teachers, who should be offered the opportunity to reflect upon the data, provide contextual information about the evaluations, obtain feedback and support for continued development, and set goals for improvement.

- Program should avoid "norm referencing": the practice of comparing individual teachers' scores to a mean or median score earned by all teachers at an institution. While those numbers can be useful for understanding how instructors are evaluated across the institution, they are not useful as an arbitrary cutoff point for determining whether an instructor is performing at an above-average or below-average level. Almost all experts on student ratings agree on this point, noting that norm referencing has "negative effects on faculty members' morale" since, by definition, half the faculty are below the norm (d'Appolonia and Abrami 1997, 1204; McKeachie 1997). McKeachie suggests a better approach: we can determine how a faculty member is doing by looking at the distribution of ratings: "How many students rated the teacher as very good or excellent? How many students were dissatisfied?" (1222).

- The use of SEI results should be part of a multifaceted approach to assessing teachers that includes other kinds of evidence. This evidence may include classroom observations by colleagues, teaching portfolios, self-evaluations, and teacher reflections on formative assessment data (see chapters 7 and 9).

- Teachers and students must be encouraged to treat student evaluations seriously. Thoughtful use of student evaluations should be part
  of a broader programmatic and campus culture in which "openness
  and sharing of information" about assessment is valued, and where
  assessment is part of a broad conversation that is "public" and "ongoing" (Braskamp and Ory 1994, 6). This sense of assessment as a public
  conversation extends to our classroom practice as well. For this reason, instructors should not merely give out student evaluation forms
  without comment. Instead, they should talk with students about the
  purposes and uses of the form, explaining how they use student feedback to shape their classroom practice.

- Finally, writing programs (as well as academic departments and other
  units) should consider creating a written policy that clearly articulates
  how they will gather, interpret, and use student evaluation data. What
  criteria will be used to interpret the results? What allowances will be
  made for teachers who are new to the institution (or who are new to
  teaching in general), for teachers of large-lecture formats or unpopu-
  lar required courses, for courses with low response rates, or for teachers whose courses are so small that they might not have a minimum
  of ten student responses? How will they use the discursive data—i.e.,
  comments from students—in relation to numerical data?

Although researchers may differ on what the studies on SEIs have
shown, they all seem to agree on one key point: SEIs should com-
prise only one part of a robust, multifaceted assessment process. They
shouldn't be reduced to a single, high-stakes score, nor should they be
over-interpreted. In light of this caution, I raise a few concluding points,
which I see as an invitation for composition scholars to think more
carefully about the role of SEIs in assessing learning and teaching, in
program evaluation, and in teacher mentoring/training. The first challenge for writing programs and teachers is to clearly articulate goals
and outcomes *before designing surveys for assessing teaching.* A second goal
is to ensure that our student evaluation forms capture a valid picture
of what we consider "learning" to be in the context of a writing course,
and to consider our course evaluations in relation to what students have
actually produced in our courses (through portfolios or other writing
assessments, for example). A third goal is to make sure that programs
and departments are using the results of student evaluations responsibly, incorporating multiple measures for teacher evaluation and programmatic assessment. Finally, where appropriate, writing programs
and individual teachers should consider ways to make the results of our
evaluations (and our subsequent teaching improvements) more transparent—both to students in our individual classrooms and, ultimately,
to the larger constituencies who are nudging us in this direction—and

to place the data in a richer context, without making student evaluations the sole indicator of how well we are doing.

Notes

1. Research across the disciplines uses a range of terms to talk about student evaluations of teaching. One of the most common is "student ratings" of instruction, or SRIs. Some researchers use the phrase "student ratings" to specifically refer to forms where students are asked to give analytic (not holistic) feedback on aspects of an instructor's performance; used in this way, "student ratings" are distinct from "student evaluations," which give holistic feedback on instructors' overall effectiveness (Arreola 2007, 112). I've chosen to use "SEI" in acknowledgement of the fact that most institutions collect more than one kind of data from students: analytic and holistic, as well as discursive and numerical. For my purposes, the term "ratings," which suggests numerical data, would be too narrow.

2. For examples of composition scholars who address student opinion surveys, see Elbow (1994) and TuSmith (2002).

3. This figure is based on a search of the ERIC database using the phrase "student evaluation of teaching performance" (Cashin 1999, 25).

4. This is not to say that all researchers across the disciplines consider the case on SEIs closed. For an example of a recent study casting doubt on the validity of student evaluations, see Carrell and West (2010). The Carrell and West study gained some traction in the national media.

5. I should note that these other measures have also been criticized for a lack of validity. Some argue that alumni surveys, when conducted long after students have graduated, are not valid sources of data. In addition, studies have shown that classroom observations do not have good reliability—that is, when teachers are observed repeatedly by different evaluators, they tend to receive highly inconsistent reviews. This problem is exacerbated when classroom observers are not well trained and normed in advance (Arreola 2007: Kulik 2001; Marsh and Roche 1997).

6. In a response to an earlier version of this essay, contributor Gerald Nelms astutely questioned what we mean by "grading leniency." In writing classrooms, instructors sometimes allow students to continue revising papers and improve their grades. Would the higher grades that result from this process-based pedagogy be considered examples of grading leniency?

7. The writing program director and first-year writing staff at my institution, University of Alabama, have successfully devised exactly this kind of survey for use in our program.

8. Another promising trend that focuses on assessing learning outcomes is represented by the Great Plains IDEA program at Kansas State, which seeks to create forms that can be tailored to individual programmatic goals and particular student demographics. The IDEA system helps universities pilot their survey instruments and refine them over time, as well as break down the data in ways that make it more comprehensible.

References

Aleamoni, Lawrence M., and Pamela Z. Hexner. 1980. "A review of the research on student evaluations and a report on the effect of different sets of instructions on student course and instructor evaluation." *Instructional Science* 9 (1): 67–84.

Arreola, Raoul. 2007. *Developing a Comprehensive Faculty Evaluation System: A Guide to Designing, Building, and Operating Large-Scale Faculty Evaluation Systems*, 3rd ed. San Francisco: Jossey-Bass.

Braskamp, Larry, and John C. Ory. 1994. *Assessing Faculty Work: Enhancing Individual and Institutional Performance*. San Francisco: Jossey-Bass.

Carrell, Scott E., and James E. West. 2010. "Does Professor Quality Matter? Evidence from Random Assignments of Students to Professors." *Journal of Political Economy* 118 (3): 409–32. http://dx.doi.org/10.1086/653808.

Cashin, William E. 1999. "Student Ratings of Teaching: Uses and Misuses." In *Changing Practices in Evaluating Teaching: A Practical Guide to Improved Faculty Performance and Promotion/Tenure Decisions*, ed. Peter Seldin and associates, 25–44. Bolton, MA: Anker.

Charney, Davida. 1996. "Empiricism is Not a Four-Letter Word." *College Composition and Communication* 47 (4): 567–93. http://dx.doi.org/10.2307/358602.

Council of Writing Program Administrators. 2000. "WPA Outcomes Statement for First-Year Composition." http://wpacouncil.org/positions/outcomes.html.

d'Appolonia, Sylvia, and Philip C. Abrami. 1997. "Navigating Student Ratings of Instruction." *American Psychologist* 52 (11): 1198–208. http://dx.doi.org/10.1037/0003-066X.52.11.1198.

Elbow, Peter. 1994. "Making Better Use of Student Evaluations of Teachers." In *Evaluating Teachers of Writing*, ed. Christine Hult, 97–110. Urbana, IL: NCTE.

Greenwald, Anthony G., and Gerald M. Gillmore. 1997. "Grading Leniency Is a Removable Contaminant of Student Ratings." *American Psychologist* 52 (11): 1209–17. http://dx.doi.org/10.1037/0003-066X.52.11.1209.

Kulik, James. 2001. "Student Ratings: Validity, Utility, and Controversy." In *The Student Ratings Debate: Are They Valid? How Can We Best Use Them?* ed. Michael Theall, Philip C. Abrami, and Lisa A. Mets. San Francisco: Jossey Bass.

Marsh, Herbert W., and Lawrence A. Roche. 1997. "Making Students' Evaluations of Teaching Effectiveness Effective." *American Psychologist* 52 (11): 1187–97. http://dx.doi.org/10.1037/0003-066X.52.11.1187.

McKeachie, Wilbert. 1997. "Student Ratings: The Validity of Use." *American Psychologist* 52 (11): 1218–25. http://dx.doi.org/10.1037/0003-066X.52.11.1218.

Naftulin, Donald H., John E. Ware, and Frank A. Donnelly. 1973. "The Doctor Fox Lecture: A Paradigm of Educational Seduction." *Journal of Medical Education* 48: 630–35.

O'Neill, Peggy, Cindy Moore, and Brian Huot. 2009. *A Guide to College Writing Assessment*. Logan: Utah State University Press.

Ory, John C. 2000. "Teaching Evaluation: Past, Present, and Future." In *Evaluating Teaching in Higher Education: A Vision for the Future*, ed. Katherine Ryan, 13–18. San Francisco: Jossey-Bass.

Ory, John C., and Katherine Ryan. 2001. "How Do Student Ratings Measure Up to a New Validity Framework?" In *The Student Ratings Debate: Are They Valid? How Can We Best Use Them?* ed. Michael Theall, Philip C. Abrami, and Lisa A. Mets. San Francisco: Jossey Bass. http://dx.doi.org/10.1002/ir.2.

Perillo, Lucia. 2000. "Why I Stopped Reading My Student Evaluations." *Chronicle of Higher Education*, July 7.

Rodin, Miriam, and Burton Rodin. 1972. "Student Evaluation of Teachers." *Science* 177 (4055): 1164–66. http://dx.doi.org/10.1126/science.177.4055.1164.

Seldin, Peter, and associates. 2006. *Evaluating Faculty Performance: A Practical Guide to Assessing Teaching, Research, and Service*. Bolton, MA: Anker.

Theall, Michael, and Jennifer Franklin. 1990. *Student Ratings of Instruction: Issues for Improving Practice*. San Francisco: Jossey-Bass.

TuSmith, Bonnie. 2002. "Out on a Limb: Race and the Evaluation of Frontline Teaching." In *Race in the College Classroom: Pedagogy and Politics*, ed. Bonnie TuSmith and Maureen T. Teddy. New Brunswick: Rutgers University Press.

4

WATCHING OTHER PEOPLE TEACH
The Challenge of Classroom Observations

Brian Jackson

When I observe someone teach, I like to go early, sit in the back, and try to blend in. The semester is half over and I am a thirty-something guy at the back of the class, wearing a tie and glasses, with a goldenrod observation sheet in front of me. Even the sleepiest of writing students will assume I'm there to spy on them and/or their teacher. Usually the students are willing to play along: They ignore me, go straight to their regular seat, and assume the unassuming position of a student waiting for some kind of learning to happen. If the students are not chatty—and it's fifty–fifty as far as I can tell—we enter a period of un-silence, that four minutes and thirty-three seconds of anxious languor before the bell interrupts the humming of the fluorescent lamps, the drone of the climate control, the one student's tap tap tapping of "Shave and a Haircut" every thirty seconds.

A few minutes into one observation, a female student, without raising her hand or looking back at me, asks, "Who's our friend?" There goes my cover. Most times everyone pretends I'm not there. I like it that way—it makes me feel like an old-school ethnographer, with the same accompanying delusions about "natural behavior" and "objective observer." Sometimes the instructor, overcome by the "nerves of the observed," introduces me and says something like, "He's my boss. He's here to observe me."

So am I friend or boss? I guess I'm both, but in this role I sometimes feel more like boss than friend, since I'm here to perform the action verbs of middle management: observe, assess, certify, evaluate, critique, report. I am in this classroom at this hour for usability testing—the usability of our program's prevailing assumptions about teaching and learning. But I'm also here to help a colleague get better

DOI: 10.7330/9780874219661.c004

at teaching students some of the most important principles they will learn in college.

In the best classes, I can barely hold back my excitement. I want to jump in and join the discussion. I find myself wanting to show off for an instructor who has designed for us—us? for the students, I mean—what the literature calls "significant learning experiences." I've seen a few excellent teachers in my days of spying: dynamic, radiant, tenacious, intuitive, more effective than most, than *me*, which is, I admit, irritating. In the worst classes, I fight the urge to hustle the instructor out of the room so students will be safe from bad teaching's blast radius. One time I observed an instructor give a forty-minute lecture on the uses and misuses of the comma. Ten minutes into it, the students already had turned inward in cocoons of contempt, their arms folded tightly as if to hug themselves to death, their eyes studying the grain patterns on the desks or watching the seconds tick away tediously. Watching bad teaching is like watching an angry parent bark at a child in the grocery store. What is our responsibility for "other people's children," the term Lisa Delpit (2006) uses to describe students?

Most often, though, I observe what could be called "generally competent teaching"—enthusiastic, well organized, and helpful. I have seen plenty of instructors who know their students' names and effectively deploy the tactics they've learned from more experienced instructors while swapping ideas in the instructor carrels. They may not have a clue about what to do with the big football player in the back of the room crouching behind his newspaper fort; they may not make essential connections between one part of a lesson and another; they may assign activities that seem more like cognitive babysitting than learning; they may lead class discussions a bit woodenly, responding to each comment with little more than "good"; they may stare blankly at the bare walls while their students write or work in groups; they may not know much about how people learn to write, about rhetoric, or even about English grammar, punctuation, or usage. But beyond all expectation, they are doing a *pretty darn good job* teaching a college-level course they've (likely) never taken, whose content they have not yet mastered. And since our program stops at the MA level, they're teaching the course *at most* for the third or fourth—and often last—time when I slip into the back with my observation sheet. These rookies receive student ratings that compete with the scores obtained by the tenured ranks of the English department. Look no further for an example of education's miracles.

But I'm not at the back of the room merely to mark my observation sheet with a "good job" stamp and send the teacher away rejoicing. Like all progressive practices, teaching puts us in a perpetual state of discontent. A *pretty darn good job* keeps the program on the rails, but rarely is it *good enough*. With tweaks and overhauls, we tinker with our programs, hoping to find the secret to teaching writing. Our discontent gives us energy. We experiment. We fail. We assess. We train. And we watch a lot of teaching. If we're honest about what we do, we do some of the teaching ourselves. Besides teaching the course that we normally hand off to amateurs, there may be no better way to get a useful diagnostic report of our programs than observing the way the program is deployed on the ground.

This collection of essays comes at a time when pressure on teachers has never been greater. Like workers in the criminal justice system, teachers are simultaneously admired and loathed. Teaching shapes the future; it's also, according to some, a government-funded shelter for the incompetent. When President Barack Obama took office, it was assumed that teaching would experience a progressive renaissance, but the President's Secretary of Education, Arne Duncan, took President George W. Bush's No Child Left Behind Act and amped it up. With around five billion dollars from the American Recovery and Reinvestment Act of 2009 (the "stimulus bill"), in 2010 Duncan launched the Race to the Top, a program designed to encourage K–12 schools to get their test scores up through more innovative teaching—or more innovative mass firings of teachers (for example, in February 2010, every teacher at Rhode Island's Central Falls High School was pink-slipped). The national conversation on effective teaching grew particularly heated when the 2010 documentary *Waiting for Superman* reinforced the old prejudice that education's crisis is a result of strong unions, spineless administrators, and tenure. (These claims were strongly refuted, and in fact disproved, by Rick Ayers, Diane Ravitch, Mike Rose, and others.) Though we should welcome passionate dialogue about teaching, the new debate tends to scapegoat teachers for all kinds of systemic problems, casting a critical shadow over the whole profession.

In the end, however, teaching is a profession that demands our best reflection and practice. Part of making it better is learning how to observe and work with other teachers to help them perform better in the classroom. I offer the following observations in the hope that they may help WPAs and teachers become more reflective observers of other people teaching writing. Observing, I argue, can be considered part of "macro teaching"—the process by which a WPA's approach to writing education will be felt at the delivery point (i.e., the single student). I view observation in this way because it reminds me that I'm not just administering a program. I am ensuring that every student has equal access to good writing teachers. I am also inviting my colleague-teachers to commit to improve. My second argument follows from the first: That observation, while serviceable as a tool for surveillance, should be used more for formative assessment to help instructors realize their potential as professional writing teachers. There is significant evidence from education scholarship that says teachers improve only when they are given the opportunity to talk with others about their work (Darling-Hammond 2010). When we watch other people teach, we commit ourselves to their growth.

* * *

Teaching is creative work. It could be considered an art—at least, people like Gilbert Highet, author of *The Art of Teaching*, believe it is. Like writing, it often carries the assumption that some people can do it and some can't, that, like Michael Keating in *The Dead Poet's Society*, it is at its best when brilliant romantics set fire to the souls of young people vulnerable to cults of personality. Yet the more organic, ineffable, mystical, or intuitive teaching is, the harder it will be to make it better. John Centra (1993), one of our leading scholars on evaluating college teaching, has said that if teaching is an art and only an art, then we can't really measure or improve it (37). Luckily, we *can* measure it, we can study it, and we can improve it. Teaching is "as much a science as an art," and for every *je ne sais quoi* we see in teaching, there are a dozen *je sais quois*, like preparation and content knowledge (38). Students and teachers alike are surprisingly consonant on what makes good teaching, and even in our own field—as softly scientific as we sometimes pretend to be—we have strong statistical data telling us "what works" in writing instruction (Dean 2010; Graham and Perin 2007).

There are five main sources for evaluating teaching: (1) student ratings, often called "client surveys," (2) student performance—a favorite of No Child Left Behind and Race to the Top, (3) teacher portfolios, (4) teacher self-assessment or reflection, and (5) classroom observation. A beyond-the-call-of-duty program will use all five to evaluate teachers, especially if the program wants to make personnel decisions based on data. All too often programs rely too heavily on student ratings to evaluate teaching; Nancy Chism (1999) voices the opinions of the experts when she writes that "the evaluation of teaching must reflect the complexity of teaching itself," and therefore it should be multidimensional (6). In addition, any evaluation system should be clear about why it evaluates teaching in the first place. In 1967, Michael Scriven gave us the distinction between summative (for hiring, firing, promoting, and punishing teachers) and formative (for helping teachers improve) evaluation (Scriven 1967, 39–83). Though Raoul Arreola (2000) argues that observation data "should play little or no part in a summative faculty evaluation," observation has become a useful, even indispensable, tool for helping teachers improve their classroom performance (75).

The first teaching observations were carried out by K–12 principals in the early 1900s as part of their role as *pater familias* to the women teachers of their school. At first an informal management tool, observation developed scientific cachet when "official instruments and rating scales" were developed in 1915, and by the 1940s observation was a widespread practice in schools, with 80% of new teachers reporting having been observed in the 1970s (Ellett 1997, 109–110; Griffith 1973, 3). It took longer to catch on in postsecondary teaching: in 1998, only 40% of liberal arts colleges were using observation, an increase of only 5% since 1978 (Minter 2002, 63). As part of the general craze for objective measurements of everything, researchers in the 1970s developed complex psychometric tools to measure what happened in the classroom. One standout in terms of its oppressive thoroughness is the Flanders System of Interaction Analysis, which requires the observer to key every peep and mutter in the class using a complex mathematical matrix (more on observation tools later). Since Ernest Boyer's game-changing study *Scholarship Reconsidered* was published in 1990, we view observation as part of our mission to study and improve teaching as an intellectual enterprise. It is an essential part of how we "own" teaching. Teaching becomes, as Lee Shulman (1993) writes, "community property" (6–7).

Since the 1970s, observations have been considered one of several basic requirements for an effective teacher-training program in composition (Flanagan 1994, 73–86; Ward and Perry 2002, 124; Wilhoit 2002, 17–27). The purpose of observation is to improve student writing by improving the quality of the instruction they receive. We can evaluate instructors from all kinds of angles, from how much content knowledge they have (sometimes not much) to the speed with which they respond to the program assistant's emails. Often WPAs ask to review syllabi before even experienced instructors teach, just to see if the course supports the program's outcomes. Learning could be evaluated at the other end as well, such as when programs assess student papers. Through observation, by contrast, we evaluate how the course is delivered to students (Jones 1994, 34).

Much of the scholarship on K–12 teacher observations is addressed to supervisors, like principals, who observe in their capacity as bosses. WPAs are in the same boat when they observe grad students and adjuncts in their programs. As necessary as it may be to do this kind of observation, it can reify the uneven power dynamic of composition work. Willerman, McNeely, and Koffman (1991) warn that when administration does the observing, teachers often feel "that their supervisors are imposing their style of teaching on them, or they may 'hide their inadequacies,' fearing that their bad teaching could be used against them later" (4). I experienced this recently when I met with a talented graduate student after an observation and he asked me, "Was that sufficient, you know, in terms of the program?" Perhaps he wanted me to assure him that he had a teaching job next semester.

To avoid this power problem, many postsecondary teaching programs approach observation *horizontally*, with peers doing the observing rather than bosses (Millis and Kaplan 1995, 137–51; Minter 2002; Shulman 1993; Wilkerson and Lewis 2002, 74–81; Willerman, McNeely, and Koffman 1991). For example, the University of Maryland–University College has a twenty-year-old Peer Visit Program that instills trust, collegiality, and a desire to improve in new faculty. This model turns the observer into a collaborator who works with the teacher in the spirit of joint inquiry; it makes both observer and observed feel like they're on the same ethnographic team, trying to figure out what helps students learn to write (Wilkerson and Lewis 2002). Deborah Minter (2002) points out that peer observation, beyond its benefits as collaborative inquiry, disrupts "the master/apprentice dynamic" at play when administrators—or even more experienced teachers, for that matter—observe teaching (58).

I don't think I have as big a problem with the master/apprentice model as Deborah Minter (though like others I'm uncomfortable with the word *master*). The peer model works well when content experts with at least a few years of teaching experience visit each other's classrooms; it may be less effective when one rookie visits another rookie, even though something undoubtedly will be gained by both. If teaching is as much science as art, there are better ways of going about it, and teachers simply will not improve unless observation can generate new knowledge about teaching and a pathway to improve it (Centra 1993). It is useful, I suggest, to think of observation in the apprentice paradigm, with the observer as an experienced practitioner—or at least a *sensei*, a word one of my grad students tells me implies an "ahead learner."

I argue that WPAs, even if they cannot fully shrug off their status as bosses, can still approach observing in the spirit of mutual collaboration and formative evaluation, with the instructor's growth as the primary goal. As I mentioned earlier, I observe teaching as an administrator, but I also observe as a fellow teacher with ten years of FYC experience. We have trade books titled *Writing Program Administrator as Researcher* and *Writing Program Administrator as Theorist,* but we do not yet have *Writing Program Administrator as Teacher.* Though I have no ambition to write such a book, I want to advance Richard Gebhardt's (2002) argument that WPA work should be seen, appropriately and productively, as "macrolevel teaching," and effective observation involves collaborative critical reflection on teaching (35). All the more reason to ensure that WPAs are not only pragmatic middle managers, but very good teachers who understand how people learn (Jones 1994, 41).

* * *

How, then, do we go about observing? Let's go to the experts first to examine an unrealistic, but potentially constructive, ideal. If you are concerned about validity, reliability, and sample size, then you will likely be disappointed with what observation has to offer. Reliability, particularly, is a challenge, since researchers have found that peer reviewers of the same teaching performance disagree "substantially" on what they are seeing (Chism 1999, 14). Nancy Chism notes that some of that disparity can be explained by the practice of sending "uninformed peers" to make "brief visits" and report back "from the perspective of their own biases" (75). Because of potential reliability problems, both Chism and Raoul Arreola (2000) argue that more than one person should observe the teacher, and more than once per course. Arreola, whose *Developing a Comprehensive Faculty Evaluation System* is indeed comprehensive, suggests organizing a "peer review team" of three or four members who then visit the class at least ten times during the semester (76). Though this approach likely is unrealistic for most programs, it points to the need for something far more sophisticated than dropping in to see what our colleagues are up to.

Observation scholars break down the process into three steps: pre-observation interview, observation, and post-observation follow-up. In the pre-interview, the teacher describes the atmosphere of the class, explains her teaching goals for the day, and asks the observer to watch for things she feels she may need to work on (Flanigan 2002, 249). The pre-observation interview—which can be either in person or in written form—is meant to give the instructor a chance to reflect on her teaching. During the observation, Flanigan argues, the observer's "primary task is to describe what happens in the class, avoiding generalizations, analysis, evaluation, imposing a structure, or drawing conclusions too early." The observer keeps track of everything that happens like a play-by-play sports announcer, filling a sample log with accurate details like "Refers to S remark from last class. 4ss come in late, chairs bang" (249).

As admirable as I think this approach is, I find myself in my own observations making evaluative judgments even before the bell rings. Call it a "blink" moment, in honor of Malcolm Gladwell (2007), but sometimes I can "sense" effective teachers by what students do when they settle into their chairs, or how the teacher interacts with them before the bell, or what's been written on the board, or even the first five words of the class period ("Okay, let's start with announcements" vs. "Let me pose a question"). Since we've been sitting in front of all kinds of teaching since preschool, we have developed a strong intuitive sense of what makes effective teaching on sight. Nalini and Rosenthal (1993) give research evidence of the phenomenon, demonstrating that students watching silent (!) video clips of college professors can give an informed judgment, which agrees with end-of-semester evaluations, in less than ten seconds. The experiment has been repeated with similar results (Wiedmann and Reineking 2006). What Flanigan is suggesting is that we reserve any evaluative judgments until we have seen the entire day of teaching, which seems reasonable if not completely possible.

We've now introduced two modes of data collecting: descriptive and evaluative. Some observation scholars give us three main approaches or systems. First, category (descriptive, analytical) systems help us classify what we see in terms of prearranged categories of behavior using check-lists or rating scales. Category tools are useful if you have specific behaviors you want to see in the teaching—behaviors that can be observed easily. Some category systems are what Susan Stodolsky calls "low inference," meaning that it is easy to determine if you've seen it (e.g., "the instructor did/did not use the tech podium"). Low inference tools can be painfully complicated, like the Flanders Interaction Analysis System I mentioned earlier that asks the observer to code teacher/student behavior (e.g., 4a = "asking questions at analysis level"). If, however, we believe that teaching is more than the sum of its parts, then we will use high-inference category tools that require more judgment on what is observed. Second, with narrative systems, we simply write what we see, with no preset categories to hamper us (Flanigan's approach). The third system uses technology: we record teaching with audio or video equipment.

Generally, in order to collect teaching data the observer needs to have some kind of sheet. Ours has been revised recently (the old sheet had been used in observations for years). At the top of the old sheet you entered your name, the instructor's name, where and when the class was being held, the number of students in the class at the bell, and the gender breakdown of the students. There was also a box where you could make hash tallies for "comments by men" and "comments by women," mostly a low-inference activity. (If I need a new research project in the future, I could go through our teaching archives and tell you approximately what ratio of women make more comments in our FYC course than men, or vice versa.) A larger box for high-inference observations asked you to describe "classroom dynamics," and my comments usually read something like this (verbatim from an observation in 2008): "A big class. 50+ seats. Students spread out. Some older-looking students. One student came in and started talking loudly, animatedly, about his roommates. Not too much energy yet, but everyone's ready to work. [The instructor] is organized and ready to teach." Finally, the bottom half of the old sheet broke up the class period into ten boxes that required the observer to keep track of "use of class time." Sometimes this section was revelatory, as when an instructor would spend fifteen minutes on announcements. Other times, less so (":15 — working in groups, instructor circulates," ":25 — still working in groups, still circulating," ":40 — yep, still in groups"). This observation sheet seems to follow Flanigan's narrative model of the objective flow sheet. From the data gathered on the front, the observer filled out three big boxes on the back that asked for "particular strengths noted," "suggestions for improvement," and "other comments."

One reason we decided to abandon this model is that the form did not help us focus on what we valued as "macroteachers" trying to help students do very specific things. We spent the entire class period documenting anything and everything that happened, and we ended up using the "suggestions for improvement" box as a catchall for random bits of teaching wisdom related to what we had seen. (An example from the observation sheet I quoted earlier: "Think about adjusting the locus of gravity—the attention and emphasis—from your left to your right, or more center.") We also caught ourselves writing the same phrases repeatedly—we could have had stamps made to save us the time. ("Be sure to engage the students in some part of the writing task you have assigned them.") Our new observation sheets are modeled after John Centra's (1993) classroom observation worksheet, a category system, which lists desired instructor behaviors on the left and asks the observer to note whether those behaviors need "more emphasis" or were "accomplished very well" (209–210). Now the front of our observation sheet lists categories of teaching strategies (like effective communication, flexibility, content knowledge) we want to see in our instructors and lets us give them a sense of how they performed those strategies. (I have included the full observation sheet in Figure 4.1, and I have registered the sheet under Creative Commons so others can use it or change it to suit their programs.)

Teaching Observation for Writing Courses

Instructor:	***Date:***
Time and Location:	***Observer:***

5= exceptional 4 = effective 3 = competent 2 = emerging 1 = ineffective

	5	4	3	2	1
Lesson Plan: began class on time and with an attention-getting activity; expressed the purpose or objectives of the lesson; created a lesson plan sensitive to student needs; used effective organization (efficient, clear transitions and an effective conclusion that summarized the lesson and looked forward to future learning); used time wisely.	☐	☐	☐	☐	☐
Teaching Strategies: used classroom space and technology effectively; used a variety of teaching activities, including student writing and collaborative groups; used materials appropriate for the situation and writing task; enhanced instruction with examples, practice, and feedback; when appropriate, revised the lesson to reinforce learning.	☐	☐	☐	☐	☐
Content Knowledge: demonstrated command of the lesson's content by citing authorities, materials, disciplinary knowledge (in both rhetoric and writing studies), or experience to support the instruction.	☐	☐	☐	☐	☐
Effective Communication: used voice and body language effectively (e.g., eye contact) and explained concepts clearly; gave clear and timely instructions for student tasks.	☐	☐	☐	☐	☐
Discussion: asked engaging questions and waited for answers; listened to student comments and responded effectively with follow-up questions, clarifications, or encouragement; managed dissent effectively; responded to nonverbal cues like confusion, boredom, or curiosity.	☐	☐	☐	☐	☐
Relationship with Students: used humor or goodwill to strengthen interest; expressed concern for student learning and well being; maintained a professional but approachable ethos.	☐	☐	☐	☐	☐
Student Engagement: The students—each student—participated somehow in a significant learning experience; most students participated in class or group discussions by asking questions and making comments; students didn't just learn principles—they practiced them; students spoke as much as, or more than, the instructor.	☐	☐	☐	☐	☐
Student Writing: students spent a significant portion of the class writing, analyzing writing, or talking about writing tasks; students were engaged for the class period—taking notes, writing, speaking, and working together; student writing was an important part of the class.	☐	☐	☐	☐	☐
Relevance: presented material directly related to the writing tasks and used learning activities to achieve the outcomes of the course; media was used to prepare students for writing; when appropriate, explained how learning relates to other classes and students' personal lives.	☐	☐	☐	☐	☐
Assessment: routinely checked the students' learning by asking questions, assigning reflective writing, or inviting groups to report on their learning; circulated among groups; expressed understanding about concerns and student progress.	☐	☐	☐	☐	☐

Figure 4.1. (Available at goo.gl/mG8qGm)

On the back of our revised sheet we keep the traditional open-ended responses that include "what I thought you did well" and "what I think you could do to improve." We feel this model helps us provide rich, specific feedback on particular teaching skills we value ("projected a professional, approachable ethos"), while still letting us spout the random teacherly wisdom ("spit out the gum," or "perhaps all the Batman trivia

What I observed

What I thought you did well	What I think you could do to improve

Figure 4.1—continued

was excessive") and shower the necessary praise ("your students seem completely acclimated to writing as a class activity—nice work!").

As I wrote an earlier draft of this chapter, I started reflecting on our observation sheet, especially in light of the excellent online source, *Rating a Teacher Observation*, compiled by The New Teacher Project (2011), a nonprofit organization working to improve public school teaching in poverty-stricken areas of the United States. So much of our observation tool focused on the instructor's behavior (rapport with students, flexible teaching strategies) that we tended to leave the most important people out of the observation: the students. The New Teacher Project argues that the observation tool must "cover the classroom performance areas most connected to student outcomes" and "focus on students" (9, 17). Since it seemed obvious to me that we need to pay more attention to what students do in the class than to what teachers do, we added a few categories that consider what students do during class, like "Student Engagement" and "Student Writing," which you will see in Figure 4.1.

One more daunting thought on observation sheets from Arreola (2000): they should "undergo standard reliability and validity studies to ensure that the resulting data are valid and reliable" (76). In a less-strenuous mood, Nancy Chism (1999) argues that observers should actually be trained to observe (76). But, either one may be too much to ask of programs already stretching to observe every instructor at least once a year.

The third, final, and likely most important part of the observation—what Flanigan (2002) calls the "post-observation follow-up conference"—is also the most rewarding and most problematic. Above I argued that we should approach observation in the spirit of mutual collaboration as teacher-colleagues trying to improve student learning. That's an appropriate sentiment, but it may be that some of the instructors would choose not to be observed, if it were up to them. I'm the one passing judgment on whether or not what happened that day in class was "competent." Fellow teacher or not, I'm still The Boss. The moment we share what we observe is fraught, since we must balance our need to train and correct with the instructor's need for commendation, empathy, and an interpersonal professional relationship (Nyquist and Wulff 1996, 9). It is also the moment most likely to be misunderstood, as Anne Flanagan (1994) points out, since authoritative and collaborative discourses operate simultaneously, and usually uncomfortably, in the act of observing (77). Though there may be no way around this tension, we have followed what Flanagan suggests by having a "two-tiered" observation plan in which "teachers of equal rank" visit each other's classes as well (83).

I try to have my observation sheet completed by the end of the class period I'm observing. That way, I can meet with the instructor immediately afterward to discuss the day's teaching. Sometimes we walk back to the carrels and find an empty office to chat in, or if it's warm enough outside we find a bench or cement curb to sit on. I ask them how the teaching is going this semester and then I ask them what they thought went well and not so well that day. Sometimes our impressions coincide perfectly; other times it seems like we both experienced completely different teaching demonstrations. I try to set a collaborative tone by talking about my own challenges or failures as a teacher, or I offer suggestions based on my own classroom experience. After about fifteen minutes of informal, free-flowing conversation, I can see in their eyes that they want "the verdict"—they want me to thumbs-up or thumbs-down the day's teaching.

Usually, I feel I have advice for them that would help them be better teachers. I encourage them to call on students to share their writing more. I notice that activities often do not help students do what they need to do to complete their major writing tasks. Ever the rhetoric evangelist, I point out opportunities missed to connect principles of rhetoric and writing with the students' out-of-class lives. I let them know about distracting performative tics (like when instructors talk to PowerPoint slides more than students, or they say "yeah, yeah, yeah" after every comment) and class management details ("avoid the slow start by saving announcements for later or online"). I encourage them to snap out of the zombie-like stare they fall into when they assign group work ("circulate!"). As politely as I can, I suggest they avoid condescension and unnecessary contention with students and instead create an ethos that communicates utmost concern about the students' success. After I make two or three suggestions, I like to end with some encouragement for the future—I want the instructors to know that I was impressed, generally, with what I saw and that they have the power to improve in the future.

From my experience, I feel we could do a better job of helping our instructors understand that the observation process is more formative than summative. From time to time an instructor will resist feedback, which is an understandable response when we consider the authoritative/collaborative dilemma. This happened to me one winter semester when I observed a highly capable instructor who I thought missed an opportunity at the end of class to let students report and reflect on the activities of the day. When I mentioned this at the end of our post-observation conference, she took it as a direct challenge rather than mentorly advice. I welcomed the dialogue, but I parted ways with her feeling like I had set the wrong tone or said the wrong things. It's going to happen again.

I want to close, however, by pointing out that I learn just as much about our program's macrolevel teaching in observations as I do about the individual instructor. Sometimes when I'm in the back of the class watching a first-year graduate instructor teach a FYC course to first-year college students, I get a visceral sense of just how hard it is to write the stuff we compel students to write, how hard it is to understand an abstract principle like rhetoric and magically apply it, for example, to an opinion editorial on carbon footprints. The best, most experienced teachers understand, from years of experimenting, the cognitive dissonance students feel when we bring in a commercial for men's body wash as a stepping stone to writing six pages of double-spaced prose on an Amy Tan essay. In my observations, I have begun to see how students can have a *notional* understanding of a principle like a logical fallacy without the *procedural* knowledge of how to *write about* the fallacies they see in artifacts. I can see how they "get" a punctuation principle that they will violate consistently in their own writing. I watch as students absorb mini-lectures on how and why to narrow a research topic, and then I cringe thinking about how the next week they'll be up at 1 a.m. clicking on the first links that come up on Google searches for "body image" or "*affects* of violent video games." Most inexperienced instructors spend too much time dispensing notional principles and not enough time practicing them. That is not necessarily the fault of the instructors, who may not move beyond teaching declarative knowledge without the help of experienced mentors who know how to teach practical or conditional knowledge. Teaching teachers—especially ones who are passing through our programs on the way to careers both in and out of the academy—is just as hard as teaching, and I need to be better at it. When I watch other people teach, I learn more about this challenge.

In the end, I am humbled by the responsibility to visit someone else's class, to intrude, it would seem, on the intellectual work of an anxious, young colleague who may never teach the course again once he or she graduates with a master's in English. They have made themselves vulnerable in an act of good will, with the hope that I can help them develop what John Dewey (1972) called "trained capacities of control" as student-teachers of rhetoric and composition. As a writing teacher myself, observation offers me moments of renewal: a new class, a new instructor, a new approach to an old pedagogical need. I'm delighted at how much I learn from watching other instructors give it their best shot, and I look forward to those moments afterward when we talk about how we can make it all better.

References

Ambady, Nalini, and Robert Rosenthal. 1993. "Half a Minute: Predicting Teacher Evaluations from Thin Slices of Nonverbal Behavior and Physical Attractiveness." *Journal of Personality and Social Psychology* 64 (3): 431–41. http://dx.doi.org/10.1037 /0022-3514.64.3.431.

Arreola, Raoul A. 2000. *Developing a Comprehensive Faculty Evaluation System*, 2nd ed. Bolton, MA: Anker.

Centra, John A. 1993. *Reflective Faculty Evaluation*. San Francisco: Jossey-Bass.

Chism, Nancy Van Note. 1999. *Peer Review of Teaching: A Sourcebook*. Bolton, MA: Anker.

Darling-Hammond, Linda. 2010. *The Flat World and Education: How America's Commitment to Equity Will Determine Our Future*. New York: Teachers College Press.

Dean, Deborah. 2010. *What Works in Writing Instruction*. Urbana, IL: NCTE.

Delpit, Lisa. 2006. *Other People's Children*. New York: The New Press.

Dewey, John. 1972. *The Early Works, 1882–1898*, Vol. 5. Ed. Jo Ann Boydston. Carbondale: Southern Illinois University Press.

Ellett, Chad D. 1997. "Classroom-Based Assessments of Teaching and Learning." In *Evaluating Teaching: A Guide to Current Thinking and Best Practices*, ed. James H. Stronge, 107–28. Thousand Oaks, CA: Corwin.

Flanigan, Michael C. 2002. "From Discomfort, Isolation, and Fear to Comfort, Community, and Confidence." In *Preparing College Teachers of Writing: Histories, Theories, Programs, Practices*, ed. Betty P. Pytlik and Sarah Liggett, 242–53. New York: Oxford University Press.

Flanagan, Anne Marie. 1994. "The Observer Observed: Retelling Tales in and out of School." In *Evaluating Teachers of Writing*, ed. Christine A. Hult, 73–86. Urbana, IL: NCTE.

Gebhardt, Richard. 2002. "Administration as Focus for Understanding the Teaching of Writing." In *The Allyn & Bacon Sourcebook for Writing Program Administrators*, ed. Irene Ward and William J. Carpenter, 34–37. New York: Longman.

Gladwell, Malcolm. 2007. *Blink*. Boston: Back Bay.

Graham, Steve, and Dolores Perin. 2007. *Writing Next*. New York: Carnegie Corporation.

Griffith, Francis. 1973. *A Handbook for the Observation of Teaching and Learning*. Midland, MI: Pendell.

Jones, Jesse. 1994. "Evaluating College Teaching: An Overview." In *Evaluating Teachers of Writing*, ed. Christine A. Hult, 30–45. Urbana, IL: NCTE.

Millis, Barbara J., and Barbara B. Kaplan. 1995. "Enhancing Teaching through Peer Classroom Observations." In *Improving College Teaching*, ed. Peter Seldin, 137–51. Bolton, MA: Anker.

Minter, Deborah. 2002. "Peer Observation as Collaborative Classroom Inquiry." In *Composition Pedagogy and the Scholarship of Teaching*, ed. Deborah Minter and Amy M. Goodburn, 54–64. Portsmouth, NH: Boynton/Cook.

The New Teacher Project. 2011. *Rating a Teacher Observation Tool*. http://tntp.org/assets /documents/TNTP_RatingATeacherObservationTool_Feb2011.pdf.

Nyquist, Jody D., and Donald H. Wulff. 1996. *Working Effectively with Graduate Assistants*. Thousand Oaks, CA: Sage.

Scriven, Michael. 1967. *The Methodology of Evaluation: Perspectives of Curriculum Evaluation*. Ed. Ralph W. Tyler, Robert M. Gagne, and Michael Scriven, 39–83. Chicago: Rand McNally.

Shulman, Lee. 1993. "Teaching as Community Property: Putting an End to Pedagogical Solitude." *Change* 25 (6): 6–7. http://dx.doi.org/10.1080/00091383.1993.9938465.

Ward, Irene, and Merry Perry. 2002. "A Selection of Strategies for Training Teaching Assistants." In *The Allyn & Bacon Sourcebook for Writing Program Administrators*, ed. Irene Ward and William J. Carpenter, 117–38. New York: Longman.

Wiedmann, Amy, and Justin Reineking. 2006. "In the Blink of an Eye: Estimates of Teacher Effectiveness from a 24-second Thin Slice of Behavior." *Journal of Undergraduate Research* 9: 1–4.

Wilhoit, Stephen. 2002. "Recent Trends in TA Instruction: A Bibliographic Essay." In *Preparing College Teachers of Writing: Histories, Theories, Programs, Practices*, ed. Betty P. Pytlik and Sarah Liggett, 17–27. New York: Oxford University Press.

Wilkerson, LuAnn, and Karron G. Lewis. 2002. "Classroom Observation: The Observer as Collaborator." In *A Guide to Faculty Development*, ed. Kay Herr Gillespie, 74–81. Bolton, MA: Anker.

Willerman, Marvin, Sharon L. McNeely, and Elaine Cooper Koffman. 1991. *Teachers Helping Teachers: Peer Observation and Assistance*. New York: Praeger.

5
SMALL GROUP INSTRUCTIONAL DIAGNOSIS
Formative, Mid-Term Evaluations of Composition Courses and Instructors[1]

Gerald Nelms

As someone who has worked both as an instructional consultant in a university teaching and learning center and as a university writing program administrator (both a first-year WPA and Communication Across the Curriculum [CAC] director), I've been struck by the irony of how little WPAs and instructional consultants share their expertise with each other, despite the fact that both maintain an abiding concern for student learning. Few instructional consultants seem to attend the Conference on College Composition and Communication (CCCC) or regularly read composition books and journals, and few WPAs seem to know that there exists a growing literature on instructional consultation and a Professional and Organizational Development (POD) Network in Higher Education (2007–2015) with an extensive website, an annual conference, and an annual journal (*To Improve the Academy*). I find this disciplinary gap disturbing, since both communities could learn much from each other. An interesting and, I believe, particularly useful example of what my fellow compositionists can learn from instructional consultants is the "small group instructional diagnostic" (SGID). The SGID is a method of gathering evaluative data about a course and its instructor from students, usually conducted around the middle of the semester. The SGID's inherently formative function and the rich data it generates make for a powerful evaluative tool.

As best as I can tell, Darsie Bowden's *WPA* article "Small Group Instructional Diagnosis: A Method for Enhancing Writing Instruction" is the only discussion of SGIDs that has ever appeared in a composition journal. Bowden's emphasis, however, is less on SGIDs' assessment value and more

DOI: 10.7330/9780874219661.c005

on using SGIDs "to foster . . . communication between students and teachers" and "to promote collegiality" (Bowden 2004, 117). These pedagogical
goals, however, are dependent on the successful use of SGIDs as formative evaluation. Moreover, emphasizing only these pedagogical goals can
diminish SGIDs' evaluative validity and, in turn, threaten these ancillary
pedagogical benefits. That said, many instructional consultants would
agree that "a SGID program (or something similar) may be the best way
to help the instructor teach and students learn" (Bowden 2004, 130). The
data generated by a mid-term SGID can help instructors improve their
teaching and can lead to important improvements in the course. Even
instructors using a common syllabus, who have no control over the organization of the course, can pass along student feedback to their WPAs.
These kinds of improvements based on formative feedback can dramatically improve scores on summative assessments.

THE VALIDITY OF STUDENT FEEDBACK

In chapter 3 of this collection, Amy Dayton provides an extended discussion of the validity of student evaluations of instruction (SEIs). Her
review of the extensive scholarship on student evaluations suggests that—
although many faculty members across the disciplines may still question
the validity of SEIs—research on SEIs has shown students to be a reliable
source of information about their courses, the teaching of those courses,
and their own learning in those courses. As Peter Seldin points out, students are, after all, "[t]he only direct, daily observers" who can speak
most authoritatively about the effects of their courses and instructors on
their own learning (Seldin 1997, 336). In his review of the literature on
student ratings, Michael Theall finds that research has shown students
to be qualified to report on "the frequencies of teacher behaviors, the
amount of work required, how much they feel they have learned, and the
difficulty of the material," along with the quality and value of lectures,
assignments, and instructor availability and assistance (Theall 2002, 2).
And while most research on student evaluations focuses on end-of-term
student ratings, we can easily see that the findings of Dayton's research
are relevant to understanding the evaluative power of SGIDs.

FEATURES AND COMPONENTS OF SGIDS

Structurally, SGIDs are defined by their use of both small group discussions and a whole-class, focus group interview. I will explore the overall
SGID process in more detail below, but for now, here is how the typical

SGID class interview works: The instructor leaves the classroom, and a "facilitator" introduces the SGID process and has students form small groups (ranging from three to eight students, depending on who is describing the SGID) (Bowden 2004, 119; Creed 1997, 4; M. R. Diamond 2004, 220; N. A. Diamond 2002, 85; Smuts 2005, 944; White 2010, 5). These small groups answer several evaluative questions, seeking consensus at some level even though the phrasing of the questions and the reported extent of disagreement vary among SGID researchers (Bowden 2004, 128, 133; Creed 1997; N. A. Diamond 2002, 84, 86; Smuts 2005, 945; White 2010). Typically, the questions ask students to identify the strengths and weaknesses of the course and its teaching and to make recommendations for changes. Each group chooses a recorder to write down the group's answers, and, after about ten minutes of small group discussion, the students come back together as a whole class for a fifteen-minute plenary discussion of their answers. Each group reports its answers, sometimes one answer at a time, in round-robin fashion. The facilitator often asks for a show of hands for each comment in order to estimate the amount of agreement or disagreement. Usually, SGID class interviews are limited to around thirty minutes total. Students are less likely to remain productively engaged after that amount of time, and instructors are less receptive to giving up more than thirty minutes of their class period. Also, it isn't clear whether the extra time actually generates much new information.

While the class interview structure is the SGID's most obvious feature, for a SGID to actually be effective, it must also adhere to certain requirements and include certain other features, which are listed below.

Anonymity

Students may not be as forthcoming or honest in their comments if they are not assured they cannot be personally identified, and the only way to assure student anonymity is to have someone besides the instructor (a "facilitator") conduct the SGID. The validity of any group of student evaluations must be considered suspect if the person responsible for grading student work is the same person collecting student evaluations. No matter how much instructors insist that they are unaffected by student comments, most students will not believe them.

Confidentiality

In the experience of UCAT (University Center for the Advancement of Teaching) instructional consultants and consultants at other institutions

(Siering, Pavlechko, and Jacobi-Karna 2010), students typically do not want to get their instructors in trouble, even when they do have complaints. Thus, SGID validity also requires the assurance that student comments will be shared only with the instructor. Some faculty members will report their SGID results to their departments and colleges on their own, but that must be the instructor's decision, not the facilitator's. Moreover, reporting SGID findings to others, such as having those findings placed in an instructor's file, typically functions summatively. Formative evaluation provides data upon which to base considerations of pedagogical changes, not personnel decisions (N. A. Diamond 2002, 84; Bowden 2004, 129). WPAs should avoid having SGID findings related to the instructor's teaching reported to anyone but the instructor, thus ensuring SGIDs remain formative.

Mid-Term Timing of SGIDs

Scheduling a SGID toward the end of a term tends to undermine its formative function. At mid-term, students have had enough time in the course to make competent judgments, but there is still enough time for workable changes to be made to improve the course. Of course, a SGID can be conducted at any time during a term and remain formative, but if done late in the term the changes would only come for future classes—and students will realize that.

Of course, WPAs increasingly face pressure to produce summative assessments, but we need to realize that formative evaluations are not intended to replace summative assessments. Research has shown that mid-term formative evaluations can improve end-of-term summative ratings (M. R. Diamond 2004, 219).

Voluntariness

Naturally, instructors are wary of any evaluation of their teaching, even when the evaluation is formative and kept confidential. As Seldin notes, "Because teaching demands a monumental investment of self, it predisposes professors to sensitivity toward criticism" (Seldin 1997, 342). Defensiveness and defiance suppress any willingness on the part of the instructor to make changes and can undermine the defining formative function of the SGID. Thus, it's best that SGIDs remain voluntary. Some research suggests that *requiring* SGIDs can compromise their effectiveness (Morrison 1995, 5, 11, 362; Penny and Coe 2004, 220–21). WPAs might strongly encourage their staff to schedule

SGIDs, but might only require SGIDs of more experienced instructors. Emphasizing their formative nature is also important.

Consultation

Although SGIDs can be represented as simply a method of evaluation, they invariably implicate the instructor and facilitator in a teaching consultation. No evaluation, of course, is ever context-free, but it's easy for summative evaluations to ignore context. Not so for formative evaluations. Formative evaluations always result in the possibility for change, and the recommendations for change that emerge from a formative evaluation must be analyzed and interpreted within the context of the course learning objectives, pedagogical decisions, and other factors. Thus, the central SGID operation, the class interview, must be framed structurally and immersed in an overarching consultation process that includes initial contact, an instructor–consultant conference, data collection, and a meeting to analyze and review the data and to plan corresponding changes.

THE ROLE OF THE SGID FACILITATOR
AND THE PURPOSE OF SGIDS

The consultative components inherent in SGIDs raise several issues, the most important being the role of the facilitator. The primary concern in selecting SGID facilitators has to be ensuring the validity of the SGID data and findings, and that requires facilitators to take on the role of impartial researchers as much as possible, a role that does not come naturally. While we might think that we can conveniently pair up writing program instructors to facilitate SGIDs for each other, or that we can assign experienced peers to facilitate SGIDs for novice instructors, both of these options can be problematic.

In various consultation situations, consultants will adopt different roles, such as that of expert authority, collaborator, or challenger (Brinko 1997, 5–6). In order to ensure that SGIDs remain focused on formative evaluation, however, SGID facilitators are advised to adopt a researcher role, as described by Nyquist and Wulff (2001). This researcher role imposes significant limitations on SGID facilitators. As a researcher, the SGID facilitator does not presume to have any decision-making authority over the course and the teaching of that course. Even when the instructor–consultant relationship is viewed as a "partnership," Kathleen Brinko notes, that partnership does not extend to any shared authority for decisions about the course or the instructor's teaching (Brinko 1997, 6). She concludes that "the client retains authority and responsibility for the process and its results" (Brinko 1997, 6).

While the researcher role does, in some ways, fit into what Brinko calls the *collaborative* consultation model, that model seems to allow for a greater empathetic connection between facilitator and instructor than the researcher role allows (Fink and Bauer 2001, 21; Lewis 2002, 68). Such empathy for the instructor will need to be deferred during the course of collecting, reporting, analyzing, and interpreting SGID data. SGID facilitators must make every effort to bracket their biases as much as possible and adopt an ethos of objectivity, even if they believe they know what changes ought to be made to improve the class. SGID facilitators must always keep in mind that they do not participate regularly in the courses under evaluation, and they cannot presume to understand enough about the contexts behind the SGIDs they conduct to make any authoritative decisions about those courses. As Nyquist and Wulff conclude, "What the instructor decides to do as a result of studying [SGID] data is her/his decision to make," not the facilitator's (Nyquist and Wulff 2001, 50). Adopting the researcher role "precludes our feeling that we must have answers about what the instructor must do" (46).

More importantly, adopting the researcher role ensures that the SGID facilitator adheres to a common precept in instructional consultation: for the instructor to fully commit to making changes to her or his teaching, "the ownership of the consultation process must be with the client, not with the consultant" (Lewis 2002, 64). Any decisions about changes must arise from an instructor's genuinely held commitment to those changes. SGID facilitators, then, must restrain themselves from offering too much expert advice and instead ask probing questions that invite the instructor to reflect on the possibilities for change and come to decisions on their own.

This emphasis on adopting the role of impartial researcher reveals the potential problems that might arise when employing peers as SGID facilitators. Bowden argues that "peer instructors, especially those who are experienced, know the writing program, the students, and a good bit about teaching writing" (Bowden 2004, 128); however, while these qualities might seem like advantages, they can in fact compromise the validity of SGID findings because of the influence of possible peer-facilitator biases. As Bridget Smuts points out, there is always a danger of "alternate agendas" skewing the data (Smuts 2005, 952). Bowden herself hints at this possibility when she mentions that, at Western Washington University, "the anxiety about the demands of teaching and the rigors of graduate school" led graduate teaching assistants into both "strong friendships" and "competition" (Bowden 2004, 125), both of which could easily create bias in peer-facilitated SGIDs. More subtly, peers might impose on a SGID their own pedagogical and theoretical commitments. Students will sense such an imposition, thus effectively undermining their trust in and their commitment to the evaluation. Yet, these instructor commitments can be strong, and can make adopting a researcher role that much more difficult.

As a research process leading to evaluations and possible changes, SGIDs clearly impose significant constraints on the roles that a SGID facilitator can adopt—constraints that test even the seasoned instructional consultant. But what if we're more interested in the *instructional* function of SGIDs and less in their *evaluative* function? Bowden, for example, stresses the improvements SGIDs can inspire in both student–instructor communication and writing program staff collegiality (Bowden 2004, 117). And Miriam Diamond's research supports the argument that SGIDs can improve "two-way communication with learners" (M. R. Diamond 2004, 226). However, while these are certainly worthwhile goals for a writing program, they are not the primary goals of SGIDs, and, in fact, these goals do not require SGIDs at all. Placing instructional goals above evaluation when employing SGIDs changes the role of peer facilitator in ways that can jeopardize both formative evaluation *and* pedagogy. For example, Bowden emphasizes how the peer-facilitated SGIDs used in her program at DePaul University provided "the opportunity to exchange ideas with other instructors on writing and teaching materials and methods, ideas that often went well beyond the specific SGID concerns" (Bowden 2004, 123). As beneficial as such exchanges might be, they also clearly shift SGID facilitators out of the researcher role. Moreover, the ideas exchanged may have little or no relevance to the immediate course at hand and may not address issues relevant to the students' comments and recommendations. Yet, the reason that SGIDs improve student–instructor communication lies in the students' belief "that their voices have been heard" (Creed 1997; see also M. R. Diamond 2004, 224, and White 2010). If their concerns and recommendations are ignored, students' trust in the process will be lost and the instructor–student rapport can be irreversibly harmed.

FINDING AND TRAINING SGID FACILITATORS

Given that SGIDs involve consultation as well as data collection and that SGID facilitators need to adopt the role of an objective researcher, those selected to facilitate SGIDs will obviously need training beyond simply how to conduct classroom interviews—they must have training that includes a basic knowledge of consultation (Bowden 2004, 118; Smuts 2005, 952; White 2010). SGID facilitators should be trained in how to ask open, probing questions; how to set aside their biases and restrain themselves from imposing their own conclusions during the SGID process; how to be patient and let instructors come to their own decisions; and how to offer options without being directive.

At this point, one might wonder whether SGIDs are too time-consuming for writing programs, especially given the need to include what appears to be extensive facilitator training. It's important to note that the hard work of establishing a SGID's initiative (identifying and training facilitators) will be done up front, and the potential improvements to the course and student learning make that early effort worth the work. As Bowden points out, in addition to providing significant evaluative data, SGIDs can dramatically improve instructor–student communication.

It's also important to note that, while peer-facilitators can compromise the validity of SGID findings—as suggested above—there are other sources for prospective SGID facilitators. WPA assistants, graduate assistants, and/or other adjunct staff can receive reduced teaching loads in exchange for facilitating SGIDs. WPAs might also work out an exchange program with other departments. Their staff can conduct SGIDs for the writing program while writing program staff conducts SGIDs for them. Another population worth culling for SGID facilitators is the full-time faculty across disciplines who have expressed an interest in the writing program. One caveat, however: faculty employed as SGID facilitators, in addition to the required training, will also need to genuinely accept the idea that student feedback can be reliable and valid data for evaluation. Finally—and perhaps most importantly—WPAs should be able to rely on their own campus instructional consultants, if their institutions have them.

Instructional consultants frequently work out of teaching and learning centers that go by names like "The Center for Teaching Excellence" or "for Faculty Development," "The Office of Instructional Consultation," "Teaching and Learning Services," and "The Teaching Effectiveness Program." Some centers/offices/programs employ multiple consultants and graduate assistants. Others may have a few or even only one such person on staff, and the staff might only be part-time. Still, no matter how large or small these centers are, those staffing them should be familiar with the literature on teaching consultation and the process for conducting SGIDs.

Some WPAs may worry about employing SGID facilitators who are not trained in writing instruction. Counterintuitive as it might seem, however, instructional consultation does not require disciplinary expertise or even much discipline-specific knowledge at all in order to effectively counsel faculty members in teaching and learning. Some instructional consultants even believe that not having subject matter knowledge actually enhances effective consultation by easing the adoption of the researcher role and reducing preconceived ideas that can undermine SGID validity.

Instructional consultants are also an excellent resource for facilitator training, such that WPAs need not become experts on SGIDs themselves. In cases where institutions do not have instructional consultants, WPAs may find individuals on campus who do such consultation work. WPAs also might look to other institutions for instructional consultants who can help with training. An excellent resource is the website of the POD Network (http://podnetwork.org), which includes links to various teaching and learning centers on its Educational and Faculty Development Websites and Programs page (http://www.dal.ca/dept/clt.html), a "site search engine" for searching faculty development websites, and a link to the POD listserv, whose members welcome questions about instructional consultation.

THE SGID PROCESS

The SGID process resembles an amalgam of four "phases of interaction" in instructional consultation, identified by Brinko (1997), and the researcher consultation process, described by Nyquist and Wulff (2001, 48–50), which involves identification of a problem, issue, or question; data collection, analysis, and interpretation; and translation of data into strategies for change. The SGID process, then, involves five stages: (1) a "pre-SGID" (i.e., pre-class interview); (2) the class interview itself (often referred to as "the SGID"); (3) the preparation of the facilitator's report; and (4) a "post-SGID" or follow-up consultation between the instructor and the facilitator that leads to (5) the post-SGID instructor–student discussion about the findings and consequences (Bowden 2004, 118–20; Creed 1997; Diamond 2002; Smuts 2005, 944–45; White 2010). Inherent in the SGID process and its requirements are the contractual relationships between all three SGID participants (the instructor, the students, and the facilitator):

- The *instructor* agrees to value student comments as honest and responsibly given and to consider student recommendations for changes to the course and the teaching of the course. In fact, students will expect changes because of the SGID, or should at least be given reasonable explanations for why their recommendations are not being acted upon (N. A. Diamond 2002, 88). In exchange, *students* agree to be forthright and honest with the instructor about their evaluations of the course and its teaching.

- The *instructor* agrees to provide the facilitator with an honest account of his or her perceptions of the course, his or her teaching methods, and the students in the class, as well as to abide by the requirements of the SGID. The *facilitator*, in turn, agrees to keep the SGID and its findings confidential and to make every effort to remain objective, professional, and impartial in the role of researcher during the SGID process. Both the instructor and the facilitator agree to constructively collaborate in analyzing and interpreting the data and translating it into strategies for change.

- The *facilitator* agrees to keep students' comments anonymous and to impartially collect this data from students. *Students*, meanwhile, agree to be honest and open with the facilitator about their views of the course and the instructor.

Facilitators must understand that if any of these contracts are violated, the validity of the SGID is brought into question.

The Pre-SGID Conversation

The facilitator needs basic information about the class (when and where it meets, its size, and its subject matter) and a date and time for the SGID interview. Typically, SGIDs are scheduled for the first or last half-hour of a class meeting, and after students have completed a major, graded assignment. First-year composition courses often begin with personal experience essay assignments, only to follow up with more academically challenging writing assignments. SGIDs should always be scheduled after a writing assignment that is representative of the difficulty and genre of writing that students can expect throughout the remainder of the course. SGIDs also should not be scheduled on test days or other days when students may have difficulty shifting their attention to course evaluation. In addition, the instructor and the facilitator should schedule a day and time to meet after the SGID class interview to discuss the findings.

Another reason for the "pre-SGID" meeting is for the facilitator to "determine how the class interview process can best be used to provide useful feedback" (Bowden 2004, 119). To that end, Bowden provides a set of heuristic questions for the facilitator to ask the instructor (132):

(1) What are your goals for the class? What do you want students to do? To know? To learn? (2) What is the general atmosphere of the class? (3) How is time spent in a typical class? (4) How do you make sure that students understand what is going on? (5) Are there any questions you want me to ask the students? (That is, are there specific things that you want to learn from your students?) (6) What do you think your strengths are? The class' strengths? What would you want to change? What will your students like best about the class?

A crucial reason for gathering "pre-SGID" information about the class is the need to determine whether a SGID is actually appropriate. Classes where students have strong negative feelings toward their instructor or the course can turn a SGID into a mere gripe session that does not produce constructive evaluations and recommendations for change, and will almost certainly put an already vulnerable-feeling instructor on the defensive, a state of mind not receptive to modifications. And once a SGID class interview has begun, there is no going back. Aborting the process in progress violates the facilitator's contract with students to be impartial, and it sends the message to students that their comments are not going to be taken seriously, a violation of the instructor's contract with students. Facilitators, then, must be trained to recognize signals that a SGID is not appropriate. If the instructor's assignments do not fit the stated goals of the course, if the general atmosphere of the course seems negative, if the instructor's attitude toward teaching and/or student evaluations is negatively charged, and especially if students have already voiced significant complaints and/or the instructor expresses an unwillingness to seriously consider making any changes to the course based on student evaluations, then conducting a SGID should at least be delayed until the facilitator can conduct a classroom observation or two and further consult with the instructor.

The facilitator should go over what the instructor should say—and not say—to students about the SGID (Diamond 2002, 84–85). An instructor should explain that he or she wants students' feedback on the progress of the course in order to consider making improvements, and, with that in mind, he or she has arranged for an impartial facilitator to interview the class. The instructor should assure students that their recommendations will be seriously considered, but should NOT promise that the course will definitely change when it may not. The instructor also should NOT tell students the exact date of the SGID class interview—some students might decide to skip class that day.

The SGID Class Interview

The class interview should be limited to thirty minutes at most. After the instructor leaves the class, the facilitator should briefly introduce her- or himself, assure the students that their instructor is not in any trouble and that the evaluation is completely voluntary, and assure students that their comments will be reported only to the instructor and will be kept anonymous. Then, the facilitator should briefly preview the class interview process, ask the students to form small groups (specifying a group size), and ask each group to identify a recorder to write down their comments (Bowden 2004, 119; Diamond 2002, 85; Smuts 2005, 944; White 2010).

Once groups have formed, the facilitator should distribute a feedback form to each group that includes the SGID questions and space for answers. (The form used by The Ohio State University's UCAT can be found in appendix 1.) It is also wise to ask each group to write down the number of people in the group and to record next to each comment the number of group members who agree with that comment. These feedback sheets should be collected at the end of the SGID class interview.

The number of questions should be limited to two or three. One or two additional questions related to the course, such as a question about the effectiveness of the textbook, might be added if the instructor wishes. The questions should focus specifically on student learning rather than on evaluating what's good and bad or strong and weak. The focus of SGIDs should always be on improving student learning.

Smuts (2005) suggests a further question that, I admit, I'm ambivalent about: "What have you, as students, contributed to the success, or otherwise, of the course?" On one hand, this question does ask students to reflect on *their* responsibility for their own learning. On the other hand, I wonder how much the answers to that question would help an instructor in making changes to the course, though I don't feel the question threatens SGID data validity in any way. If a composition course includes other reflective assignments, and especially if it concludes with a student portfolio with a reflective essay, I might be disposed to include the question, but an important consideration in any decision about SGID formatting is the time limitation. Having students metacognitively reflect on their own responsibility for their learning may require considerably more time than a SGID normally allows. Also, this question is one that the instructor could ask when discussing the SGID findings with the class or in a longer reflective writing assignment.

Plenary sessions should be structured around the SGID questions. Facilitators, typically, will ask the recorder from each group to report one point that the group listed on its feedback form, and the reporting continues group by group, round-robin fashion, until all the points have been made. If time becomes a factor after several rounds, a facilitator may ask the whole class whether there are other significant points, including dissenting opinions, that need to be made. Usually, there will not be that many different points between the groups, and typically related points can be summarized into one point. When facilitators summarize student comments, they should always ask students to affirm that their summaries accurately represent the point(s) they want to make. Sometimes, too, points made by a group may need clarification or might be something the instructor has no control over (Smuts 2005, 945). In these cases, facilitators can ask for clarification or probe for a deeper understanding of the point, asking questions such as: "Do you mean X?" or "Does your instructor have the authority to do something about that?" It's important, however, that students not get the impression at any time that the facilitator is taking sides with the instructor.

An important issue for which there is no consensus in SGID literature is, ironically, how much consensus among students to require. Some consultants strongly emphasize consensus. The original rationale for seeking consensus was to help instructors distinguish between the issues that really need addressing and those that are less important to most of the class, and Nancy Diamond points out that "conflicting remarks" from students can diminish their value with some instructors (Diamond 2002, 86). On the other hand, as White (2010) argues, "Often, students see the course and instructor from very different perspectives." From a researcher standpoint, the facilitator should not presume to begin interpreting the data by selecting what is or is not important. The facilitator, then, should take down all relevant comments to ensure the facilitator–student contract is not breached. That said, it is also a good idea to ask for votes on agreement with each comment via a quick show of hands as a way of generating even richer data. After all, dissenting comments from one group might be mirrored in other groups, forming a significant minority that reveals meaningful disagreement among the students. That disagreement itself might be important information for the instructor.

The SGID Report

Scholars differ somewhat on the function of the report of the SGID class interview. Generally, the report is intended to simply provide class interview data to the instructor in an organized way—it is NOT intended to be *the* interpretation of the data. Making recommendations prior to actually reviewing the data with the instructor presumes more knowledge of the course and its teaching than the facilitator may have. The facilitator, in fact, walks a fine line at this point in the process. It would seem responsible to err on the side of caution.

UCAT SGID reports follow Nancy Diamond's suggestion to organize and locate student comments under the three SGID questions and indicate the amount of agreement regarding each comment within the group (Diamond 2002, 87). Thus, UCAT facilitators continue to adopt the role of impartial researcher even at this stage in the process. UCAT reports also distinguish between comments from the various small groups and comments made in the plenary session. The report lists the instructor's name, position, and department; the course number and name; the date of the SGID class interview; the number of participating students; and the name of the consultant/facilitator, followed by a brief description of the SGID class interview process used. Then, each question is listed with a summary of the comments made during the plenary session discussion, followed by the comments for each of the small groups, exactly as written on the feedback forms. Each group is assigned an arbitrary number. This transcription of student comments into digital form ensures anonymity. No effort is made to interpret the data at all.

That said, some categorizing of comments can be helpful. Sara Jane Coffman (1998) identified seven categories of student comments from her study of SGIDs across six different disciplines at Purdue University: (1) testing and grading (including comments on help sessions and fairness); (2) course procedures; (3) instructor characteristics (including comments on professionalism, helpfulness, availability, warmth, and enthusiasm); (4) instructor's teaching techniques; (5) activities and interaction (including comments on how active classes are and what's done in class); (6) course content; and (7) written assignments and readings (including comments on prompts, number of assignments, etc.). Employing these categories as a formula for classifying all SGID student comments is probably too reductive—they have not been thoroughly tested as an analytical or heuristic tool. Still, they do provide a way to *begin* classifying and summarizing comments. If some comments don't easily fit in one or more of the categories, however, then obviously new categories should be identified.

The Post-SGID Consultation

The post-SGID meeting between the instructor and the facilitator involves a brief review of the process by which the data was gathered; an analysis and interpretation of that data by the instructor in collaboration with the facilitator; a discussion of what changes to the course and its teaching the instructor should make (and is willing or not to make and why); and finally, the development of a plan for the instructor–student discussion of the SGID findings (Bowden 2004, 120; Creed 1997, 8; Diamond 2002, 87; Smuts 2005, 945; White 2010, 15–16).

UCAT instructional consultants go over the student comments orally, focusing primarily on those made during the plenary session, leaving the written comments of the small groups to be read by the instructor later. Also, the facilitator withholds the written report from the instructor until the very end of the post-SGID consultation. That way, the instructor's attention is not divided between hearing what's being said and reading what's in the report.

Again, the role of the facilitator here is unsettled among instructional consultants. UCAT consultants generally adopt the role of impartial researcher all the way through the review of student comments, restraining any urge to interpret the data and letting the instructor interpret instead. As Nancy Diamond writes, "Instructors can shed light on comments you, as the interviewer, might not have fully understood" (Diamond 2002, 87). With that in mind, too, UCAT consultants reject the idea that some comments should be emphasized over others, or that some can be ignored (Diamond 2002, 88). And, even after the data has been reviewed, the interpretation of that data remains a collaboration between the instructor and facilitator, with the final authority for any decisions about the course and its teaching lying with the instructor. Even when offering interpretations requested by the instructor, UCAT consultants typically frame them as hypothetical: "In other courses, this point has meant X. Do you think it could mean that in your class?" "When students say this, it's been my experience that they mean X, but you tell me, could that be the case here?"

UCAT facilitators only tend to adopt other consultant roles when the conversation turns to the changes the instructor is willing to make. Typically, at this point, facilitators move from the researcher role into a collaborative consultation. Some instructors will be ready and willing to make changes, while others may need more time to digest and consider the comments. The facilitator should reaffirm that the students will be expecting the instructor to seriously consider their comments and recommendations. The instructor is not obliged to make any changes, of course, but he or she *is* obliged to have good reasons for not making recommended changes and to explain those reasons to his or her students. The facilitator may need to ask the instructor to articulate those reasons. Rarely, the facilitator may need to adopt the confrontational model of consultation if the instructor appears unwilling to accept the validity of the student comments. Nancy Diamond notes that "another goal for the [post-SGID consultation] is that the instructor realize that student comments are true from the students' viewpoints and that they have to be evaluated from the instructor's perspective as well" (Diamond 2002, 88). Both viewpoints have value, even if they sometimes seem at odds. Diamond offers a set of questions for the instructor to reflect on as a way of moving toward such an understanding (88). Below are my reworkings of Diamond's questions:

- With regard to each comment or recommendation, is it valid? Is there a legitimate reason why students might believe this?
- Is it within my control to make a change that addresses this comment, if I am willing to make the change?
- Are there good reasons for making a change to address this issue or concern?
- Am I willing to make that change? If not, what good reasons do I have for not making that change?

Introducing these questions with regard to each suggested change will push the instructor to genuinely consider the student comments. And answering these questions can be framed as "a collaborative venture [between instructor and facilitator] in problem-solving" (White 2010).

The Post-SGID Instructor–Students Discussion

The SGID report needs to be written within a day of the SGID class interview, and the post-SGID consultation should be held soon after the completion of that report, usually anywhere from one to three days afterward, so that the students will not be kept waiting too long to hear the instructor's response to their feedback. At the end of the post-SGID consultation, the instructor and the facilitator should discuss a plan for how the instructor will talk to the students about the SGID findings. As Nancy Diamond notes, "The SGID process raises students' expectations that changes for the better will occur" (Diamond 2002, 88).

Nancy Diamond suggests several tips for instructors when they discuss SGID findings with their classes, to which I add several more. First, the instructor should genuinely thank students for providing feedback to help improve the course, and the instructor needs to assure students that he or she has seriously considered that feedback. Then the instructor should acknowledge some of the positive comments. It's important to recognize that these positive comments actually represent recommendations for things about the course that students don't want changed. They are as genuine as any criticisms the students might make. The instructor should then individually address the suggestions for change and state whether or not these suggestions are going to lead to change—for those changes he or she is unwilling to make, explanations should be given. Sometimes, the criticisms of the course may lead the instructor to changes that differ from the ones the students recommended. These also need to be discussed. Sometimes, too, students may not have been entirely clear about exactly what they recommend. In those cases, the instructor should ask for clarification. Instructors should be counseled to avoid rushing the post-SGID discussion with their students. Again, much good comes from letting students know that their opinions about their learning are genuinely valued. Also, this metacognitive discussion can reveal further gaps in students' learning.

CONCLUSION

As Smuts (2005) points out, SGIDs are not an easy method of course and teacher evaluation. They can be time-consuming, and they require trained facilitators (952). On the other hand, the benefits that can be derived from SGIDs are well worth the time and effort. The primary benefits ensue from the inherently formative nature of SGIDs. SGIDs provide evaluative data that both instructors and students can feel confident are valid, and from which instructors can make significant improvements to the current course (Creed 1997; White 2010). This confidence on the part of students that their voices are being heard and that they can actually influence their own learning will facilitate instructor–student communication, (Bowden 2004, 123; Diamond 2004, 226) and, as Smuts points out, can create "a platform" for further discussions about the course, the teaching of the course, and students' responsibility for their own learning (Smuts 2005, 945). Students come to value the care and effort that instructors put into their teaching, and instructors come to realize that students really do want to learn. In sum, small group instructional diagnoses promote an understanding that education is built not on conflict between teacher and student but on collaboration.

APPENDIX

Sample Small Group Student Feedback Form
(The University Center for the Advancement of Teaching,
The Ohio State University)

Student Group Feedback

Number of people in your group: _____
Indicate how many in your group agrees with each comment you record under each question.

What are the strengths of the course and instructor that assist you in learning?

What things are making it more difficult for you to learn?

What specific changes would you recommend to the instructor that would assist you in learning?

Thank you for your comments.

Note

1. For their instruction in conducting SGIDs, I want to acknowledge the other instructional consultants who staffed the University Center for the Advancement of Teaching (UCAT) at The Ohio State University during my tenure there: Kathryn Plank, Teresa Johnson, Laurie Maynell, Stephanie Rohdieck, UCAT director Alan Kalish, and then graduate student intern Spencer Robinson. I also want to thank Spencer Robinson and then graduate administrative associates Lindsay Bernhagen, Glené Mynhardt, and Sharon Ross for their valuable feedback on an early draft of this chapter.

References

Bowden, Darsie. 2004. "Small Group Instructional Diagnosis: A Method for Enhancing Writing Instruction." *WPA: Writing Program Administration* 28 (1/2): 115–35.

Brinko, Kathleen T. 1997. "The Interactions of Teaching Improvement." In *Practically Speaking: A Sourcebook for Instructional Consultants in Higher Education*, ed. Kathleen T. Brinko and Robert J. Menges, 3–8. Stillwater, OK: New Forums Press.

Coffman, Sara Jane. 1998. "Small Group Instructional Evaluation across the Disciplines." *College Teaching* 46 (3): 106–11. http://dx.doi.org/10.1080/87567559809596250.

Creed, Tom. 1997. "Small Group Instructional Diagnosis (SGID)." *The National Teaching & Learning Forum* 6 (4).

Diamond, Miriam R. 2004. "The Usefulness of Structured Mid-Term Feedback as a Catalyst for Change in Higher Education Classes." *Active Learning in Higher Education* 5 (3): 217–31. http://dx.doi.org/10.1177/1469787404046845.

Diamond, Nancy A. 2002. "Small Group Instructional Diagnosis: Tapping Student Perceptions of Teaching." In *A Guide to Faculty Development: Practical Advice, Examples, and Resource*, ed. Kay Herr Gillespie, Linda R. Hilsen, and Emily C. Wadsworth, 82–91. Boston: Anker Press.

Fink, Dee, and Garbriele Bauer. 2001. "Getting Started in One-on-One Instructional Consulting: Suggestions for New Consultants." In *Face to Face: A Sourcebook of Individual Consultation Techniques for Faculty/Instructional Developers*, ed. Karron G. Lewis, and Joyce T. Povlacs Lunde, 21–43. Stillwater, OK: New Forums Press.

Lewis, Karron G. 2002. "The Process of Individual Consultation." In *A Guide to Faculty Development: Practical Advice, Examples, and Resources*, ed. Kay Herr Gillespie, Linda R. Hilsen, and Emily C. Wadsworth, 59–73. Boston: Anker Press.

Morrison, Diane. 1995. "Opening Doors to Better Teaching: The Role of Peer-Based Instructional Consultation." PhD diss. CA: Claremont Graduate University.

Nyquist, Jody D., and Donald H. Wulff. 2001. "Consultation Using a Research Perspective." In *Face to Face: A Sourcebook of Individual Consultation Techniques for Faculty/Instructional Developers*, ed. Karron G. Lewis, and Joyce T. Povlacs Lunde, 45–61. Stillwater, OK: New Forums Press.

Penny, Angela R., and Robert Coe. 2004. "Effectiveness of Consultation on Student Ratings Feedback: A Meta-Analysis." *Review of Educational Research* 74 (2): 215–53. http://dx.doi.org/10.3102/00346543074002215.

Professional and Organizational Development (POD) Network in Higher Education. 2007–2015. http://podnetwork.org/.

Seldin, Peter. 1997. "Using Student Feedback to Improve Teaching." *To Improve the Academy* 16: 335–46.

Siering, Greg, Gary Pavlechko, and Kathleen Jacobi-Karna. 2010. "Midterm Feedback: Moving from Student Complaints to Meaningful Recommendations." POD (Professional and Organizational Development) Network 35th Annual Conference, St. Louis, MO, November 5, 2010.

Smuts, Bridget. 2005. "Using Class Interviews to Evaluate Teaching and Courses in Higher Education." *South African Journal of Higher Education* 19 (5): 943–55.

Theall, Michael. 2002. "Student Ratings: Myths vs. Research Evidence." *Focus on Faculty* 10 (3): 2–3. http://studentratings.byu.edu/info/faculty/myths.asp.

White, Ken. 2010. "Mid-Course Adjustments: Using Small Group Instructional Diagnoses to Improve Teaching and Learning." In *Assessment in and of Collaborative Learning*, ed. The Washington Center's Evaluation Committee, Evergreen State University. http://www.evergreen.edu/washingtoncenter.

6

REGARDING THE "E" IN E-PORTFOLIOS FOR TEACHER ASSESSMENT

Kara Mae Brown, Kim Freeman, and Chris W. Gallagher

Teacher portfolios, and now electronic portfolios, are well established in K–12 teacher education and in the scholarship of teaching movement in higher education, inaugurated by the Carnegie Foundation for the Advancement of Teaching and the American Association for Higher Education. Researchers and practitioners tout teacher e-portfolios as valuable tools for making teaching and learning visible; sponsoring teacher reflection and inquiry; promoting professional development; allowing rich representations of teacher identity; supporting constructivist and situated learning models; helping teachers market themselves to potential employers; and facilitating curricular investigation and revision (Avraamidou and Zembal-Saul 2003; Boyer 1990; Cambridge et al. 2001; Hutchings 1998; Kilbane and Milman 2003; Kreber 2001; Minter and Goodburn 2002; Mullen, Bauer, and Newbold 2001; Seldin 1991; Seldin et al. 2010; Sunal, McCormick, and Sunal 2005; Wilferth 2002; *Journal of Adolescent and Adult Literacy*; for taxonomies of teacher portfolios and e-portfolios according to their purposes, see Barrett 2013; Kilbane and Milman 2003; Wray 2008). For these reasons, e-portfolios seem a natural fit for teacher assessment.

However, if there is one thing compositionists know about assessment, it's that there is no perfect assessment instrument. As scholars such as Brian Huot (1996), Asao Inoue (2009), and Michael Neal (2011) have argued, assessment is a complex technology that includes but is not reducible to its instruments. Context matters. We should not be surprised to learn that research has revealed a variety of shortcomings in e-portfolio programs for teacher assessment. In a study of three such programs, Delandshere and Arens (2003) found problems that included low-quality evidence, a paucity of explanatory material, and a tendency

DOI: 10.7330/9780874219661.c006

toward parroting preset standards. The researchers describe the portfolio activities as "some sort of empirical data collection venture built on key words from the standards but missing the broader theoretical perspective indispensable to making sense of these data" (71). In a study of electronic teaching portfolios, Wilson, Wright, and Stallworth (2003) found that the e-portfolios offered little evidence of meaningful reflection and included limited connections among artifacts. Other scholars, such as Tompkins (2001), have noted that the digital affordances of electronic portfolios may lead to style over substance. These problems have led some researchers in K–12 (e.g., Beck, Livne, and Bear 2005) and higher education (e.g., Schendel and Newton 2002) to suggest that e-portfolios should not be used for the summative assessment of teachers, at least not at the same time they are used for formative purposes.

As WPAs and teachers who have participated for three years in a teacher assessment program using electronic portfolios, we recognize both the enormous potential and the considerable challenges of using e-portfolios for teacher assessment. We contend that electronic teaching portfolios can be an effective part of a meaningful teacher assessment system, but only when certain enabling conditions are in place.

To be clear: the "e" in e-portfolios is critical to our argument. Curiously, little of the considerable literature on electronic teacher portfolios explicitly takes up their digital affordances. Most of the literature treats e-portfolios as extensions of print portfolios and therefore echoes well-established themes in portfolio literature: the need for multiple artifacts, the importance of reflection, the complexity of identity construction, and so on.[1] While we can imagine effective uses of print portfolios for teacher assessment, we believe that e-portfolios can aid us (administrators and teachers) in productively negotiating a set of key tensions long recognized in teacher—indeed, in all—assessment.

The primary tension we have in mind revolves around the traditional distinction between summative and formative assessment. In the teacher e/portfolio literature, this tension often manifests as a struggle between the reflective and the rhetorical functions of e-portfolios (see chapter 7; Anson 1994; Anson and Dannels 2002; Leverenz 2002; Newton et al. 2002; Robinson, Cahill, and Blanchard 2002). Put simply, teacher-composers are often torn between honest, warts-and-all reflection for the purpose of professional growth and a desire to put their best foot forward in order to earn a positive evaluation. While we acknowledge this tension, our argument is that the affordances of e-portfolios, when exploited under the right conditions, can help us make formative and summative teacher assessment complementary.

Similarly, we think e-portfolios have the potential, under the right conditions, to help us negotiate other tensions that are endemic to teacher assessment, specifically:

- between the kind of integrated, synthetic thinking teachers must do to ground themselves in coherent theory and practice and the kind of networked, associative thinking they must do to remain flexible and intellectually alive;
- between broad, holistic judgments that allow teachers to understand the arc of their careers and the close, analytical work with specific texts, practices, or moments that allow them to mine their experiences for meaning; and
- between independent, reflective practice and participation in communities of reflective practice, both hallmarks of mature and resilient teachers.

We believe e-portfolios can be vehicles for bridging these divides. As the examples that follow will show, e-portfolios allow us to take a both/ and approach rather than an either/or approach to these seemingly competing goods in the following ways:

- As multimodal compositions, e-portfolios provide a rich evidence base for institutional decision-making *and* they provide valuable opportunities for ongoing professional development.
- As display interfaces, e-portfolios are ideal vehicles for showcasing competence *and*, as continuing sites of reflection, they are ideal vehicles for exposing ongoing difficulties and challenges.
- As single compositions comprised of multiple artifacts, e-portfolios encourage symphonic, integrative thinking *and*, as "web-sensible" (Yancey 2004) texts, they encourage associative, networked thinking.
- As flexible collection and reflection sites for artifacts, e-portfolios promote holistic judgment *and* close work with specific texts, practices, or moments.
- As deeply personal, reflective compositions, e-portfolios put learning in the hands of composers *and*, as easily circulated texts, they provide opportunities for sharing with various audiences.

We have arrived at this collective stance on teacher e-portfolios through our experiences with them in a teacher assessment system over the past three years.[2] This system applies to all full-time lecturers (fifteen in all) teaching within a large writing program at a private research university in the northeast.[3] Chris, as writing program director, was the primary architect of the system. Kim and Kara Mae, both of whom hold administrative positions in the writing program, are full-time lecturers and have been assessed by the system. While our *stance* on e-portfolios for teacher assessment is shared, our *experiences* with them have been varied. For this reason, we highlight both our individual and collective perspectives.

CHRIS

When I arrived at Northeastern University in 2009, the full-time lecturers were assessed via an annual "portfolio," submitted electronically, that included a set of Word files: a list of courses taught, syllabi, sample assignment sequences, and summaries of student evaluations. The evaluation criteria were public but tautological: a "good" rating included "good" student evaluations, for instance, and a "very good" rating included "very good" student evaluations. (A "superior" rating, curiously, included "excellent" evaluations but "superior" teaching materials.) Working with the Writing Program Committee and the lecturers, we designed a system using an e-portfolio platform. We enlisted a colleague in our teaching technology center to offer some crash training and a set of screencasts to help instructors learn about composing e-portfolios. Because many of the instructors—and some of the reviewers—were new to e-portfolios, we set up a simple template and asked lecturers to provide the following:

1. Overall reflection on teaching (~500 words). This reflection should provide your overall assessment of your teaching for the year in the context of your teaching philosophy and goals. Where have you improved? What do you need to continue working on? The subcommittee is looking for thoughtful, candid self-assessment.

2. Syllabi and major writing assignments for each course.

3. Student evaluation tallies and teacher reflections on each course.

4. (Optional) Teacher-chosen artifacts: up to fifteen pages (or equivalent) of handouts, responses to student writing, course sites or other teaching-related web texts, evidence of conference program contributions, curricular or assessment materials, brief explanations of trainings or other professional development experiences, etc.

In addition to incorporating more opportunities for reflection, we wanted to allow more room for the selection of materials—hence the optional section. We also spent a good deal of time drafting and revising the evaluation criteria, eventually arriving at the following:

- careful course design within the context of program goals
- cultivation of a challenging and supportive classroom learning environment

- respect for students' cultural and linguistic diversity
- clear communication of course goals and expectations
- appropriate use of class activities, assignments, and teaching strategies to support student learning
- regular engaged, helpful, and fair feedback and evaluation of student work
- ongoing reflection on teaching and experiences with students, including meaningful and responsive engagement with student evaluations

The call for e-portfolios each year has included these criteria. Reviewers—the personnel subcommittee of the Writing Program Committee—use these criteria to guide their feedback and their determination of a holistic rating. As tenured or tenure-track compositionists, members of the subcommittee have expertise in both teaching writing and teacher evaluation. When we implemented the e-portfolio system, though, we did not all have experience with e-portfolios. We, too, have made use of our teaching technology center's expertise. Some of us have begun using e-portfolios in our classrooms and reading the literature on them. We've also "trained" ourselves and each other. In various ways, we have had to learn, over time, how to read and respond effectively to these compositions. As I mention above, the template was as much for us as it was for the lecturers.

Over time, as we all became more comfortable composing and reading digital portfolios, we moved away from required use of the template. Also, the lecturers have effectively expanded the reflective element, routinely surpassing the 500-word guideline, as well as the optional element, often including well in excess of 15 pages. Although this obviously increases reviewers' time commitment, we are glad to see lecturers participate in the redesign of the e-portfolios.

At a recent meeting with lecturers and reviewers, we collectively confirmed our commitment to the criteria—even those we recognized as difficult to measure—and to making the template an option, not a requirement, for teachers. We also decided that at least one example of written response to student writing would be required in order to provide a richer representation of feedback. While we all believe the system works well overall, it continues to be a work in progress.

KIM

Over the course of constructing e-portfolios over the last three years, I've grown more comfortable with the digital medium, and I increasingly find it enables me to negotiate tensions between departmental expectations and my own. The evaluative criteria provided by the program help enable me to negotiate these tensions; they create a lens through which I can view and shape my artifacts.

While the evaluative criteria are clear, we have flexibility in how we meet them. The optional section allows us to include artifacts of our choosing. Also, the digital medium itself allows us to construct our portfolios to shape our audience's reading in ways that a print portfolio cannot. Some of the criteria, such as "clear communication of course goals and expectations," seem easily addressed by the required documents. However, others are more difficult to represent, such as the "cultivation of a challenging and supportive classroom learning environment." However, the e-portfolio, because of its potential to display a wider array of media from my classroom, allows us to demonstrate how we meet these criteria.

For my first e-portfolio, I simply uploaded all of the required documents, much like the print portfolios I'd done in the past. The program had provided a template for us to use, but, in my confusion with the new medium, I didn't use it. Instead, I attached one giant Word document—seventy-nine pages—that opened with a reflective essay, followed by my syllabi, assignments, responses to course evaluations, and some sample papers with my comments. There was nothing "e" about it at all. I was mostly trying to demonstrate that I'd met the basic criteria.

The second time, I wanted to make more use of the electronic space, though it was still somewhat rudimentary. I used the template, which divided up portfolios into three sections: course syllabi and assignments, course evaluations, and supplemental materials. I pasted documents into the electronic space rather than merely attaching them, thus working more with the medium.

I added a Prezi and a few links to supplemental sources and provided navigation through the space. In putting the e-portfolio together this time around, I began to be aware of how much material my teaching generated. In a way, the digital space flattened out that seventy-nine pages, and in doing so it made the heft of the materials more apparent than the linearity of the print portfolio. Perhaps, in a way akin to the flattening of dimension the cubists experimented with on canvas, the e-portfolio allowed me to view my teaching materials in ways I hadn't considered before. I was surprised by how much material there was, and I began to see some patterns—most importantly a tired similarity between materials. I wanted to differentiate my writing classes more, and I wanted to use more media in my teaching. I set out to do so the next year.

The third time around, I was eager to put more "e" in my e-portfolio. Instead of following the structure suggested by the required artifacts, I structured the e-portfolio according to each class, and, most importantly, I included a wider array of artifacts (a video lecture, a podcast discussion, and screen shots).

In my third e-portfolio, I used more of the potential of the multi-modal medium, including audio and video. The screencasts enabled me to show how I have conversations with my online students on Facebook. Also, because the electronic space seems better suited to shorter texts that can be read without a lot of scrolling, I chose to include a larger number of shorter assignments. This approach showed a greater range of papers with comments—something from each class. In these small glimpses of instruction, I hope my teaching personality comes across more fully.

On the flip side, constructing the e-portfolio has allowed me to see criteria I am not demonstrating very well—in particular, "careful course design within the context of program goals" and "respect for students' cultural and linguistic diversity." I do think I am doing these things, but I don't think they're apparent in the e-portfolios, yet. One critique I receive is that my assignments appear too "boilerplate." I'm conflicted about this critique. On one hand, I agree. As I've noted above, the e-portfolio has heightened my awareness of the lack of variety in some of my major assignments from year to year and course to course. Yet on the other hand, they are working—as student evaluations and student writing seem to suggest—so I am hesitant to change them for the sake of change. I hope in future e-portfolios to take more advantage of the medium to show more of my teaching than might come across on the syllabus or the formal assignments, to show how I make those boilerplate assignments my own in the classroom. I might be able to record lectures or use another visual medium that will suggest how I use these assignments.

I've already seen a way I might represent the even more challenging criterion of respecting "cultural and linguistic diversity." Three students from my most recent semester included multiple languages in their own e-portfolios, without my suggestion that they do so. While I can't pinpoint something I've done as an instructor to encourage this, they clearly felt not only comfortable with doing so but also compelled to. I think this is because the e-portfolio, and my teaching methods, helped them realize it was appropriate and necessary to make visible those parts of their identities—such as writing in other languages—that aren't often seen in classes where they're allowed to write only in English. This last point is important because it shows how my experience constructing e-portfolios returns to my classroom—the more comfortable I am with digital media, the more comfortable I am teaching and encouraging my students to work within them, and thus my students gain benefits from them too.

Randy Bass and Bret Eynon suggest that using digital genres, such as e-portfolios and websites, enables students to make "visible" learning that is usually "invisible." By invisible, Bass and Eynon (2009) mean both those intermediate aspects of learning between drafts or not evident in final projects and "the aspects of learning that go beyond the cognitive to include the affective, the personal, and issues of identity." I would extend Bass and Eynon's ideas to the teaching e-portfolio—it has the potential to make those "invisible" aspects of my teaching more visible to others and myself. I am thinking of transparency in two ways here: transparency of expectations *for* the e-portfolio and transparency *of* the e-portfolio itself—what it makes visible. And not just visible: the digital medium provides a richer embodiment than print, involving not only words or still images but also sound and moving images. This different embodiment allows me to see and present my teaching practices in fuller ways than I can in a print portfolio.

* * *

Kim's experience demonstrates that the digital affordances of e-portfolios allow her to negotiate the tensions we describe at the beginning of this chapter. Over time, she is able to take advantage of the e-portfolio platform for her own formative purposes while fulfilling the institutional requirement for annual summative evaluation; to showcase her integrative thinking (looking for patterns across teaching experiences) while highlighting her networked thinking (working with students on Facebook); to gain a holistic view of her teaching ("tired similarities") while analyzing discrete moments (students incorporating language other than English); and to practice independent reflection while putting herself in conversation with both her reviewers and the program at large. Her experience demonstrates two key advantages of the e-portfolio: its function as an archive and as a digital composing and reading space. As an archive, the e-portfolio allows for a diachronic view of her teaching, in which she can address evaluators' responses to previous e-portfolios, thus creating a conversation about the summative demonstration of her teaching that leads to formative reflection. As a digital composing and reading space, the e-portfolio provides a rich, synchronic experience through a greater variety of media and artifacts, thus creating a broad, holistic view of her teaching while also showing those smaller moments where her individuality emerges.

KARA MAE

When we began using e-portfolios for teacher assessment, I had never composed a teaching portfolio, "e" or otherwise. However, I had been working with my students on reflective e-portfolios for a few semesters and was beginning to have a clear idea of what made an e-portfolio successful—meaningful and honest reflection, thoughtfully selected artifacts, clear organization and contextualization, and effective use of the "e" aspect of the e-portfolio. (After all, why chose to digitize a portfolio if one is not going to take advantage of the affordances of the medium?)

As a reader of many student e-portfolios, I found that I responded positively to organizational schemes that revealed something of the writer's thinking, images that helped convey important information or ideas, and, when possible, artifacts shown on the screen rather than attached. In short, I responded well to e-portfolios that functioned more like a website than a digital file repository. I wanted to make sure that I followed these same guidelines in the composition of my own e-portfolio. In fact, I think that the first e-portfolio I created is perhaps the strongest in terms of design. I used colorful charts to show the quantitative results of my teaching evaluations. I used screenshots of my course websites and hyperlinks to demonstrate my teaching materials. I used images of the journals in which I published that year. The e-portfolio was well organized. Even the "optional" materials were categorized into different sections, each with well-developed contextual introductions to inform the reader about what they were seeing and why it was included.

The comments I received from the assessment committee for that e-portfolio were very positive, though one comment in particular stuck out to me, which stated that I should have stuck to the template. However, I found the whole idea of using a template contradictory to what I knew about e-portfolios. Not only had I been working with e-portfolios with my students, but I had also been working closely with a small group of colleagues who were using e-portfolios in their classrooms. All of our conversations about what makes an effective e-portfolio suggested that agency, ownership, and choice were key. After all, particularly in an e-portfolio, where elements can be connected through links or through the hierarchy of the menus, the structure becomes a key rhetorical element. The connections are not just a matter of organization; they give insight into how the composer of the e-portfolio understands the connections between different artifacts. I felt that the structure I had developed for my e-portfolio said much about how I think about my classes and my work. Imposing a template seemed to take away from the reflective nature of the e-portfolio. The structure *was* part of my reflection.

The comment gave me insight into what the assessment committee valued in our e-portfolios. It seemed to me that the design and structure mattered very little. Instead, what seemed to matter were the course materials and the reflections on those course materials.

The next year, I spent much less time thinking about the design of the e-portfolio and instead focused more on the reflection. In my opinion, this e-portfolio was not as strong. I followed the template, although it disrupted my composition process by forcing me to use an organizational strategy that did not feel right. I ended up with "blank" pages at the beginning of each new section, which I was not happy with, but I was nervous to include anything on those pages since the template did not explicitly call for any content. I didn't bother with nice charts or screenshots as I had the previous year. While the reflections were perhaps a bit stronger, this e-portfolio was simply not as reader-friendly. This second e-portfolio relied much more on attachments and the template organization did not allow for the kinds of connections that I would have liked to make.

Despite all that, out of the three e-portfolios I have completed to date, this one earned the highest score from the assessment committee. The year represented in this e-portfolio was also the one in which I received the most positive feedback in my student evaluations. Furthermore, that year I mostly taught courses I had taught before and for which I had well-polished materials. Given that the portfolio is meant to be a measure of the instructor's year of work, the result makes sense, since the materials are the representation of that work and the e-portfolio the medium for conveying them. However, my ratings raised the question of how much the medium does, or should, matter. I felt I was missing an opportunity to use the affordances of the e-portfolio to my full advantage as a reflective teacher—again, for me (but not necessarily for all of my peers), the e-portfolio design is itself an act and artifact of reflection—but I also recognize that I was being assessed on more than my ability to compose an e-portfolio.

Moving into the composition of my third e-portfolio, and keeping this tension in mind, I felt I had learned a lot about both what the personnel subcommittee needed out of my e-portfolio and what made the process meaningful for me. Both of those concerns seemed to converge around the idea of reflection. I resorted to a simple, straightforward design, organizing the e-portfolio by course and semester, and I focused much of my energy on my written reflections. For me, the most significant aspect of creating the teaching e-portfolio has always been the way it forces me to reflect on my own teaching practice. Reflection is an integrated part of my practice as a teacher, if only in informal ways. I take notes after each class on what worked and what didn't, I discuss classroom activities and assignments with my colleagues, and I constantly revise lessons, activities, and assignments in light of that critical awareness. However, when composing the e-portfolio for a particular audience—in this case, the reviewers—and therefore making that reflection more formal, my reflection changes. As I compose the written reflection for my e-portfolio, I find myself thinking about audience. I am able to grant my audience the kind of dispassionate perspective and programmatic context that I am often unable to grant myself when I consider my own teaching. And, by anticipating that audience, I also absorb their perspective. I find that in my e-portfolio I am able to be honest with myself (and by extension with the committee) about both my successes and my challenges in the classroom. Of course, in doing so, I am engaging in a significant act of trust. I have to trust that the committee will understand that by working through challenges in writing I am able to work toward solutions. I have to trust that they won't read those challenges as failures, but instead as part of the process of being a critically engaged educator.

Over the years, I have sensed that this trust has developed more as expectations have become more transparent. Each e-portfolio I have composed has worked in some ways like a draft. With each iteration I am better able to understand what my readers' expectations are and how best to communicate my ideas. Along with that negotiation, the process itself has been revised to better suit both the assessment committee's and the instructors' needs: the criteria have been clarified, more resources have been provided for creating the e-portfolio, and there have been more formal and informal conversations about the process.

Such trust is perhaps most evident in the way that I am able to reflect on students' evaluations of my classes. Usually, I, like many instructors, find reading student evaluations to be emotionally taxing. However, when I tally the quantitative responses from my course evaluations and reflect on my students' comments, I am able to do so not so much from my own anxious point of view, but from the point of view I anticipate from the readers of my e-portfolio—a point of view that I assume is, to some degree, disinterested. Because I know my e-portfolio will be read in the company of other instructors' e-portfolios, the process of thinking through the evaluations becomes less personal. I am able to imagine how my own evaluations might fit in among the many others. There is a kind of safety in numbers, or in community. I begin to imagine my own evaluations and reflections not only in terms of whether or not I, personally, am doing a good job, but I consider how they might fit into the program as a whole. While I don't see the e-portfolios of my colleagues, I am more able to imagine the successes and challenges that they face, and this helps me put my own in perspective.

In fact, e-portfolios offer opportunities for instructors to make their teaching practices public. By opening up their audience from just the assessment committee to the other instructors in the program, instructors could shape the way that those e-portfolios are written. Aside from the institutional assessment, there would be opportunities for more formative assessment through peer review. Also, just as the trust I put in the assessment committee has developed over time, it seems that the same thing could happen among a community of teachers, who could all benefit from such sharing.

* * *

Kara Mae's experience with teacher e-portfolios, like Kim's, involves a series of challenging but ultimately successful negotiations. Through some struggle, and some adjustments both by her and the program, she is able to use her e-portfolios to engage in the kind of reflection that serves her formative needs *and* the summative requirements of the program. She creates e-portfolios that are highly synthetic, featuring careful contextualizing annotations for reviewers, *and* highly associative, providing many links to other sites on the web. Her e-portfolios show her engaged in broad, holistic thinking about the arc of her career *and* close analytical work on particular moments (via her daily notes, for instance). Her e-portfolios are uniquely hers, featuring her independent reflection, *and* they are an artifact of her ongoing engagement with her readers, the program, and, to some extent, her peers.

ENABLING CONDITIONS

While Kim and Kara Mae's experiences and their reflections on them demonstrate that e-portfolios *can* function as productive vehicles for negotiating key tensions in teacher assessment, they also show that certain *enabling conditions* must be in place in order for that to happen:

- Both the institution's and the teachers' purposes must be honored. To be sure, Kim and Kara Mae feel a responsibility to demonstrate they are meeting programmatic expectations and standards, but they also feel responsible for their own pedagogical growth. They both feel increasingly free to experiment with the e-portfolio platform, just as they feel free to experiment (or not) with their pedagogies. They are fully engaged and invested participants in the assessment process.

- Rigid adherence to preset expectations and standards must be avoided. Kim and Kara Mae approach the composing of their e-portfolios as meaning-makers. While they are mindful of programmatic expectations and standards, they do not allow them to hamstring or short-circuit their reflection; rather, they use the criteria, and their readers, for their heuristic value—as a prompt for inquiry into their teaching.

- Criteria for evaluation must be public, shared, and subject to periodic review and perhaps revision. In order for Kim and Kara Mae to use the criteria as heuristics, the criteria need to be known and clear to them. While not all criteria will be equally easy to represent, as Kim notes, they should be publicly and clearly stated. If they are not, they must be revised. For this reason, the criteria should be subject to occasional—and preferably collaborative—review.

- Teachers must have some opportunity to shape the context and design of their e-portfolios. Participating in collective review and revision of the criteria is one way to accomplish this. We are also thinking here of the design of the e-portfolios themselves. Kim and Kara Mae offer different perspectives on the decision to provide teachers with some unfettered choice in designing their e-portfolios. In any event, we agree that, while "some opportunity" will need to be defined by each program according to its local circumstances, teachers must be active shapers of their e-portfolios, not just compilers of documentation.

- Honest, searching reflection on both successes and challenges must be encouraged and rewarded. Kim and Kara Mae both indicate that trust is key: teachers must feel that their readers/evaluators will not penalize—and indeed will reward—thoughtful reflection on failures and challenges as well as successes. Otherwise, the natural human tendency will be to sweep problematic experiences under the rug, a process by which reflective teachers lose significant opportunities to learn and grow.

- A culture of collaboration and community, rather than competition and compliance, must emerge from e-portfolios. Competition and compliance encourage sweeping those problematic experiences under the rug. By contrast, collaboration and community facilitate honest, open exchanges that lead to learning. Kim and Kara Mae clearly feel they are in ongoing conversation with their reviewers and the program. Although, as Kara Mae notes, e-portfolios do not (yet) circulate in the peer community, it is clear that the generally collegial climate of our program promotes thoughtful reflection among instructors.

- Teachers must know how to take advantage of the possibilities, and account for the limitations, of the multimodal, digital e-portfolio genre. As teachers who use electronic portfolios in their own writing classrooms, Kim and Kara Mae quickly learned how to exploit the digital affordances of the e-portfolio genre (a few of their peers did not). As they did, they were better able to represent their teaching in rich, multimodal ways and to reflect thoughtfully on that teaching. Still, both could have used more support as they learned about specific technologies related to their e-portfolio work. Programs that use electronic portfolios must find ways to help teachers—no matter their current level of knowledge and ability—learn about the specific affordances and limitations of digital portfolios.

- Teachers must be provided with adequate time and reward for composing effective e-portfolios. Kim and Kara Mae both show through their developmental narratives that learning how e-portfolios work, and learning how to *make* them work effectively, take time and effort. This time and effort must be provided, recognized, and rewarded by programs using electronic portfolios for teacher assessment.

- Audiences for the e-portfolios, including institutional reviewers, must know how to read and respond effectively to them. Kara Mae describes using her audience itself as an enabling condition: in effect, she reads her e-portfolio *through* them, which allows her a different perspective on her work. In order for her readers to serve in this capacity, they must know how to read and respond in meaningful and productive ways. Even though both Kim's and Kara Mae's opinions sometimes differ from their reviewers, they trust and count on them to read with care and discrimination and to provide them with meaningful feedback.

- E-portfolios must be both archivable and revisable. Both Kim and Kara Mae return to their e-portfolios each year, rereading them and the feedback they received before revising for the current year. In order for teachers to engage in this kind of reflection—not just semester to semester but year to year—it is critical that the e-portfolios be retrievable and changeable.

CONCLUSION

As we hope readers can see, this chapter does not offer a model program to be emulated. Kim and Kara Mae offer several critiques of the e-portfolio process, pointing to problems that include less-than-useful feedback, constraining templates, inadequate training, and insufficient community building around the e-portfolios. Also, we still struggle to strike several balances—for instance, providing enough freedom for technologically adept teachers such as Kara Mae while still providing enough scaffolding and support for those teachers who are less experienced with multimodal and multimedia composing.

Although we're somewhat hesitant to expose these shortcomings and ongoing challenges, we know that we must reflect and act on them in order to learn and grow as a program. We also know that what we have to offer from our experience is not a set of "best practices" so much as a heuristic that other programs can use to negotiate key tensions in teacher assessment. The conditions listed above may not be the *only* enabling conditions for teacher assessment through e-portfolios, but they strike us as an excellent place to start.

Notes

1. There are exceptions. In an early example, Tompkins (2001) identifies several distinct affordances of digitality: nonlinearity, direct and unmediated contact with evidence, interactivity, integrated author and video displays, portability, and power [of web-based data tools] (103). Similarly, Bauer and Dunn note that web-based environments allow both composers and readers/viewers to access portfolios from any computer; that multimedia platforms offer rich representations of learning and development; that HTML is based on international standards and therefore stable; that web-based files are portable across the web and distributable in other forms; and that e-portfolios are easily accessed for asynchronous assessment by a wide variety of stakeholders. Avraamidou and Zembal-Saul (2003) also mention a few advantages: accessibility from any place at any time, a potentially broadened audience, nonlinearity, and hyperlinking, which (in contrast with Delandshere and Arens's [2003] findings) allowed the teachers in their study to make "connections between their coursework and field experience and between their claims, evidence, and justification statements, which resulted in an interconnected presentation of their learning experience" (435). In some cases, particular affordances of electronic portfolios are experienced as challenges. Barkley, for instance, writes that "[b]ecause of the multilayering and navigational options of the Web, constructing documents suitable for this environment forced me to think in a nonlinear manner" (121). She also notes that she had to learn to write with the kind of brevity that befits web pages and screen reading and to think in unaccustomed ways about design.
2. The platform we use for teaching e-portfolios is TaskStream.
3. Full-time lecturers are reviewed annually and are on annual contracts, though the expectation is that contracts will be renewed. No instructor has been denied a contract on the basis of the annual review, and many lecturers have been working in the program for several years. There is currently talk of moving lecturers to three-year contracts and instituting a ladder system within their ranks.

References

Anson, Chris M. 1994. "Portfolios for Teachers: Writing Our Way to Reflective Practice." In *New Directions in Portfolio Assessment*, ed. Laurel Black, Donald A. Daiker, Jeffrey Sommers, and Gail Stygal, 185–200. Portsmouth, NH: Heinemann.

Anson, Chris M., and Deanna P. Dannels. 2002. "The Medium and the Message: Developing Responsible Methods for Assessing Teaching Portfolios." In *Composition, Pedagogy, and the Scholarship of Teaching*, ed. Deborah Minter and Amy Goodburn, 89–100. Portsmouth, NH: Boynton/Cook.

Avraamidou, Lucy, and Carla Zembal-Saul. 2003. "Exploring the Influence of Web-Based Portfolio Development on Learning to Teach Elementary Science." *Journal of Technology and Teacher Education* 11 (3): 415–42.

Barrett, Helen. electronicportfolios.org. Accessed May 14, 2013.

Bass, Randy, and Bret Eynon. 2009. *Capturing the Visible Evidence of Invisible Learning.*

Academic Commons.

Beck, Robert, Nava Livne, and Sharon Bear. 2005. "Teachers' Self-Assessment of the Effects of Formative and Summative Electronic Portfolios on Professional Development." *European Journal of Teacher Education* 28 (3): 221–44. http://dx.doi.org /10.1080/02619760500268733.

Boyer, Ernest L. 1990. *Scholarship Reconsidered: Priorities of the Professoriate: A Special Report.* Ewing, NJ: The Carnegie Foundation for the Advancement of Teaching.

Cambridge, Barbara, Susan Kahn, Daniel Tompkins, and Kathleen Blake Yancey. 2001. *Electronic Portfolios: Emerging Practices in Student, Faculty, and Institutional Learning.* Washington, DC: American Association of Higher Education.

Delandshere, Ginette, and Sheila A. Arens. 2003. "Examining the Quality of the Evidence in Preservice Teacher Portfolios." *Journal of Teacher Education* 54 (1): 57–73. http://dx.doi.org/10.1177/0022487102238658.

Huot, Brian. 1996. "Toward a New Theory of Writing Assessment." *College Composition and Communication* 47 (4): 549–66. http://dx.doi.org/10.2307/358601.

Hutchings, Pat. 1998. "Defining Features and Significant Functions of the Course Portfolio." In *The Course Portfolio: How Faculty Can Examine Their Teaching to Advance Practice and Improve Student Learning*, ed. Pat Hutchings, 13–18. Washington, DC: American Association for Higher Education.

Inoue, Asao B. 2009. "The Technology of Writing Assessment and Racial Validity." In *Handbook of Research on Assessment Technologies, Methods, and Applications in Higher Education*, ed. Christopher S. Schreiner, 97–120. Hershey, PA: IGI Global. http:// dx.doi.org/10.4018/978-1-60566-667-9.ch006.

Journal of Adolescent & Adult Literacy. 2007. 50 (6): 432–519. Accessed May 14, 2013.

Kilbane, Clare R., and Natalie B. Milman. 2003. *The Digital Teaching Portfolio Handbook.* Boston: Allyn & Bacon.

Kreber, Caroline. 2001. *New Directions for Teaching and Learning: Scholarship Revisited: Perspectives on the Scholarship of Teaching.* San Francisco: Jossey-Bass.

Leverenz, Carrie Shively. 2002. "The Ethics of Required Teaching Portfolios." In *Composition, Pedagogy, and the Scholarship of Teaching*, ed. Deborah Minter and Amy Goodburn, 100–120. Portsmouth, NH: Boynton/Cook.

Minter, Deborah, and Amy Goodburn. 2002. *Composition, Pedagogy, and the Scholarship of Teaching.* Portsmouth, NH: Boynton/Cook.

Mullen, Laurie, William Bauer, and W. Webster Newbold. 2001. "Developing a University-Wide Electronic Portfolio System for Teacher Education." *Kairos* 6 (2).

Neal, Michael. 2011. *Writing Assessment and the Revolution in Digital Texts and Technologies.* New York: Teachers College Press.

Newton, Camille, Tracy Singer, Amy D'Antonio, Laura Bush, and Duane Roen. 2002. "Reconsidering and Reassessing Teaching Portfolios: Reflective and Rhetorical Functions." In *Composition, Pedagogy, and the Scholarship of Teaching*, ed. Deborah Minter and Amy Goodburn, 3–13. Portsmouth, NH: Boynton/Cook.

Robinson, Julie, Lisa Cahill, and Rochelle Rodrigo Blanchard. 2002. "Looping and Linking Heuristics for Teacher Portfolio Development." In *Composition, Pedagogy, and the Scholarship of Teaching*, ed. Deborah Minter and Amy Goodburn, 14–21. Portsmouth, NH: Boynton/Cook.

Schendel, Ellen, and Camille Newton. 2002. "Building Community through Reflection: Constructing and Reading Teaching Portfolios as a Method of Program Assessment." In *Composition, Pedagogy, and the Scholarship of Teaching*, ed. Deborah Minter and Amy Goodburn, 121–31. Portsmouth, NH: Boynton/Cook.

Seldin, Peter. 1991. *The Teaching Portfolio: A Practical Guide to Improved Performance and Promotional/Tenure Decisions.* Bolton, MA: Anker.

Seldin, Peter, J. Elizabeth Miller, Clement A. Seldin, and Wilbert McKeachie. 2010. *The Teaching Portfolio: A Practical Guide to Improved Performance and Promotion/Tenure*

Decisions. San Francisco: Jossey-Bass.

Sunal, Cynthia, Theresa McCormick, and Dennis Sunal. 2005. "Elementary Teacher Candidates' Construction of Criteria for Selecting Social Studies Lesson Plans for Electronic Portfolios." *Journal of Social Studies Research* 29: 7–17.

Tompkins, Daniel P. 2001. "Ambassadors with Portfolios: Electronic Portfolios and the Improvement of Teaching." In *Electronic Portfolios: Emerging Practices in Student, Faculty, and Institutional Learning,* ed. Barbara Cambridge, Susan Kahn, Daniel Tompkins, and Kathleen Blake Yancey, 91–105. Washington, DC: American Association of Higher Education.

Wilferth, Joseph. 2002. "Private Literacies, Popular Culture, and Going Public: Teachers and Students as Authors of the Electronic Portfolio." *Kairos* 7 (2).

Wilson, Elizabeth, Vivian Wright, and Joyce Stallworth. 2003. "Secondary Preservice Teachers' Development of Electronic Portfolios: An Examination of Perceptions." *Journal of Technology and Teacher Education* 11 (4): 515–27.

Wray, Susan. 2008. "Swimming Upstream: Shifting the Purpose of an Existing Teaching Portfolio Requirement." *Professional Educator* 32 (1).

Yancey, Kathleen Blake. 2004. "Postmodernism, Palimpsest, and Portfolios: Theoretical Issues in the Representation of Student Work." *College Composition and Communication* 55 (4): 738–761.

SECTION II

*New Challenges, New Contexts
for Assessing Teaching*

7

TECHNOLOGY AND TRANSPARENCY
Sharing and Reflecting on the Evaluation of Teaching

Chris M. Anson

In my work helping writing instructors create teaching portfolios (Anson 1994), I began to discover an interesting irony hidden in small fissures between the portfolios' formative and summative functions. In displaying various materials from their classes—student evaluations, syllabi, writing assignments—these instructors knew they were being judged on the quality of their teaching. After all, the portfolios were partly designed to showcase their best efforts. But in the secondary documents—the ones that *reflected* on their materials and gave voice to their concerns—some teachers revealed a kind of tentativeness and speculation that no longer positioned them as displaying the finest products of their instruction. Instead, their entries disclosed what they were actually *thinking* as teachers.

Over time, I was increasingly drawn to these more reflective entries and the interesting instructional puzzles they explored. In contrast, the more confidently the teacher presented his or her successes, the more suspicious I became that closure had set in—a kind of methodological complacency. I started valuing the risks teachers took when describing and reflecting on something that didn't meet their expectations, such as the failure of a strategy or a mismatch between what they felt students learned and how the students performed. Teachers who brought to the surface deeply complex issues (such as how to respond to an ideologically distasteful but well-argued paper) seemed more intellectually engaged in their work and more likely, I thought, to be continuously searching for excellence. In disclosing the formative process of evaluation *as* summative, they created trust in their instructional abilities.

In this chapter, I argue that summative evaluation is ideally made in the context of, or with access to, the kind of formative self-reflection

DOI: 10.7330/9780874219661.c007

that demonstrates teachers' interest in continuous improvement—a process that Donald Schön (1983) has called *reflective practice*. As important, digital technologies now allow us to make the results of that work widely accessible, a process that allows for personally-managed accountability. After briefly theorizing the spaces between the formative and the summative in the evaluation of teachers' work, I'll turn to two digitally-enabled methods that make these spaces transparent for classroom and public audiences through students' evaluations of their experiences in a course. This "opening up" of the usually private dimensions of evaluation forces teachers to adopt productive, critical stances about their work, rather than stances that are defensive, obfuscating, or self-congratulatory. In publicly reflecting on their own teaching, instructors take control of the processes of critique and judgment, showing that they are just as interested in evaluating and improving themselves as other stakeholders are in doing that for them.

RESISTING STASIS

Summative evaluation of teaching is based on "a judgment which encapsulates all the evidence up to a given point" and is seen as a "finality" (Taras 2005).[1] Because it often profoundly affects a teacher's life and career, the process of summative evaluation usually arouses fear and apprehension. Even if they are only committee members who serve in an advisory role to someone who implements their recommendations, colleagues who conduct summative evaluations wield great power, their judgments often deciding the fate of the teacher whose materials they are reviewing. Because the stakes are high, the evaluative process is carefully regulated and rendered in legalistic language intended to protect all parties' interests. But, practically, these constraints only unnerve the person being evaluated and interpersonally distance the ones doing the evaluating. A formal classroom observation, for example, often follows a protocol and uses an established rubric and rating scale to make judgments on qualities such as "the success with which the teacher coordinates class discussion of the material at hand." Bearing the stamp of judgment, the resulting report is signed, dated, and entered into the teacher's permanent file, subject thereafter to all regulations governing personnel records. Although such information has potential value for the teacher's improvement, its immediate purpose is to judge, weigh, or rank the outcome of the teacher's ability at a particular career stage.

In contrast, formative evaluation focuses not on stasis but on development. In the strictest sense, it reveals the distance between current performance and some kind of standard or benchmark for achievement (Harlen and James 1997). However, in teaching-related contexts, formative evaluation has no consequence for the teacher beyond learning and improvement. Anyone can provide it, and there is no necessary power differential between the teacher and the person offering the feedback. A teacher and a close colleague invited to sit in on her class have social parity. The colleague's purpose is not to judge the outcome of the teacher's ability but to provide *input* that encourages thoughtful reflection, subsequent experimentation, and higher levels of awareness and knowledge (see Kolb 1984). The very concept of self-reflection is a kind of internalized formative evaluation—a teacher might start by reflecting on what he or she *does*, but then move to "an account of what happens when he or she does something explicitly *different*. It is not, that is, a report of what *is*, but a purposeful experiment and investigation . . . into what *might* be" (Hutchings 1998, 15).

Just as students learn little about their writing from final-draft grades, teachers rarely use the results of a summative evaluation to improve their instruction. Teachers are also more likely to experiment with new practices and work toward improvement from information provided formatively. For example, during a casual observation of a teacher, I noticed that he favored the left side of the classroom, both in his eye contact and in his pattern of calling on students. When we met later, he was surprised to learn about this tendency, and we reflected on its causes. He pointed out that two or three of the most diligent and verbal students sat on the left side, and that he must have been unconsciously acknowledging them or expecting their insightful responses. We then explored some of the complexities of class discussions and how to democratize them. Instead of simply calling on and making more eye contact with students on the right side of the room, he began to experiment with his entire method of leading discussion. Now made consciously aware of the balance of comments from the students, he was able to draw out otherwise reticent participants and value their contributions, improving not just his own "performance" but the level of his students' engagement.

Unfortunately, such insights rarely make it into the materials used to judge teachers' instruction. When teachers are asked to demonstrate their teaching ability, their products are most often *primary documents* (Anson 1994), the necessary artifacts of their instruction: course overviews and syllabi, descriptions of policies and processes, handouts, assignments and any supporting materials that accompany them, or samples of graded papers. If they are institutionally required, student evaluations of instruction and peer observations of teaching become some of the most important documents used to evaluate the quality of instruction, even though they are not generated by the teacher.

Less common but sometimes included in teaching portfolios are *secondary documents* (Anson 1994), those that reflect on the primary documents or on teaching more generally: philosophies or statements of teaching goals, annotations of the primary documents, or explorations of grading or commenting practices (see Seldin 1991). In most of the literature on the improvement of instruction (especially through teaching portfolios), reflection is said to be central, helping teachers to "unearth new discoveries about themselves" (Zubizarreta 2004, 24). Because teachers produce primary documents as part of their contractual obligations, presenting them for evaluation involves little more than a quick error hunt or a bit of reformatting. In contrast, teachers need to invest additional time to write secondary documents, and the thoughtful reflection expected in such documents doesn't come easily or quickly. For many theorists, such reflection represents a scholarly side of teaching that ought to be promoted and rewarded across the entire landscape of education (Boyer 1990; Edgerton, Hutchings, and Quinlan 1991).

Freestanding secondary documents such as teaching philosophies can be useful in portraying an instructor's beliefs about learning, their attitudes toward students, or broader ideologies of education. But they're notoriously difficult to write, falling prey to platitudes and generalizations or reflecting popular ideas without any evidence of enactment. Routinely, I have read teaching philosophies that invoke important theorists such as Paolo Freire and strongly profess student-centered approaches to instruction in which, for example, the teacher claims to provide a classroom atmosphere that makes learning exciting, that engages all students, and that shows them that learning is a lifetime activity. But on visiting their classes and looking at their syllabi, I've been alarmed to find a much more controlling disposition, more teacher-centered practices, and a less engaging atmosphere than was promised in the philosophy. Without a deliberate connection to other evidence, such documents don't always encourage the kind of reflective stance that leads to further improvement in teaching. In contrast, reflection that accompanies and focuses on primary documents or classroom data is rooted in the artifacts of teaching. Especially when the data originate from students' own sense of what's happening in the class and how they're progressing as learners, the teacher's reflection takes on richer and more exploratory characteristics that lead to experimentation, new theoretical constructs, and improved classroom practice.

THE PARADOX OF PRIVACY IN TEACHING

In addition to its manifestation in primary or secondary documents, reflection on teaching is also strongly affected by audience. Early scholarship on teaching portfolios described them as spaces where teachers can speculate about their instruction—in collaboration with other teachers—in order to "foster a culture of teaching and a new discourse about it" (Edgerton, Hutchings, and Quinlan 1991, 6) and "think about . . . teaching in a social context" (Edmonds 1992, 1). This idea was and still is problematic to many teachers because it violates a history of teaching as an autonomous and private activity.

By default, teaching takes place in a highly social context, where experts and learners gather and work together to gain knowledge and expertise. But a disequilibrium between the expert and the learners defines the nature of the "social": the teacher makes most of the curricular and pedagogical decisions, judges the students' progress, sets the parameters for participation, and orchestrates all the activities. A curious privacy exists within this public nature of the profession: the teacher can hide most of the daily routines of instruction from the view of faculty, peers, and everyone beyond the institution (Lieberman and Miller 1978). When their peers observe their classes, faculty often script their sessions more deliberately and thoughtfully for the visit, putting on a better (but less authentic) show. Personnel files documenting teaching, which may be seen by colleagues during review periods, often contain the bare rudiments of instruction (syllabi and student evaluations). Comments on students' work, which reflect various approaches to student learning, rarely surface, and they remain some of the most private of all teaching activities (Anson 1999). Classroom doors, through which we might glimpse teachers and students at work, often remain closed.

Creating wider audiences for one's reflections on teaching, then, stands in opposition to dominant ideologies of instruction that see teaching as the manifestation of individual effort. Any attempt to scrutinize it is always driven by the disagreeable and reluctantly acquiesced need for summative assessment. As Trigwell et al. (2000) suggest, the likelihood of a teacher engaging in the scholarship of teaching may be closely tied to their willingness to share their reflections with others. Teachers less likely to systematically explore their own instruction tend to use informal theories of teaching and learning to inform their practice and are more teacher-focused than student-focused. They reflect more on what they do than on what students experience. And they are more likely to "keep their ideas of teaching and learning to themselves and to see teaching as a personal, private activity" (163–64). In contrast,

> Teachers who are more likely to be engaging in the scholarship of teaching . . . seek to understand teaching by consulting and using the literature on teaching and learning, by investigating their own teaching, *by reflecting on their teaching from the perspective of their intention in teaching while seeing it from the students' position, and by formally communicating their ideas and practice to their peers.* (Trigwell et al. 2000, 164; emphasis added)

In an effort to create lively, productive contexts for collaboration, many institutions provide opportunities for faculty to work together on complex issues that arise from their instructional experiences (see Anderson 1993). Among the most popular are teaching teams or circles, reciprocal classroom visits and observations, collaborative inquiry and pedagogical scholarship, and intercampus collaboration (Hutchings 1996). But such activities still occupy niche-like spaces on most campuses. The fear that opening the door to one's teaching may expose uncertainties and struggles—signs mistakenly believed to be associated with instructional weakness—still weighs heavily against public disclosure. In a post to the *Chronicle of Higher Education*'s blog, "ProfHacker," Janine Utell (2010), a professor at Widener University, publicly admits to feeling that one of her courses had "gone horribly wrong" and reflects on the consequences of doing so:

> Being able to talk about failure is a crucial part of overcoming the dark place that acknowledging it can create. At the same time, it's scary for us as individual teachers, and as a profession overall. How can you reflect on your failure, let alone acknowledge it, when doing so means admitting you might not be an expert, and may put your very job in jeopardy—a state of affairs I acknowledge is quite real?

In an effort to bring these "dark places" to light, Utell set up workshops for colleagues that allowed them to explore the ways in which they felt they had failed as teachers during the semester and, more importantly, how their failures became learning experiences that changed the way they taught.

Utell's confession joins a growing number of books, articles, and blog contributions arguing that we can improve only by openly exploring the conundrums and complexities of teaching, by legitimizing reflection, and by giving credibility to narratives of perceived failure as well as success (see, for example, Dressman 1999; Dressman 2000; Power and Hubbard 1996; Tassoni and Thelin 2000; and The Failure Project n.d.). Yet, sharing such reflections with audiences beyond small groups of sympathetic colleagues or readers of educational periodicals remains mostly untheorized and, I would argue, seldom practiced. More troubling is our tendency to collect information from one major group of

our "publics"—the students we teach—yet never collaborate or recipro-
cate with them in the interests of improvement. Aside from (or perhaps
including) the ubiquitous and highly formalized student evaluations of
teaching administered on most campuses, faculty generally distrust students' opinions of their instruction. When these opinions are offered
outside the sanctioned forms, they become anathema. Opinion websites
such as ratemyprofessors.com, myedu.com, professorperformance.com,
and pickaprof.com (now defunct) have drawn heavy faculty criticism
for promoting consumerist attitudes toward education and providing
unreliable, selective information from students motivated, often negatively, to enter opinions. Some faculty profiled on these sites have even
created "revenge" rants, either through videos on YouTube or mtvU's
"Professors Strike Back" (MacDonald 2010). In the context of increasing public demand for transparency in higher education, these tensions
are bound to exist until faculty participate in shaping sensible dialogue
about their own teaching and students' experiences in their courses.

"Going public" with data about their teaching and then reflecting on
it offers one way for faculty to turn a summative process largely beyond
their control into a thoughtful display of the way that they think as
instructors and the continuous work they do to improve their teaching.
Before the Internet, there was no practical way for teachers to share
such displays beyond their immediate settings. Today, however, the
Internet provides many tools for teachers to show their work *and* reflect
on it, including:

- keeping an online electronic teaching portfolio available to either the
  world or select audiences;
- creating online course portfolios accessible to other teachers of the
  same or similar courses (Seldin 1994) and posting them to
  courseportfolio.org, an international repository of course portfolios
  (part of the Peer Review of Teaching Project);
- setting up a publicly accessible teaching blog for the ongoing
  exchange of ideas and the exploration of puzzles and problems;
- creating an open wiki to showcase good teaching practices and provide links to other resources; and/or
- posting podcasts or "vodcasts" that reflect on specific aspects of teaching and learning.

Two further digitally-enabled methods stand out in the ways that
they value *students'* experiences in every class, thereby rooting reflection
deeply in the continuous cycles of instruction—and in the individual,
social, and pedagogical contexts—that make up the professional lives
of teachers.

OPENING UP CLOSURES: TWO METHODS

Student evaluations of instruction are usually administered at the end of a course, either on scannable forms in class with the instructor not present, or online during a designated period before grades are assigned. Too late to be of any use in the course, the results of these evaluations end up in the instructor's personnel file, where they're eventually used for performance reviews. But more formative student evaluations of instruction range from the dynamic and highly revealing "small-group instructional diagnosis (described in chapter 5 of this volume) to methods that are relatively easy to design and administer.

Online Midterm Course Assessments

The first method of inviting student input and making it transparent involves creating online midterm assessments of course progress based on clearly articulated goals or outcomes for students' learning. This process hinges on pre-articulated goals or outcomes, in the absence of which students can write only what they feel rather than measuring their progress against the knowledge, skills, and self-awareness that the course is supposed to give them. Although colleges and universities are increasingly requiring that all courses include statements of goals, outcomes, or objectives, this is not a universal practice. Creating them voluntarily represents an important part of reflection because it refocuses attention from what the *teacher* will do to what the *students* are ultimately supposed to take away from the course (see Biggs and Tang 2007). Instead of asking himself which favored plays students will read, the Shakespeare instructor now asks what perspectives, appreciations, insights, skills, and historical knowledge the students will acquire (such as making sense of the difficult syntax and lexicon of early modern English, or being able to discern universal and deeply human themes of conflict). Rather than devoting all her attention to deciding which cultures to cover in her general-education course, the teacher of introductory anthropology now asks how learning about them can help students "develop a command of the most important theoretical and methodological approaches to the study of culture." Students are thoroughly briefed on the goals or outcomes at the start of the term, and told how everything in the course is designed to realize them.

Halfway through the course, students complete an anonymous online survey. The first part asks them to rate how well they think the course has been accomplishing the published goals or outcomes to that point, based on their own efforts and those of the instructor. The excerpt below shows the first two outcomes-based questions (of five) from one such midterm assessment in a general education history course.

EXCERPT FROM MIDTERM COURSE ASSESSMENT, HISTORY 266
HIS 266 Students

Thanks for taking a minute to complete this survey.

First, please realize that this survey is for us; it's not a Departmental, College, or University survey. The first part is designed to assess how well you think we're accomplishing the course outcomes. The second part is a space for you to react to how the course is going so far, so we can make any needed improvements. The survey is completely anonymous.

1. Please rate how well you think we are accomplishing the following course outcome so far:

   "Be able to analyze and explain the impact of major historical forces and events that shaped the region, with which special attention to human rights abused and issues."
   - ❏ Strongly agree
   - ❏ Agree
   - ❏ Neutral
   - ❏ Disagree
   - ❏ Strongly Disagree

2. Please rate how well you think we are accomplishing the following course outcome so far:

   "Be able to evaluate and critique primary and secondary historical sources, including those on the Internet."
   - ❏ Strongly agree
   - ❏ Agree
   - ❏ Neutral
   - ❏ Disagree
   - ❏ Strongly Disagree

In addition to the course goals or outcomes, the survey may include questions about the more general features of the course: quality of the class sessions, helpfulness of the teacher's responses to students' work, nature of the reading material, how readily students are understanding the material—in short, anything of importance to the success of the class and the progress of students' learning. These can take the form of scaled questions to give a numerical average of students' opinions. The survey might also include one or two boxes for more open-ended comments and suggestions, with guiding questions such as, "Please comment on what's standing out for you positively in the course," and "Please comment on what adjustments can be made in the course—without any major overhauls or shifts in its structure, expectations, etc.—to help facilitate your learning."

After the students have taken the electronic survey, the teacher prepares a synthesis of the responses. The digital form makes it easy to create numerical averages in the form of grids or graphs, as well as bullet-point summaries of narrative comments and suggestions. In class, the teacher reports the results and engages students in a discussion of which areas need continued (or additional) emphasis before the course is finished. Responses that criticize other students, wander completely off-topic, or provide only unhelpful, acerbic rants can be left out (though typically these are rare, perhaps because the students know their comments are meant to be useful and have only the class as audience). Because the students discuss the implications of the survey results in class, the teacher is drawn toward an instructional ideology that sees students as participants in their own education. Designed to promote minor adjustments to the course, the assessment helps the teacher ensure—from the students' perspective and experience—that the course is doing what it promises.

Table 7.1 shows the statistical results of the midterm course assessment from the students enrolled in HIS 266. In these results, students were satisfied with their progress in meeting several of the outcomes, but were less sanguine about "being able to write logical, interpretive historical essays phrased in clear, logical, active-voice prose" (from the HIS 266 outcomes). Having shared these numbers, the teacher can then draw more information from the students in class in the form of concerns and suggestions for improvement. The class discussion doesn't provide anonymity, but it's a way to turn individual, anonymous responses into a collective improvement effort. In reflecting on the results, this teacher could also think of ways to support students' writing more fully, perhaps by working an online peer review into the course, providing mini-lessons on how to structure historical essays, or showing anonymous, "interestingly problematic" samples of papers from a previous course and having students apply the grading criteria to those papers in order to further internalize the teacher's expectations (see Anson, Davis, and Vilhotti 2011).

In a narrative comment box, students write responses and suggestions ranging from general praise to concerns about the readings, class

Table 7.1 Averaged Results of Midterm Survey, History 266

Course Outcomes	
"Be able to analyze and explain the impact of major historical forces and events that shaped the region, with special attention to human rights abuses and issues."	4.3
"Be able to evaluate and critique primary and secondary historical sources, including those on the Internet."	4.0
"Be able to organize logical historical arguments, supported by specific evidence."	3.8
"Be able to write logical, interpretive historical essays phrased in clear, logical, active-voice prose."	3.2
"Demonstrate growth in critical thinking (the higher levels of Bloom's taxonomy) and in cognitive level (based on William G. Perry's model).	4.1
Other Course Features	
Class sessions: variety, level of engagement, productivity, etc.	4.5
Feedback on your work (peer and teacher).	3.9
Communication with you and the class (email, etc.).	4.8
Nature and learning value of the various assignments and projects.	3.7
Readings (theory essays, outside articles).	3.2
Breadth of coverage of topics, issues, strategies, and perspectives.	3.7

discussions, and assignments. The following comment focuses on the way the instructor uses time at the start of class to go over various logistics such as due dates, assignments, readings, etc.

> I feel like some of the time we spend at the start of class is wasted on housekeeping and questions, especially as they relate to rehashing the requirements of assignments. All questions are not necessarily important to air during class time and maybe students who have questions could see you after class if everyone else gets it. Then you could simply e-mail the question and your response to everyone.

For economy, it's helpful to synthesize all such narrative comments into a series of bullet points or brief statements. This allows some comments to be reworded (if they're phrased problematically or reveal the person's identity, or if several comments say the same thing). The following synthesis pulled together the narrative comments in HIS 266:

> *Things working well:* professor's desire for feedback (this survey) is refreshing; info is new and really interesting; blog is great/enjoyable; low-stakes papers are fun to write; class sessions are enjoyable; visual aids are helpful.

> *Things to work on:* Website is a little overwhelming; blog criteria seem a little unclear; reading material can be challenging; lots of time spent on logistics each class period; some students talk with each other/have cell

phones go off; better connectors needed between chapters/class topics; more even participation in class would help.

Clearly, some comments in this class could be accommodated immediately, such as clarifying the criteria for the blog entries or calling attention to occasional disruptions (notice how the survey results themselves can help in such an effort because the concerns are coming from the disrupters' peers rather than the teacher). Other concerns, such as the complexity of the website, could be partly addressed during the term (e.g., through a five-minute demonstration of how to navigate the site), but could also have implications for longer-term improvements to the course.

Toward the end of the course, the midterm assessment can be readministered to gauge how well the identified gaps were filled and give students an opportunity to reflect again on their initial concerns and suggestions. The results of both assessments can then be posted to the instructor's website as a visible, public display of interest in students' experiences and the success of their learning in the course. In this way, two kinds of public audiences have access to the teacher's thoughtful and intentional efforts to create an excellent learning environment and reach the stated course outcomes: first, the class members, who see and experience the teacher's efforts to map their progress and attend to their learning; second, a broader public, who are invited to value the teacher's ongoing commitment to improve and excel.

Reflections on Student Evaluations of Instruction

The public display of teacher-generated course assessments becomes the driving force behind the second digitally enabled strategy. In this strategy, the teacher reflects on the final, institutionally-administered student evaluations of teaching, both the numerical results and the students' narrative comments, and then creates a written commentary that addresses the students' concerns with ideas about course revisions. The teacher then places the numbers, narrative comments, and teacher commentary on a personal or (depending on institutional and other regulations) departmental website to make them publicly accessible for all to see. In this way, student opinions play a role in the teacher's continuous reassessment of teaching (especially in the context of specific courses), while also publicly demonstrating an interest in formative, continuous improvement as a function of reflective practice.[2]

At my personal website, links from the teaching page lead to evaluation data from each of my courses. To orient a potentially wide variety of readers to the purpose of this disclosure, at the start of every course page I include a couple of paragraphs explaining why I'm sharing the results and how my reflection on them helps me to continually improve my instruction.

> *Before you begin: I strongly believe that teaching well is a lifelong pursuit—an art to be explored and developed, and a science that constantly presents new challenges and opportunities for analysis and growth. As a teacher, I am very much a learner. I need to reflect on what I'm doing and how I'm doing it. Student evaluations are one source of information for me to reflect and improve. As such, I use them formatively, as information helpful in the improvement of a significant part of my professional life: teaching students and teaching other teachers.*
>
> *But student evaluations can also have a more public function, displaying areas of my teaching that students find to be strong and areas in need of improvement. Below, you will see evaluation data from the course and term indicated above, along with a bit of reflection from me about what I see in these numbers and comments. Please use this information responsibly. If you're deciding whether to take a course from me, consider what you see here not only as evidence of ability, but as evidence of my willingness to listen to your peers and improve my teaching in ways that respond to their justified concerns and needs. If you're a fellow professional looking at these data because you want to learn more about or evaluate my work, please consider them only as one part of an overall plan for teacher effectiveness and a lifelong pursuit of excellence.*

In some cases, where appropriate, I have included anonymously written comments from the students in the course. In so doing, I have created a kind of "dialogue" from some of these comments by interspersing my own (italicized) thoughts and reflections on ways to address specific concerns the next time I teach the course. By working on areas of concern, I can then match student opinions in future courses against earlier ones to see whether the changes are having a positive impact on the course and its students.

Consider, for example, the evaluation data from one of my recent sections of "Literacy in the United States," a service-learning course designed for juniors and seniors, most of whom are pursuing careers as schoolteachers. The data show the averaged results of twenty-eight student evaluations from this section of the course for each of the fourteen questions ("The instructor was receptive to students outside the classroom: 4.6," "The course readings were valuable aids to learning: 4.2," etc.). The numerical data are followed by my reflective comments. The first part of those comments, "What these numbers are telling me," considers the statistical averages of the course evaluations. After explaining that this is the fourth time I have taught the course, which I designed and got approved as a permanent offering in the Department of English, I describe its general design and purpose, and point out that this particular section had the largest enrollment of the four times it has been taught. I then try to make sense of the score averages:

> *Overall, the evaluations are relatively strong; but once again, I sense that the students feel they are asked to do more than in a typical course because of the tutoring requirement—and I have held the course to typical standards for three credits. The elimination of oral presentations two sections ago again seems like it was a good move, as it gave us more time to discuss the course material and provided better pacing. One somewhat puzzling result is the average for Question #14 ["Overall, this course was excellent": 4.0], because it's lower than any of the individual scores. Some holistic judgment is not getting captured in any of the other more specific questions, and it will be worth trying to gauge why, perhaps in an anonymous midterm course assessment, which I administer in every class. I have never found an ideal book or collection of readings, a fact continuously indicated in the scores for Question #10 ["The course readings were valuable aids to learning: 4.2"], and I may need to do some special surveys of individual readings or discuss opinions of the current book more fully with future classes. No matter how overtly I refer to the course outcomes, including in a midterm assessment in which students must gauge how well they think they are accomplishing them, this score never reaches 5.0, and it should. I may need to think of some way to help students realize that we refer to these repeatedly in the course.*

Following the numerical evaluation scores and my reflection on them, I include all narrative comments that I deem worthy of disclosure, both positive and negative. Thoughtful observations—supported by details of the class or revealing insights from a personal perspective—get more attention than comments that share only a simple opinion ("I loved this class") or falsehoods ("All we did was work in stupid groups," when frequent presentations, large-group discussions, and whiteboard demonstrations balanced out the small-group work). Also noted are comments made by several or more students, which reveal some consensus about a particular strength or weakness.

One student in this class wrote the following: "Didn't get much out of the course. The readings were too long to read, and when I did read them, I felt like I had wasted an hour of my life." Although such a comment expresses a legitimate sentiment, without further probing it doesn't promote the kind of dialogic thinking and reflection that would be worth my own time or the time of outside readers, and commenting on it would only lead me down the path of blaming the student for not wanting to put more energy into his or her learning. More insightful and constructive comments, however, beg for reflection, such as the following:

> Sometimes the class got too loud and talkative. I understand it is college, but sometimes he needed to step in and take control sooner. As the

semester went on, we had more mini-group discussions. I liked the interactions with students better than just a full-group discussion.

To me, this comment raises an interesting instructional question about how strongly a teacher should control a discussion, and how different students interpret the messiness of highly engaged interactions. In "response," I wrote the following, posted in italics below the student's suggestion:

There were definitely times when discussion became animated, and lots of people wanted to express opinions. This is the kind of class discussion that I adore—when every student is engaged and immersed in the ideas we're considering, even if they are simply taking in what others are saying. I tend to let such discussions go for a while before exerting control over the group and reining it in. In this way, lots of ideas can be put on the table, and we can then begin to sort through them and see patterns and relationships among them, and work toward greater coherence, if only to lay out several alternative ways to think about the issues. However, as this student's comment suggests, some students may feel that too many ideas, expressed too passionately, get in the way of their understanding—that the discussion becomes "noisy" both literally and symbolically. I need to study this phenomenon more fully and try strategies that keep the energy going (and keep me off center stage) while at the same time bringing a stronger sense of direction, even initially. I often have students write down their ideas first, which then offers a way to control the follow-up, but simply reading the freewrites aloud doesn't often lead to the kind of dynamic discussion that throwing out a controversial idea does. This student has opened up an interesting area for further speculation and experimentation in the context of the course.

Creating a publicly accessible reflection on the students' opinions of a course, such as this one, requires a delicate rhetorical stance—neither acquiescing completely to students' views nor defensively justifying practices that they dislike or object to. In essence, it says, "Students' opinions are valuable; after all, they're the learners. My expertise as a teacher also helps me to interpret their opinions and judge how accurate they are and how well they reflect an understanding of the learning process. I take all credible responses seriously—teaching is extremely complex, and these data are one way for me to make sense of my instruction and strive continuously to improve it."

THE POLITICS OF GOING PUBLIC

"Going public" with digitally accessible evaluation data is not without political and interpretive significance. An anecdote will illustrate this point. In the context of a teaching portfolio required in a writing program, an ambitious, young, non-tenure-track instructor I had taught earlier in a graduate course reflected thoughtfully on her teaching, including two or three occasions when her classes didn't work out as she'd planned. The newly-appointed administrator of the program, unschooled in teaching portfolios and their use as a space for formative evaluation, immediately seized on these disclosures as signs of weakness in her teaching and gave her a low rating among a substantial cohort of non-tenure-track instructors—which earned her no merit pay for that year and placed her on a list of faculty who were at risk of being eliminated if the next fiscal budget couldn't support them (see Anson and Dannels 2002). The moral of this story is that, while going public with reflection can positively affect how deeply teachers consider their instruction, the evidence of thoughtfulness shared in those reflections can also go right over the heads of misinformed or ignorant audiences.

The value an institution places on support for teaching improvement can strongly affect teachers' decisions to go public with evaluation data and disclose the ways they are thinking about their instruction. On campuses with toxic climates or serious rifts between the faculty and administration, it may not be prudent to provide *any* information beyond what is strictly required, and then just to hope for the best as that (usually minimal) information gets translated into a verdict about promotion, merit pay, or reappointment. Administrators at such institutions may think that their imposition of the strictest standards and the most draconian measures for judging success will lead to excellence. But sadly, because they deny everyone the opportunity to work collectively and transparently on their individual and shared performance, they're often the least successful at improving teaching. Compare campuses that encourage reflective practice, collaboration, and a climate of shared responsibility. At such places, faculty know that their performance is based on richer, deeper, and more nuanced information than the statistical results of student evaluations, and they are more encouraged to display their teaching in multiple ways, including occasions when something that fell short of success begs for further analysis and experimentation (see Bain 2004).

Being reflective in the context of an unsupportive institution also means having the courage to speak out and model certain practices. For tenured faculty, this takes less risk. But, those for whom it may be too risky to disclose anything beyond what's required can still make reflection a routine and personally meaningful (if concealed) part of instruction. Simultaneously, these faculty need the courage to help inform their administrations, urging them to adopt new ideologies of teaching, learning, and evaluation. It's not difficult to make a strong case for the role of reflection in the improvement of education—both theory and research support it—and these arguments can be used to help unprepared administrators recognize their own shortsightedness or the need for a stronger orientation toward the formative in the evaluation of teaching. Changing evaluative procedures and the beliefs that inform them can often open up possibilities for the collective disclosure of teaching practices and the kinds of thoughtful, pedagogically-sensitive reflection that improves those practices.

Perhaps more importantly, current trends suggest that the public disclosure of summative teaching evaluation will not be an option for anyone working at institutions funded even partly by taxpayers. Consider the case of the Texas legislation requiring universities to post data on faculty members' cost (salary and benefits) relative to a revenue formula linked to teaching (Simon and Banchero 2010; see chapter 1). Such rough-hewn measures—which do not tell the full story about the many and varied contributions of faculty—distort the mission and workings of the institution, mislead the public, and lead to equally illogical and wrongheaded reactions among administrators. As other states impose similar kinds of misguided accountability, it may not be long before the public will also demand information about teaching performance. Fourteen states protect the privacy of personnel records, including performance reviews and student evaluations of instruction, and four more states exclude the access of public-records to just faculty. However, seventeen other states require that personnel records of faculty be made public without exception, and seven more have only general exceptions to public access (Arreola 2007). Legislation can always modify and refine records-protection laws, allowing, for example, sensitive or privacy-invading personnel actions to be kept off-limits while still insisting that evaluations of instruction be made available for all to see. States that already provide public access to personnel records can follow the Texas model and require that records such as student evaluations be made available more easily than by navigating Byzantine websites or requesting each faculty member's data from the institution. If such legislation succeeds, allowing university administrations to provide access to our evaluation data may be an even less desirable prospect than taking control of the process and ensuring data are not revealed without an opportunity for the faculty member to explore, interpret, and comment on them productively. As Edward White (2005) has quipped, "Assess *thyself* or assessment will be done unto thee" (33).

Although I have focused on two ways that faculty can use digital technologies to generate and/or take control of student evaluation data through reflective practice, broader institutional initiatives have even greater potential to encourage reflection and its public display. Working with teaching evaluation committees, faculty senates, divisions of undergraduate instruction, teaching and learning centers, and other such bodies can lead to revised policies about teaching and its evaluation, as well as new resources, such as interactive campus websites where faculty can post information about their teaching. Getting into the practice of owning our own evaluation—so that no one owns it for us—both contextualizes the data by placing it back into its socially dynamic and pedagogically rich contexts, and provides a much-needed opportunity for us to continue to improve and not assume that, as a couple of my more closure-oriented colleagues sometimes say, "We already know how to teach."

Notes

1. See chapter 1 for a fuller discussion of the differences between formative and summative evaluation.
2. Before any public display of institutionally gathered data, it's important to contact a campus office of legal affairs to learn about any regulations concerning such disclosure.

References

Anderson, Erin. 1993. *Campus Use of the Teaching Portfolio: Twenty-Five Profiles*. Washington, DC: American Association for Higher Education.

Anson, Chris M. 1999. "Reflective Reading: Developing Thoughtful Ways to Respond to Students' Writing." In *Evaluating Writing: The Role of Teachers' Knowledge about Text, Learning, and Culture*, ed. Charles R. Cooper and Lee Odell, 302–24. Urbana, IL: NCTE.

Anson, Chris M. 1994. "Portfolios for Teachers: Writing Our Way to Reflective Practice." In *New Directions in Portfolio Assessment*, ed. Laurel Black, Donald A. Daiker, Jeffrey Sommers, and Gail Stygall, 185–200. Portsmouth, NH: Heinemann.

Anson, Chris M., and Deanna Dannels. 2002. "The Medium and the Message: Developing Responsible Methods for Assessing Teaching Portfolios." In *Composition Pedagogy and the Scholarship of Teaching*, ed. Deborah Minter and Amy M. Goodburn, 89–100. Portsmouth, NH: Heinemann.

Anson, Chris M., Matthew Davis, and Domenica Vilhotti. 2011. "'What Do *We* Want in This Paper?': Generating Criteria Collectively." In *Teaching with Student Texts*, ed. Joseph Harris, John Miles, and Charles Paine, 35–45. Logan: Utah State University Press.

Arreola, Raoul A. 2007. *Developing a Comprehensive Faculty Evaluation System*, 3rd ed. Bolton, MA: Anker.

Bain, Ken. 2004. *What the Best College Teachers Do*. Cambridge: Harvard University Press.

Biggs, John, and Catharine Tang. 2007. *Teaching for Quality Learning at University*, 3rd ed. New York: McGraw-Hill Education.

Boston, Carol. 2002. *The Concept of Formative Assessment*. ERIC Document Reproduction

Service ED470206. http://www.vtaide.com/png/ERIC/Formative-Assessment.htm.

Boyer, Ernest. 1990. *Scholarship Reconsidered: Priorities of the Professoriate*. Stanford, CA: Carnegie Foundation for the Advancement of Teaching.

Dressman, Mark. 1999. "Mrs. Wilson's University: A Case Study in the Ironies of Good Practice." *Language Arts* 76 (6): 500–509.

Dressman, Mark. 2000. "Theory into Practice?: Reading against the Grain of Good Practice Narratives." *Language Arts* 78 (1): 50–59.

Edgerton, Russell, Patricia Hutchings, and Karen Quinlan. 1991. *The Teaching Portfolio: Capturing the Scholarship of Teaching*. Washington, DC: American Association for Higher Education.

Edmonds, Anthony O. 1992. "The Teaching Portfolio: An Idea Whose Time Has Come?" *Faculty Development* 5 (3): 1.

The Failure Project. n.d. http://thefailureproject.tumblr.com.

Harlen, Wynne, and Mary James. 1997. "Assessment and Learning: Differences and Relationships between Formative and Summative Assessment." *Assessment in Education: Principles, Policy & Practice* 4 (3): 365–80.

Hutchings, Pat. 1998. "Defining Features and Significant Functions of the Course Portfolio." In *The Course Portfolio: How Faculty Can Examine Their Teaching to Advance Practice and Improve Student Learning*, ed. Pat Hutchings, 13–18. Washington, DC: American Association for Higher Education.

Hutchings, Pat, ed. 1996. *Making Teaching Community Property: A Menu for Peer Collaboration and Peer Review*. Washington, DC: American Association for Higher Education.

Kolb, David A. 1984. *Experiential Learning: Experience as the Source of Learning and Development*. Englewood Cliffs, NJ: Prentice-Hall.

Lieberman, Ann, and Lynne Miller. 1978. "The Social Realities of Teaching." *Teachers College Record* 80 (1): 54–68.

MacDonald, Gail Braccidiferro. 2010. RateThisFacultyEvaluationSite.com. *Academe* (July–Aug): 31. http://www.aaup.org/article/ratethisfacultyevaluationsitecom.

Power, Brenda Miller, and Ruth Shagoury Hubbard, eds. 1996. *Oops: What We Learn When Our Teaching Fails*. Portland, ME: Stenhouse.

Schön, Donald A. 1983. *The Reflective Practitioner: How Professionals Think in Action*. New York: Basic Books.

Seldin, Peter. 1991. *The Teaching Portfolio: A Practical Guide to Improved Performance and Promotional/Tenure Decisions*. Bolton, MA: Anker.

Seldin, Peter. 1994. "The Course Portfolio as a Tool for Continuous Improvement of Teaching and Learning." *Journal on Excellence in College Teaching* 5 (1): 95–105.

Simon, Stephanie, and Stephanie Banchero. 2010. "Putting a Price on Professors." *Wall Street Journal*, Oct. 22. http://online.wsj.com/home-page.

Taras, Maddalena. 2005. "Assessment—Summative and Formative—Some Theoretical Reflections." *British Journal of Educational Studies* 53 (4): 466–78.

Tassoni, John, and William H. Thelin, eds. 2000. *Blundering for a Change: Errors and Expectations in Critical Pedagogy*. Portsmouth, NH: Heinemann.

Trigwell, Keith, Elaine Martin, Joan Benjamin, and Michael Prosser. 2000. "Scholarship of Teaching: A Model." *Higher Education Research & Development* 19 (2): 155–68.

Utell, Janine. 2010. "Using Failure to Reflect on our Teaching." *Chronicle of Higher Education*, July 20. http://chronicle.com/blogPost/Using-Failure-to-Reflect/25435/.

White, Edward. 2005. "The Misuse of Writing Assessment for Political Purposes." *Journal of Writing Assessment* 2 (1): 21–36.

Zubizarreta, John. 2004. *The Learning Portfolio: Reflective Practice for Improving Student Learning*. Bolton, MA: Anker.

8

TELLING THE WHOLE STORY
Exploring Writing Center(ed) Assessment

Nichole Bennett

Writing centers and writing programs are scholastic, and often programmatic and departmental, bedfellows. Similar resources fill the bookshelves of both writing program administrators and writing center directors. Assessment is one scholarly topic where our fields also converge. Writing program faculty, writing centers, and writing tutors all rely on assessment. At the heart of the teaching and tutoring of writing is a continual movement among an assessment of the writer and his or her needs, a sharing of knowledge and strategies to meet those needs, and a reflection on what the writer has learned. The challenge (that both writing programs and writing centers share) is that neither has been able to leverage assessment to tell the whole story.

For writing centers, and perhaps writing programs, a solution to this problem becomes apparent through reviewing the scholarship. Despite the many well-respected and oft-cited assessment resources, writing center work has long neglected an essential and foundational element of assessment: our writing tutors. The challenge is not that we fail to use assessments to change our programs, but that we ignore an inherent element of the process. Our conversations about the assessment process must be built on a shared language between and among tutors and their directors. Without such a language, implementing effective changes becomes a top-down edict from the director to the tutors, a move that is antithetical to the very nature of writing center work.

The challenge we face in developing a shared language on assessment is compounded by the existence of two distinct scholastic spheres within the writing center field. Those who direct and administer writing centers are, for the most part, well versed in composition theory and assessment research, while the tutors, who work directly with the

DOI: 10.7330/9780874219661.c008

learners we serve, are trained primarily through practical guides that often completely ignore rhetoric and composition theories and assessment practices. Though the responsibilities of administrators and their tutors do require different resources, the stark division between the theoretical works promoted among our administrators and the practical guides encouraged for our tutors have limited our field's growth through assessment.

Although the divide is palpable, it is permeable. Writing center administrators can and do find value in, for example, *The Dangling Modifier* (2010), "an international newsletter by and for peer tutors in writing produced in association with the NCPTW (the National Conference on Peer Tutoring in Writing)." Similarly, both peer and professional tutors actively read peer-reviewed articles by eminent scholars of our field in *The Writing Center Journal.* The most dedicated administrators and tutors mediate between both scholarly worlds and pull from the resources available in each sphere of research.

Admittedly, straddling two sets of resources has encouraged writing center scholars to develop a deeper understanding of the tutoring experience from every angle—tutor, administrator, faculty member, and even tutee. But a separation has been maintained in the discussion of assessment. Since each set of resources has a distinct audience with its own needs, it could be argued that a collaboration and conversation about assessment is unnecessary. Such a claim would have more merit if both administrator and tutor assessment were equally flourishing. Instead one thread—the thread most read and contributed to by administrators about programmatic assessment practices—has grown exponentially; the other thread—the one most read and contributed to by tutors about practical assessment practices applied during tutoring sessions—appears to have grown little, if at all.

Programmatic assessment is essential to writing center work, especially in light of the recent focus on accountability and assessment in higher education. We have cultivated a culture of data collection and analysis. Writing centers purchase programs like Tutortrac and WCONLINE develop elaborate in-house database and spreadsheet systems to monitor contact hours and courses supported in order to track who uses our centers. We painstakingly compile retention data, graduation rates, grade comparisons, and tutor and tutee GPAs in order to support our claim that we positively impact student learning. We cull student and faculty opinions through surveys and focus groups in order to identify strengths and explore opportunities for continued growth. And yet, we have all but ignored the informal, difficult-to-track assessments that are a central element of the work of our writing tutors. The formative assessment tools our tutors use in their sessions can be just as, if not more, telling. Building an assessment practice that utilizes data from both the formal, programmatic assessments and the informal, individual assessments will help us tell our whole story.

Unfortunately, writing center scholarship perpetuates the schism between the language that administrators use for assessment and the language that our tutors use in their work with learners. One of the results of this lack of a shared language is that, despite a discussion of assessment in early tutor training manuals, more recent works have all but ignored the role of the informal assessments inherent to tutoring sessions.[1] The exclusion of overt discussions of assessment in tutor training manuals is purposeful—tutors are not supposed to wield the red pen. A narrowly defined and accepted conception of assessment has made assessment, evaluation, and grading synonymous. If we do not begin to develop a shared understanding of assessment and its role within our centers and tutoring sessions, then we will miss the opportunity to connect our program-wide assessment practices with the day-to-day work of our centers. If we ignore the opportunities to train our tutors in the uses and applications of assessment in the tutoring session, then we will neglect to provide a full array of tools for the tutoring session. If we do not begin to build a shared conversation of assessment, then we will leave our tutors alone in trying to balance the very real need to use informal assessments to guide their collaborative conversations with the learners who visit our centers and the expectation that tutors not assume the role of evaluator or grader of writing.

The shift in assessment is not purely a concern for writing centers. The field of assessment in general is shifting to garner a deeper understanding of the impact our services and classes have on student learning. In an interview for the *Journal of Developmental Education*, Rosemary Karr, former president of the National Association for Developmental Education (NADE), shared a similar sentiment regarding the focus of assessment in developmental education. For Karr, "the opportunity to critically examine the DE [Developmental Education] field makes this an exciting time, as it is providing the data which is necessary to begin to explain what is happening in the classroom and how various instructional interventions—as well as systems beyond instruction—affect student learning outcomes" (Diaz 2010, 21). Writing center scholarship is particularly well placed to begin to explain what is happening in the tutoring sessions to affect student learning. In order to achieve the in-depth understanding Karr suggests is possible, we will have to change more than how we collect, analyze, and present our assessment work. In order to take advantage of this moment in research and assessment, we need to do more than simultaneously promote two threads of the same discussion. We must do more than acknowledge that there are two parallel assessment conversations in our writing centers. We must begin to build bridges between the assessments that occur in our tutoring sessions and the assessments of our tutoring programs. We must move toward integrating our tutors and their experiences with assessment into the assessment plans of our centers. If we want to begin to understand the learning that happens within our centers, then we must first cultivate a language of assessment within them.

The primary means of building a program-specific, shared language of assessment is to incorporate assessment topics in tutor training and professional development opportunities. Tutor training provides an ideal means for beginning to develop a shared vocabulary that translates assessment into a language our tutors know, understand, and can comfortably apply to their work. The inclusion of assessment conversations into tutor training does not have to be an additional topic to cover in an already crowded writing tutor course or workshop schedule. Specifically, assessment conversations can be used not only to develop a shared understanding within the program, but also as an exploration of important tutor training and tutoring concepts. Including assessment activities and conversations that add complexity and real-life applications to otherwise abstract tutoring concepts is the ideal practice for assessments in general.

Three activities that blend assessment and tutor training topics to achieve such a nuanced activity are included in this article, but, before exploring these, I suggest a framework for this discussion of assessment. "Formative Assessment in Higher Education: Moves towards Theory and the Enhancement of Pedagogic Practice," an article by Mantz Yorke (2003), may focus on one kind of assessment, but the concerns that Yorke raises deserve our attention as we move to integrate assessment into the work of our centers. Exploring Yorke's four concerns and their connection to writing center work, as well as Brian Huot's (2002) *(Re) Articulating Writing Assessment for Teaching and Learning*, provided the foundation for understanding the role of assessment in my center, my philosophy as a tutor trainer, and my practice in developing activities that include assessment in tutor training. Thus, a brief review of both Yorke and Huot is necessary before examining the three assessment activities I would like to share.

The first of Yorke's (2003) list of issues in assessment is "an increasing concern with attainment, leading to greater emphasis on the (summative) assessment of outcomes" (483). Writing center administra-tors often focus on end-of-semester summative assessments that reveal patterns in usage and satisfaction of tutoring services. Representative of such work is Reinheimer and McKenzie's (2011) recent research on the correlation between tutoring and student retention. Their work lays the foundation for other centers to use data to make similar claims that academic support programs do impact student retention, a key outcome of higher education. Although the data they present clearly supports their claim that "tutoring has been shown to enhance the undeclared students' possibility of becoming more academically and socially inte-grated," their work does not explore how or why that statement is true (34). Such a focus on summative, outcomes-based assessment—to the exclusion of formative, student-centered assessment—is exactly what Yorke cautions us against. This is exactly the assessment trap many of us find ourselves in. It is not that summative assessments are not neces-sary or that good work is not occurring in our centers, but that a focus on summative program assessments limits our ability to fully understand and share the practices that support our tutors.

Despite budget issues, writing centers are particularly well placed to address Yorke's second concern. Since the bulk of a center's daily work occurs in one-on-one writing conferences, Yorke's concerns over "increasing student/staff ratios, leading to a decrease in the atten-tion being given to individuals" seems irrelevant (483). Writing tutors are trained to focus their informal assessment practices on individual learners, and individual meetings with the same learner. Paula Gillespie and Neal Lerner's relatively recent tutor training manual, *The Longman Guide to Peer Tutoring*, may not use assessment terminology, but it does ask tutors to develop important, informal assessment skills to assist their work with individual writers. Gillespie and Lerner (2008) are, in essence, advocating for assessment when they suggest that "the impor-tant thing is to approach a session with a curious and open mind and, once again, to develop control of the strategies that you might offer writers and the flexibility to know what's working in a session and what adjustments *you* need to make. What you'll often find to be your most important source isn't what you can tell writers, but instead what you do instead of talking. In other words, by listening and observing, by look-ing at body language and uncovering what the writer is doing and why" (59; emphasis added).

In order to listen and observe, the tutor has to initiate the conversa-tion. Open-ended questions lead to the greatest insights into the writer's past writing experiences and current writing concerns. The conversation itself is an informal assessment that helps the tutor better understand where the writer is and where the writer needs to be at the end of the tutoring session. The initial exchange of open-ended, probing questions and the writer's answers set the stage for informal assessments throughout the tutoring session. Informal assessments used during tutoring sessions are as much about the constant act of self-reflection and self-awareness required of our tutors as they are about assessing individual writers' concerns about their writing projects. The informal assessments that we model in our tutor training and apply throughout our sessions are difficult, but not impossible, to capture.[2] Indeed, paying attention to the informal assessments used in our centers is just as important as paying attention to programmatic assessments because the informal assessments tell us much more about the individual exchanges—the one-on-one conversations—between writers and tutors. Using assessment to better understand these individual exchanges would bring our assessment emphasis in line with our philosophical emphasis—helping individual writers. In some ways, we are constantly informally assessing learning. The challenge then is not to collect data from every informal assessment, but to identify the informal assessments that will help us recognize our programs' strengths and weaknesses.

Yorke's third concern touches directly on the tension between the predominantly summative, programmatic assessments of writing center administrators and the predominantly formative, individual assessments of writing tutors. Although the cause for the tension is different for Yorke (2003), the result is the same, as he finds "curricular structures changing in the direction of greater unitization, resulting in more frequent assessments of outcomes and less opportunity for formative feedback" (483). Our focus on summative assessment and the development of the universal has led to a neglect of the formative assessments that are at the heart of our tutoring. For example, Dolores Perin's (2004) ambitious field study of academic support at fifteen community colleges identifies universal or shared areas of interest for academic support centers that deserve our increased attention. Perin's list includes a variety of universal concerns, from professional development opportunities for tutors to understanding the student characteristics that positively impact student success (580–81). While her call for additional research on and discussion of the role of learning assistance centers is heartening, her research does not include the student learner's or the tutor's voice. Such exclusion ignores the heart of our work and underscores the lost opportunities when we focus primarily on programmatic assessments. Moreover, Perin's list of universal concerns misses an attempt to understand what happens in a tutoring session, including the formative, informal assessments used by tutors to negotiate the tutoring session.

Yorke's (2003) final concern is at the heart of my focus on bringing assessment into the center, and it is directly connected to the split between scholarship for writing center administrators and scholarship for writing center tutors. The claim seems innocuous enough: "the demands placed on academic staff in addition to teaching, which include the need to be seen as 'research active,' the generation of funding, public service and intra-institutional administration" impacts assessment practices (483). The same could be said of any field. However, the schism within our field of research has led to a division of assessment labor. Writing center administrators focus on quantitative assessments, while writing tutors focus on qualitative assessments. There is a practical element at work here. Access to the data, the purely quantitative reports our databases churn out with a point and click, is typically limited to administrators and full-time staff, who need such information to complete annual reports, provide accrediting bodies with required documentation, and undertake special projects. Moreover, the sensitive nature of that data, especially in relation to grades and course or college success, make it difficult to grant unlimited access to the data and databases, especially as many of our tutors are undergraduates at our institutions. Access to the tutees, the primary source of our qualitative assessments, is typically the domain of the mostly part-time tutors. Since the tutors are the ones who closely interact with the tutees on a regular, if not daily, basis, they become the eyes and ears of the writing center. They hear and see the tutees' reactions to tutors, they learn which approaches to sharing knowledge are appreciated, they witness the struggles with assignments, and they celebrate successes in learning. In order to use assessment to tell our whole story, we must share the responsibility for both quantitative and qualitative assessments among all of our staff.

Such a call for shared responsibility becomes increasingly important if we consider Brian Huot's (2002) revisioning of assessment in relation to our development of writing tutor training. Huot's exploration of the role of assessment in the teaching of writing is built upon one essential truth: "assessment is everywhere" (61). Assessment is more than formative "judgments [about writing] that allow a student to improve" (65). Assessment is more than final draft evaluations, course grades, or other summative assessments that "exist outside of a context in which a student might improve her work." Instead, Huot argues that our goal should be instructive evaluation, which "requires that we involve the student in all phases of the assessment of her work" (65). Assessment then becomes something that the writer can internalize, a process through which students develop "the critical consciousness necessary for a developed, evaluative sense about [their own] writing" (79). Most importantly, it requires conversations with the people that are at the very heart of the work we do in our centers.

If instructive evaluation is the goal of our work with students, then writing centers are particularly well placed to meet Huot's vision for writing assessment. However, many writing centers would be ill-prepared to dive into such assessment work because they have yet to overcome the divide within our scholarship. Inviting tutors to begin to think critically about and reflect on the role of assessment in the center is essential to encouraging a greater consciousness within our centers. Thus, tutor training becomes an essential means for inviting our staffs to join the assessment conversation from the first moment they enter our centers. While there are many ways to include assessment conversations in tutor training, I would like to share three activities. All three exercises may be equally appropriate for the faculty and staff of writing programs. Often the undergraduate, peer writing tutors from our writing centers will become our graduate and new faculty for our writing programs. Sharing the tactics I found helpful in the development of the paraprofessionals in my writing center may help in the development of training for full- and part-time faculty.

In order to create worthwhile assessments, we must have a strong understanding of what we do and what we are trying to assess. The first step toward collaboration between writing center administrators and tutors must be the development of a shared understanding of the center's mission statements, visions statements, program goals, and learning outcomes. Developing a shared understanding requires more than simply sharing this information during tutor training; it requires thoughtful exchanges about such statements, which are central to the center's purpose.

An hour-long training activity, used as part of my center's College Reading and Learning Association training program for both writing and content tutors, highlights one possibility for pairing assessment with mission statements in interactive tutor training activities. During this workshop, we ask tutors to critically consider the center's mission statement. First, tutors are asked to create a personal mission statement for themselves as tutors. We share our personal mission statements and discuss their implications and the many roles tutors play as suggested by their statements. We then move to a discussion of the mission statement of the department. We ask tutors to consider how their personal tutoring mission statement connects to and disconnects from the department mission statement. We discuss ways to simultaneously respect both their individual mission statements and the department mission statement. Finally, we ask tutors to work in groups to revise the center's mission statement. In this revision, they must consider the purpose of the center, the center's role within the college, and the various personal mission statements they have shared and discussed during the training. The use of prompted, reflective writing and collaborative revisions allows for conversations about writing, and the sharing of the tutors' personal mission statements encourages reflection on the multiple hats we must wear as tutors.

Most important, by connecting their personal mission statements to the center's mission statement, we begin to connect the tutors' daily work with the assessment work of the center. They begin to see how they are actively engaged in the larger purpose of the center. By encouraging tutors to analyze both personal mission statements and the department's mission statement, we are doing more than simply telling them what it is that we do and why we do it—we are asking them to critically think about how their individual tutoring sessions are part of a larger conversation that we should return to regularly. As tutor trainers and center administrators, we must remember—regardless of the preferred tutoring techniques and philosophies of the center—to emphasize that the individual and department mission statements cannot be merely archived. They are a living, and hopefully symbiotic, element of the center. This hourlong activity encourages reflection about assessment at its most fundamental level—the individual tutor within the center. By including tutors in the conversation about our department's mission statement, we begin to develop a shared understanding of our tutors' experience, training, and identities. We begin to build a vision of assessment that is with and for tutors rather than of and about tutoring. We begin to tell our whole story as a center constantly evolving through the growth and development of individual tutors' identities within the center.

In a separate training workshop specifically for writing tutors, we turn to the often-overlooked connections between the writing process and the assessment process.[3] Through this tutor training activity, I model the good behavior Geller et al. (2007) advocate for in *The Everyday Writing Center*. I am "work[ing] with tutors in the ways tutors should work with writers" (30). By using my writing tutors' prior knowledge of the writing process to explore a new topic—or at least apply a familiar topic, assessment—I am modeling both the role prior knowledge can play in a tutoring session and one means for breaking down difficult or new concepts. In addition, using a simple graphic organizer to help keep track of the ideas generated during the training session, I model the role graphic organizers can play in writing, especially in the drafting and brainstorming stages. By blending tutoring techniques into a theoretical conversation about two important processes—writing and assessment— tutors can begin to see the skills they will need to develop and use during tutoring sessions.

This training session begins with a discussion of the writing process. Tutors and facilitators are asked to complete a reflection on their habits as a writer. They share their reflections and we discuss the similarities and differences, noting how all of us have developed our individual writing process to rely on our strengths and overcome our weaknesses. I divide the whiteboard or chalkboard in half, and on the left side of the board we brainstorm a possible master writing process that uses broad sweeping labels or categories in order to capture all of the stages shared through our reflections and discussion. We also include references to our conversation about our individual writing processes and strategies in order to remind ourselves of what happens at each stage. Such a list typically includes brainstorming, drafting, revising, and editing. I usually have to add three elements that writing tutors often overlook:

> **Peer review** — I encourage peer tutors to discuss writing tutoring appointments they have had and professional tutors to share moments when they collaborated with their professional colleagues to develop a writing project.
>
> **Assessment** — Like many centers, I dissuade my tutors from making comments about grades and writing on the learner's paper. Tutors quickly learn and understand the rationale for such policies. However, they also often hesitate to discuss the role of assessment in our conversations about writing tutoring.
>
> **Reflection on the feedback received from the reader** — Modeling how to constructively use feedback to develop as a writer is often an essential skill to share with the learners who visit the center.

Such additions open the conversation to a discussion of the purpose of the writing process—to refine our ideas so that they can be shared with an audience. Adding the assessment process to the conversation becomes easier now that we have developed a shared understanding of the stages of the writing process (see Table 8.1).

The messy reminders of all the different strategies we have shared for each stage of our master writing process make connecting the writing and assessment processes easier. Tutors begin to realize that writing's

Table 8.1 Stages of the Writing Process

Writing Process	Assessment Process
Brainstorming	Information gathering
Drafting	Assessment design
Peer review	Piloting of assessment
Revising	Refining of assessment
Editing	Editing
Assessing	Assessing
Reflection on feedback	Analysis of results

brainstorming and assessment's information gathering steps are similar, and that both writing assignments and assessment projects require thinking and planning time before any writing or assessing even begins. It becomes easier to see that both the drafting and assessment design processes include writing and planning, often with a graphic organizer similar to the one we used to organize our conversation. Peer review and the assessment pilot may occur on different scales—peer review is typically limited to one or two reviewers, while a pilot typically includes a larger sampling—but their purposes are the same: to collect feedback critical to the development of the project. The parallels between revising, refining, and editing are easily teased out through conversations.

The acts of assessing and reflecting on feedback as well as the analysis of results often require considerable attention because they seem beyond the scope of the writing tutor's role. While writing tutors may not be actively engaged in the formal assessment of writing, they *are* engaged in frequent informal assessments—often more than one assessment per tutoring session—that determine how to best support a writer as he or she develops a particular writing project. It becomes easier for tutors to see the connection between assessment and reflection when the conversation focuses on the formative assessments they use during tutoring sessions. The challenges of developing and implementing programmatic assessments that capture those formative assessments are illustrated when they see the assessment process and writing process side-by-side. It is like asking someone to assess everything before the final draft without putting evaluative pressure on any of the writing process stages. Writing tutors begin to see the connection between their everyday work and the assessment projects of the center.

Unfortunately, the gap between tutoring work and scholarship has often excluded our staffs from the assessment process. However, a discussion of the administration of past, present, and future assessment projects and the tutors' potential role in those projects—everything from distributing student satisfaction surveys to completing their own assessments of the center—helps to build a shared interest in and responsibility for center assessments. Moreover, such conversation yields important insight into our own assessment practices. The first post-assessment process conversation with the tutors in my writing center revealed a huge oversight. Although my center had always shared assessment results with tutors, the administrators had rarely involved tutors in the analysis of those results. Thus, an opportunity arose for the tutors to critically consider how to use the assessment data to develop our strengths, address our weaknesses, identify opportunities for growth, and overcome threats to our tutoring program.

Another example of missed opportunities in my center is lack of attention we gave to student satisfaction surveys. It is not that we did not read, collect, collate, and report the comments, but that we missed an opportunity to use the student satisfaction surveys to improve the daily work of the center. My center was not alone in this oversight. A significant element in the challenge of using assessment to tell our whole story is that we are still struggling to make sense of the role of and appropriate use for assessment in higher education. David Boud's (1990) article, "Assessment and the Promotion of Academic Values," may be over twenty years old, but his challenge to higher education assessment practices is still largely unaddressed, especially in the academic support field. In particular, he argues that faculty and staff in higher education should "place a high value on critical analysis of our own work, but we are in general uncritically accepting of assessment practices," a trap we can all too easily slip into (101). The complication within my center was that we ignored both the potential for critical analysis of our own work and critical reflection built upon the student satisfaction surveys.

Student satisfaction surveys have long been a means of assessment in many academic support centers. They are comparable to course evaluations in that the forms ask the tutees to evaluate our services. In my center, evaluations of both the tutor and the center are completed on a regular basis. Learners often complete the form multiple times, and often multiple times for one tutor, during the course of one semester. The completed forms are usually turned in at our front desk or our suggestion box so that the student's anonymity is protected. In the past, these forms have followed a linear filing process. The office staff collected the forms and submitted them to the director, the director reviewed the forms and submitted them to the coordinators, the coordinators read the forms and shared them with the tutors, the tutors returned the forms to their coordinators after reading, and the forms were filed away by semester and year. The tutors rarely revisited the forms; in fact, to do so was problematic because the forms were not filed in the tutor's personnel file but by the academic calendar year. Such practices only served to "encourage a narrow, instrumental approach to learning that [emphasizes] the reproduction of what is presented, at the expense of critical thinking, deep understanding, and independent activity" (Boud 1990, 101). The student satisfaction surveys were left to gather dust on shelves and in filing cabinets after they were included in our annual reports. Their potential to help tutors improve their practice was forgotten.

Addressing such oversights has been relatively simple. At the end of the semester, after the data have been compiled and patterns of comments are cited in end-of-semester reports, the evaluations are placed in the tutors' personnel files. By filing the paperwork by tutor instead of semester, tutors and their coordinators can more easily access their evaluations. When the tutor meets with his or her coordinator to prepare for an observation of a tutoring session, the personnel file, including all completed student satisfaction surveys, is reviewed. The form is no longer some abstract assessment practice that has no relevancy to the daily workings of the center. By using the completed forms to guide conversations about the tutor's development, the assessment gains purpose and relevancy for both the tutors and the coordinators. Most important, the voices of the learners we support have a greater impact on our development as a program because the surveys they complete are now regularly reviewed and thoughtfully considered by the tutors and the coordinators.

There is still much assessment work to do within my own center, the larger writing center context, and writing programs in general. In many ways, we will continue to do what we have always done. We will continue to track data on student usage, the academic success of tutees, and satisfaction surveys. We will continue to make claims about the impact of our centers on the learning that goes on at our colleges and universities. But we have begun to move in a new direction that will hopefully lead us toward a better, deeper understanding of the learning exchanges that are integral to tutoring.

By developing a shared language of assessment within my center, the scholastic division that has driven tutors and administrators into two separate spheres of assessment is slowly becoming less distinct. By revisiting and critically considering the assessment practices already in place within my center, we have begun to discuss ways to make the learning that occurs in our center more visible. By blending summative and formative, individual and programmatic, and quantitative and qualitative assessment practices, we are moving closer to capturing the learning that happens in our center. We have begun to use assessment to tell our whole story. How will you begin to tell yours?

Notes

1. In *The Practical Tutor*, Meyer and Smith (1987) observe that "a tutor must almost necessarily evaluate a writer's work . . . in order to decide how to proceed. However these judgments should not be voiced; rather, they should be converted into questions to deduce from the writers whatever material is required" (31). Gillespie and Lerner's (2008) more recent tutor training manual, *The Longman Guide to Peer Tutoring*, does not explicitly refer to assessment in its discussion of best practices in tutoring.
2. This is not to say that no attention has been given to the informal assessments negotiated during a tutoring session. The International Writing Center Association's 2010 conference in Baltimore, Maryland, showcased several panels and presentations based on dissertations that demonstrate an increasing finesses, if not ease, with exploring the role of assessment in a tutoring session.
3. I presented a cursory exploration of the comparison between the writing process and the assessment process at the Mid-Atlantic Writing Center Association's annual conference in West Chester, Pennsylvania (Bennett 2011). I do not mean to imply that either process is limited to one set of stages, but to share one means I have found successful in discussing the role of assessment in writing center work.

References

Bennett, Nichole. 2011. "Addressing the pain in the @$$essment: Strategies for planning and implementing a meaningful assessment project." Paper presented at the Mid-Atlantic Writing Center Association Annual Conference, April.

Boud, David. 1990. "Assessment and the Promotion of Academic Values." *Studies in Higher Education* 15 (1): 101–11. http://dx.doi.org/10.1080/03075079012331377621.

The Dangling Modifier. 2010. http://sites.psu.edu/thedanglingmodifier/.

Diaz, Cristella R. 2010. "Transitions in Developmental Education: An Interview with Rosemary Karr." *Journal of Developmental Education* 34 (1): 20–22, 24–25.

Geller, Anne Ellen, Michele Eodice, Frankie Condon, Meg Carroll, and Elizabeth H. Boquet. 2007. *The Everyday Writing Center: A Community of Practice*. Logan: Utah University Press.

Gillespie, Paula, and Neal Lerner. 2008. *The Longman Guide to Peer Tutoring*, 2nd ed. New York: Pearson Longman.

Huot, Brian. 2002. *(Re)Articulating Writing Assessment for Teaching and Learning*. Logan: Utah University Press.

Meyer, Emily, and Louise Z. Smith. 1987. *The Practical Tutor*. New York: Oxford University Press.

Perin, Dolores. 2004. "Remediation beyond Developmental Education: The Use of Learning Assistance Centers to Increase Academic Preparedness in Community Colleges." *Community College Journal of Research and Practice* 28 (7): 559–82. http://dx.doi.org/10.1080/10668920490467224.

Reinheimer, David, and Kelly McKenzie. 2011. "The Impact of Tutoring on the Academic Success of Undeclared Students." *Journal of College Reading and Learning* 41 (2): 22–36. http://dx.doi.org/10.1080/10790195.2011.10850340.

Yorke, Mantz. 2003. "Formative Assessment in Higher Education: Moves towards Theory and the Enhancement of Pedagogic Practice." *Higher Education* 45 (4): 477–501. http://dx.doi.org/10.1023/A:1023967026413.

9

ADMINISTRATIVE PRIORITIES AND THE CASE FOR MULTIPLE METHODS

Cindy Moore

By now, the idea that teaching, like learning, is a complex activity—and should be evaluated as such—is common knowledge among educators. We've known for decades that, in order to draw accurate, fair conclusions about a teacher's effectiveness, we need to both "consult" a variety of information "sources" (e.g., students, colleagues, administrators, the teacher herself) and use "multiple measures" of teaching effectiveness, including teaching materials, class observation reports, and actual student work (Seldin 1984, 132; see also Seldin et al. 1990). With respect to rhetoric and composition, these principles informed early assertions that "teachers should never be evaluated only by student perceptions," nor by a single "class visit" (White 1989, 168), as well as the field's gradual endorsement of the teaching portfolio as a "means of documenting and reflecting on teaching practices" (Minter and Goodburn 2002, xvii).

Yet, as this volume shows, despite a collective understanding of how we ought to assess teaching, we often have trouble translating that understanding into actual assessment practice. Perhaps the best evidence of the gap between theory and practice is the "common and consistent" reliance on "student ratings of instruction" for "evaluation of instructors and instruction" across our campuses (O'Neill, Moore, and Huot 2009, 144). Even when evaluators invite other means of demonstrating teaching effectiveness, they still tend to focus on the less direct, typically more quantitative evidence provided by student course evaluations, using it as the standard against which all other evidence is interpreted. That is, despite the now-impressive body of scholarship on the importance of using many types of data from diverse sources to evaluate teaching, it is still too often the case that instructors are evaluated by a single method from a single source: course surveys completed by students. Further,

DOI: 10.7330/9780874219661.c009

when other information *is* considered, often it is not examined along with—and at the same "level" as—student-survey results.

Assuming most evaluators know by now that—in addition to asking for diverse kinds of evidence from a variety of sources—they should consider each "stone" of information as part of a larger "mosaic" (Seldin, Miller, and Seldin 2010, 45), it seems clear that resistance to using a true multiple-methods approach cannot simply be addressed through reminders about what the experts say and why. Many experts, including those in our own field who have written about faculty evaluation, struggle themselves to match theory with practice when placed in a supervisory role. So, while it is tempting to build the case for best evaluation practices on theoretical grounds, we must acknowledge that this approach does not always inspire observable change.

My assertion in this chapter is that we would get farther faster if we considered the primary obstacle to adopting a multiple-methods approach to evaluating teaching and then addressed this obstacle within a pragmatic framework based on typical administrative priorities. That is, we need to work more *rhetorically*, just as we've done for years to change the nature of student writing assessment, "think[ing] carefully about administrators as audience," including "what they do" and "what they want" (Haswell and McLeod 2001, 173). In my experience as an administrator of various types at several different universities, the main obstacle to a full embrace of a multidimensional approach to faculty evaluation is the sense that it requires far more time than less comprehensive methods. The best way to alleviate this concern is to appreciate it, meet it head on with time-saving strategies, and justify any additional time needed in terms of other administrative concerns, such as money and accreditation.

THE GREATEST CHALLENGE: TIME

Obviously, reading a list of student ratings and calculating the average can be done quickly. Reading a stack of teaching-related materials—of different types and from different sources—takes much longer, even when that stack is as compact and well organized as possible. The challenge isn't just about reading *more*; it's also about reading *differently*. A multiple-methods approach requires reading an array of materials holistically. It demands a kind of analysis that we often practice as researchers and teachers (particularly when we require student portfolios) but still seems strange to us in a faculty-evaluation context. This type of reading can be especially difficult if we aren't sure what exactly we are looking for in the documents, which is often the case when universi-ties—or departments—have not established clear evaluation guidelines. The potential interpretive challenges of a multiple-methods approach are well illustrated by discussions of the teaching portfolio, which, according to Anson and Dannels (2002), is best considered as "a collec-tion of genres" that includes not only reports of student course evalua-tions and peer observations but also "narratives, teaching philosophies, speculative journal entries, course syllabi, assignment sheets, [and] eval-uative rubrics," composed by different people for different purposes and audiences (92).

In terms of the course evaluations that are typically discussed in a teaching portfolio, for example, Halonen and Ellenberg (2006) claim that students may have in mind a number of purposes beyond assessing instruction, including attempting to "suck up" to the instructor, despite being told that evaluations will not affect course grades; questioning "heritage, breeding, intelligence, sense of humor (or lack of it), and income" as a way "to try to inflict psychological pain as revenge for their perceptions that the class disappointed them"; supporting other stu-dents who are unhappy about a course or instructor; criticizing physical attributes like "hair, fashion style"; and advocating for (or against) the professor (154–55). Further, students' sense of audience may vary. Do they have the faculty member in mind? Fellow students? A presumed supervisor? Because we do not know how students are thinking about purpose and audience as they complete course surveys, we cannot inter-pret, with any certainty, their responses.

Likewise, peer evaluations of instruction have "a wide range of pur-poses," which makes them similarly difficult to interpret without addi-tional contextual information (Millis 2006, 83–87). Beyond the most obvious purposes (e.g., to evaluate for tenure and promotion and to support faculty development), classroom visits may be used to gather information for departmental assessment discussions, identify candi-dates for teaching awards, and/or to build rapport among faculty (83). In addition, faculty conducting observations and writing reports may have purposes other than those articulated by a department or pro-gram. As with student surveys, various personal biases may influence the peer-observation process. Bain (2004) suggests, for example, that peer observers—consciously or not—want the observation process to affirm their own teaching strengths and preferences. Professors "tend to give high marks to colleagues who teach the way they do and lower ratings to those who do not—regardless of the learning," he explains (168–69). Such a tendency can mask legitimate reasons for differing approaches, including disciplinary differences and differences in early-career train-ing. In addition to "subjective impressions," Arreola (2007) offers other factors that can influence peer evaluators, including "friendships" and "hostilities" (93). The intended purpose of peer evaluation can be fur-ther complicated by faculty resistance to a process that, when engaged appropriately, can be "prohibitive" in terms of "the cost in time and effort" (97). Similar to student surveys, the audience for peer-observation reports may not be clear to the observer. Will the report be seen by the faculty member only? By the faculty member and a supervisor? By a group of colleagues? Audience assumptions can impact both the con-tent and the tone of a report.

Materials provided by the faculty member also reflect specific con-texts, each with different rhetorical expectations, making them similarly difficult to interpret at times. Syllabi, assignments, and sample student work will look different depending not only on the level of the course/student, but also on the degree of curricular consistency and the depart-mental and/or disciplinary expectations for both style and content. Even the instructor-composed reflective analysis—which is often intended to help evaluators make sense of teaching materials—is complicated with respect to purpose and audience. Anson and Dannels (2002) offer the example of an instructor who thought that the purpose of the self-reflection was to demonstrate professional development by "exposing and reflecting on a problem in a recent course" (91). The administra-tor charged with evaluating the instructor had a different purpose in mind—to demonstrate "unequivocal success." The instructor, thus, was rated low because the problem was seen as "a sign of weakness" (91). In terms of audience, Ruth Mirtz (2002) explains that teaching reflec-tions (in this case a "teaching philosophy") will resonate differently with evaluators depending on their "understanding of good teaching" (e.g., whether they see it as "a matter of performance and knowledge of one's field" or as "support for learning") (45).

With respect to concerns about time, those who are in the position of evaluating teaching may resist a multiple-methods approach because they are not convinced that the evaluation story constructed from care-ful consideration of various types of evidence will end differently from the one based on a quick calculation of student-rating averages or a ratio of positive to negative student (or peer) comments. Those of us who have evaluated faculty know that sometimes the stories will *not* end differently. Even Peter Elbow (1994), an enthusiastic critic of one-dimensional faculty evaluation, admits that when student evaluations of faculty are at one end of a spectrum (either "strikingly strong or strikingly weak") and other evidence supports these ratings we can feel confident in our "verdict that someone is an excellent or poor teacher" (101). The problem is that most teachers do not land squarely on either end of the student-evaluation spectrum, especially if answers to individual questions are considered apart from the overall rating. Rather, they "fall somewhere in the middle and get a mixed bag of results: a mixture of strong-, middle-, and weak-rated features and probably many mixed opinions or disagreements among students" (101). Without considering other information about instruction, Elbow argues, it is difficult to know what these mixed results mean. As he puts it, *"In teaching, as in writing, it is possible to be good in very different ways. A teacher might be warm or cold, organized or disorganized, easy or hard and still be good"* (104–5; emphasis original).

ADDRESSING THE TIME FACTOR

There is no getting around the fact that carefully considering evaluation information from a variety of sources can take more time than simply scanning the results of student surveys. However, the overall time spent judging faculty performance during a single semester or year does not *necessarily* have to take more time. An important part of advocating for change is to help evaluators see how challenges related to time might be effectively minimized. Scholars who promote a multidimensional approach to faculty evaluation have offered strategies to alleviate anxieties about time. With regard to teaching portfolios, such strategies include "put[ting] a ceiling on the number of pages" submitted (e.g., eight to twelve each for the analytical "narrative" and for "documentation" of "claims made in the narrative") and limiting the kinds of evidence collected by establishing no more than three basic categories (e.g., "material from oneself," "material from others," and "products" of teaching and learning) (Seldin, Miller, and Seldin 2010, 19–20). Still, if a twenty-five-page portfolio of different types of materials is posed against the easily gathered and readily analyzed numerical reports from student evaluations, administrators may still resist the more comprehensive portfolio approach. Another solution is to evaluate tenured and long-term non-tenure-track faculty less frequently—for example, on a rolling two- or three-year basis (i.e., 33% of such faculty would be evaluated one year, 33% the next, etc.). Elbow (1994) offers this type of approach to chairs and WPAs who perceive "dealing with" a "pile of qualitative data" as "daunting" (104). If there's a system in place for ensuring that instructors are regularly collecting materials and soliciting feedback from students and peers, he explains, the "official judging mechanism need only occur every two to three semesters for untenured faculty and every four to five semesters for tenured faculty— not an impossible job" (105). In fact, many experts on faculty evaluation recommend that decisions about faculty (whether in the area of teaching, research, or service) be made based on a "pattern of performance over time," "preferably several years"—an approach that universities tend to use only for tenure and promotion and not for other personnel decisions (Arreola 2007, 76).

If annual review of faculty is necessitated by an entrenched merit-pay system or fluctuation in staffing needs (making it necessary to base decisions to rehire on limited data), a more flexible approach—one resembling student learning-outcomes assessment—can be used. With their program director, chair, or dean, a faculty member articulates a small set of teaching goals or questions that are then evaluated each year based on different types of evidence (e.g., peer observation reports one year, revised syllabi and assignments another year, sample student work the next year, and so on). To alleviate worry among evaluators about how particular types of evidence would add up over several years, faculty can be asked to compose a brief reflective narrative to both contextualize the particular type of data they are submitting during a given year and draw connections between the analysis of that data and data submitted in previous years.

Alternatively, faculty who teach a variety of courses might select one course to highlight in an annual course portfolio, which requires fewer documents than a comprehensive portfolio. Again, for untenured faculty, data and analyses for single courses can be briefly synthesized each year so that—if/when necessary for tenure, promotion, or, in the case of non-tenure-line faculty, contract renewal—the full narrative for a teaching portfolio would, in essence, already be written. This approach also works well for part-time and short-term, full-time faculty because it requires simply filing extra copies of course handouts during the semester, copying a handful of sample papers, and writing a brief reflective narrative. As with full-fledged teaching portfolios, however, care must be taken to limit the amount and/or kinds of materials submitted.

With respect to evaluators outside of a program or department, another way to save time would be to accept that, like scholarship, good teaching is discipline-specific and rely more on disciplinary experts (i.e., faculty hired because of their expertise and experience in particular fields) to determine the quality of their colleagues' teaching performance. In this way, evaluating teaching using multiple methods becomes similar to evaluating the research efforts of faculty who write in various genres, including, for example, poetry, fiction, and academic argument. It is often the case that the "self" or persona of these different publication types may seem different (as they might across various kinds of teaching materials). Yet, since we are basing our judgment on the overall quality of the work (as defined by the reputation of the publisher, the rigor of the peer review, competiveness, citations by other scholars, etc.), who the writer "is" (or "is not")—as reflected in written work—is far less important than consistency in the *quality* of the work produced, as assessed against criteria agreed upon by the particular disciplinary community.

Just as universities (departments, programs) ask members within a particular discipline to decide what the criteria should be for evaluating research (within general parameters provided in their tenure and promotion documents), so too should they be asked to articulate specific teaching evaluation criteria based on current best practices of their fields. Faculty members anticipating evaluation should be asked to frame their teaching accomplishments in terms of these criteria, offering evidence for their claims about teaching whenever possible. Beyond student commentary, peer/supervisory testimony, and samples of student work, such evidence might include references to disciplinary best practices, invitations to speak about teaching at a disciplinary conference, teaching citations/awards, and/or pedagogical publications. In this way, the case for effective teaching resembles the more familiar "scholarly case," requiring a "coherent" argument supported by "evidence" (Bain 2004, 168).

In fact, clear, specific criteria, reflective of current theory and research and sensitive to disciplinary differences, help ensure not only the appropriateness of evaluation but also the efficiency that evaluators desire. Ideally, these criteria are developed and discussed by the faculty at large and guide all aspects of teaching, all formative and evaluative responses to teaching, and all of the data-gathering methods upon which responses are based. They are used by faculty as the basis for their annual review (or tenure, promotion) case for teaching effectiveness, thus addressing the reviewers' need for guidance on "how to read" the "pile of stuff" submitted for evaluation, as one member of my school's Board of Rank and Tenure put it. If these criteria represent a comprehensive picture of good teaching—including attention to "content expertise"; skills in instructional design, delivery, and assessment; and "course management skills" (Arreola 2007, 19)—and if they are accompanied by a rubric specifying levels of performance, evaluators will have an easier time reconciling the multiple "selves" represented in different types of materials. In addition, the use of clear, faculty-designed criteria will enhance the "functional validity" of the evaluation process, or its perceived "fairness and utility" (xxviii), bringing other administrative benefits, as discussed below.

HELPING ADMINISTRATORS SEE THE VALUE OF TIME SPENT ON MULTIPLE METHODS

In their discussion of the importance of writing administrators and faculty understanding not only upper-level administrative priorities but also administrative discourse ("admin-speak"), Joyce Kinkead and Jeanne Simpson highlight a number of salient concerns. Budgetary issues, discussed in terms of "faculty full-time equivalents" ("FTEs") and institutional/programmatic "productivity," are certainly priorities, but so are institutional goals (i.e., "mission"); "assessment" (particularly the kind required for accreditation); and "accountability" (e.g., to the "institution's governing board, the state governing body, the commissioner for higher education, the governor, or the legislature") (Kinkead and Simpson 2002, 69–72). Just as we have done with student assessment initiatives related to placement and graduation readiness, those of us in a position to influence local conversations about faculty evaluation can use administrative concerns like these to help promote change.

The Costs of Single-Source Evaluation

Again, because writing faculty and program administrators tend to justify practices in terms of writing (teaching, learning) theory, when we think about the costs associated with potentially problematic practices, we often think about theoretical costs (e.g., oversimplification, misunderstanding, misapplication of concepts) when people ignore or discount our theory-based arguments. In my experience, what works better than counting theoretical costs with empathetic colleagues, however, is to enumerate for wary administrators the resource-based costs of using a one-dimensional process to evaluate a complex endeavor like teaching.

It helps to point out, for example, that any single-source method of evaluation is prone to error, and that errors can be costly. Even the producers of standardized, nationally normed course evaluation forms make clear the problems of relying exclusively on survey-generated data to make personnel decisions. For example, after outlining "several weaknesses inherent in the rating process" (e.g., the "halo effect," the "Error of Central Tendency," the inability of students to judge certain aspects of instruction), the IDEA Center (n.d.) asserts that their widely used student evaluation surveys "are most useful when they are a part of a more comprehensive program *which includes additional evaluation tools*" (emphasis added). Our theories aside, caveats like these make common sense to us as teachers and researchers; we don't evaluate students based on a single type of performance on a single day, and we don't make scholarly claims based on a single source of evidence.

Such cautions also imply real institutional costs. Just as there are financial costs associated with erroneous decisions about student performance (placement in non-credit-bearing courses, requirement to retake a course, delayed graduation), there are costs associated with personnel decisions made because of questionable faculty evaluation practices. Administrators who evaluate faculty need to be reminded of these costs. Faculty cost money to hire and support. The usual costs can increase substantially if the faculty member is not rehired or, in extreme cases, sues because of a theoretically unsound evaluation process. Obviously, faculty who are not rehired cost the university money because another person must be searched for and hired, sometimes at a higher base salary rate than was in effect during a previous hiring cycle. In addition to the actual dollars needed for increased salaries, search activities, and start-up costs, any funds used to support research-release time for tenure-track faculty who leave a university are also lost. Beyond the "real costs," there are also costs associated with the administrative and faculty time needed for conducting another search and for mentoring and supervising another new faculty member. This is not to say that poor teachers should be retained, but rather that a determination of "poor teaching," like any important decision, should be based on thoughtful considerations of as much, and as varied, information as possible—and with a clear sense of what is at stake not only for the individual faculty member, but for the university as a whole.

Another cost associated with faculty evaluation has to do with historically underrepresented faculty, who, according to recent scholarship, can be particularly disadvantaged by a single-source evaluation process. Administrators who are resistant to changing an approach that seems to work well enough, generally, can often be persuaded by the practical reality that faculty from underrepresented groups may not be faring as well as their mainstream colleagues. Beyond struggling with feelings of isolation, "tokenism," and stress associated with higher service expectations and "denigration" of "research interests" (Turner and Myers 2000, 83–112, 26–27), such faculty often experience skepticism and "hostility" from students who are uncomfortable with differences in teaching "behaviors" that often "reflect race, gender, nationality, or socioeconomic class" (Merritt 2007, 254). This hostility is sometimes expressed through student course surveys, which, again, too often play a significant role in renewal, tenure, and promotion decisions. The cost of making an error in judgment about the teaching performance of, for example, faculty of color may include not only the costs outlined above, but—because potential applicants will research the campus climate for diverse faculty, including retention rates—also a decreased ability to recruit additional historically underrepresented faculty, which, for many universities, compromises stated vision, mission, and strategic diversity initiatives, including those related to recruitment of under-represented students.

Another potential cost of a questionable evaluation process is a legal one. Many academics believe that the courts are resistant to getting involved in the business of universities. Historically, this is true. Writing in the 1980s about legal challenges to faculty evaluation outcomes, Seldin (1984) explains that the courts "generally stay out of the meth-ods-and-criteria arena in the judging of faculty performance" (21). In a more recent discussion of the negative impacts of "flawed personnel decisions," however, Fite (2006) notes the "significant" increase in both the number of formal faculty grievances and the willingness of courts to involve themselves in faculty evaluation decisions, especially those that seem discriminatory (185). Citing an article by A. Franke, Fite adds that judges are sending more such cases to juries, "who are regarded as more skeptical of institutions and sympathetic to the individual faculty member" (186). Fite suggests that schools wishing to "minimize the pos-sibility of legal complications in personnel decisions" follow "certain guidelines" for evaluating faculty, based on the work of scholars such as Peter Seldin. These guidelines include providing, "in writing," detailed criteria to faculty and employing "evaluation systems [that] use multiple evaluation sources" (Fite 2006, 187). Like Fite, Arreola (2007) under-scores the legal value of using multiple methods, given the "legal liabil-ity" posed by student course surveys, which are heavily relied upon by evaluators but "have generally not undergone the rigorous psychometric and statistical procedures required" to support claims of validity and/or reliability (100, 110). Though a faculty member is unlikely to sue due to concerns about time, money, or retaliation, just one legal case can cost a university tens of thousands of dollars, even if the case is eventually dismissed or settled out of court. In fact, the very threat of a lawsuit can cost thousands of dollars in consultation fees. Negative publicity is an additional potential cost worth considering.

While it is harder to document, another cost of not using a multiple-methods approach is compromised faculty morale. Whether the ubiquitous, single-source measure of teaching effectiveness—the student course survey—accurately reflects teaching ability or not, faculty often perceive that it does not. Despite many attempts to alleviate faculty concerns about potential biases that may affect the validity of student surveys (e.g., Harris and Cullen 2012, 143–45; Kulik 2001; Wachtel 1998, 192–93), the fact is that faculty often *believe* that "factors" such as expected course grade, the "faculty member's personal characteristics," and the "difficulty of work required" have a "significant effect" on student evaluations and, thus, should not be relied upon for making high-stakes personnel decisions (Baldwin and Blattner 2003, 28). Mistrust in the evaluation process can translate into much broader, and potentially more costly, feelings of mistrust, discontent, and malaise among the faculty at large. As Fite (2006) explains, personnel decisions that are "flawed" (or perceived as such) not only "undermine faculty and administrator relations," but they "threaten the sense of shared purposes that underlie the complex yet fragile bones of academic community and which support productive teaching, research, and student engagement" (185). Further, they "may affect the decisions faculty make about their own roles and workload and deflect the pursuit by faculty . . . of their institution's stated missions and educational goals" (185). In other words, if community morale declines because of perceived problems with the evaluation process, faculty may be less likely to support and participate in initiatives important to administrators—initiatives like recruitment, curricular revision, and assessment that can have clear financial consequences.

Connecting with Accreditation

Though administrators have always cared about the quality of academic programs, they have not always been asked to think about quality in terms of learning outcomes that can be objectively assessed. Further, until fairly recently, they have not been challenged to specify what a postsecondary education "delivers" to graduates (Jaschik 2013). Current accreditation standards and practices, which both reflect a theoretical shift in higher-education conversations and attempt to answer increasingly insistent public calls for accountability, offer ways to help administrators see the value of alternative faculty-evaluation methods.

Those of us who were teaching in or administering writing programs during the mid-to-late 1990s started to see a shift in how accrediting agencies were approaching assessment. Instead of being asked by university institutional-research offices to supply numbers and educational credentials of part-time versus full-time faculty—and, perhaps, a representative syllabus or two—WPAs and other campus administrators began to be required to provide information about course objectives, or "outcomes," and "evidence" of how these objectives would be met by students. Depending upon our region and accrediting group, we may have even been asked to design program assessments that involved collecting and evaluating actual student writing rather than simply reviewing syllabi and surveying students, faculty, and alumni as we had done in the past. Directions for reporting information started to change, too. Instead of just explaining what we were doing, we were asked to discuss why we were doing it and how what we were doing supported or "aligned with" broader university objectives, which, in turn, were supposed to be directly linked to a school's specific educational mission.

This shift in accreditation approach, prompted by public calls during the 1980s for colleges and universities to be held more accountable (to tuition-paying students and families, taxpayers, and state governments), is typically explained as a "pendulum swing" from an inputs-based definition of educational "quality" to an outputs-based definition (Braskamp and Braskamp 1998). This swing coincided with a "subtle but profound" "paradigm shift" in higher education, generally: from a focus on *instruction* (and the resources needed to support instruction) to a focus on actual *learning*, or the "product" of instruction (Barr and Tagg 1995, 13–14). Within an "instruction paradigm," a university's primary responsibility is to "deliver instruction" by way of knowledgeable faculty and "a series of discrete, largely unrelated, three-credit classes" (19). Success is measured in terms of the ability to attract high-quality students and faculty; to develop and expand curricula; to improve resources; and to increase enrollment and, with that, revenue (16). A "learning paradigm," on the other hand, requires special attention to whether and how all students (not just the best ones) are learning from both in- and out-of-class instruction and experiences. Curricula, classes, schedules, and other institutional "structures" are adjusted to accommodate "any learning method that works" in order to "clear the way for every student's success" (20, 23). Success within this paradigm, then, is determined by looking at the extent to which students meet "learning and student-success outcomes" and the development of environments and technologies that improve learning (16). Because learning can only be gauged by examining what students are able to *do* (at the end of a course, by graduation, etc.), there was a necessary shift in the type of evidence required to support claims of success: from "indirect" evidence, like syllabi or alumni surveys, to "direct" evidence, like student papers or projects. Ideally, schools would provide "a variety of evidence" collected through "multiple measures," resulting "in a collage of student performance" (Braskamp and Braskamp 1998).

While most administrators are now aware of this shift from inputs to outcomes, from an exclusive emphasis on instruction to consideration of learning, they don't often apply that shift to other campus-wide assessment activities, such as faculty evaluation. This is really no surprise because, despite what seems an obvious connection between what teachers do in the classroom and the extent to which students learn, accrediting agencies have been slow to suggest that processes used to evaluate higher-ed instruction should be aligned with processes used to evaluate higher-ed learning. That is, while we have been encouraged for years to engage in "ongoing systematic collection and analysis of meaningful, assessable, and verifiable data" about student learning (Northwest Commission on Colleges and Universities 2010, 4.A.1), collected through "multiple direct and indirect measures" (Higher Learning Commission 2007, 3a), they typically have not asked us to demonstrate teaching effectiveness in the same manner—that is, with a broad range of both indirect and direct data that are analyzed, verified, and put to good (i.e., "meaningful") use. Further, while we have been encouraged to use the results of student learning assessments to "improve instruction"—through, for example, faculty development initiatives—or fulfill the school's "mission" (New England Association of Schools and Colleges 2011), we haven't been asked to consider how individual instructors might reflect on their own role in student achievement of learning outcomes. This is true even for accrediting agencies whose criteria for evaluating faculty performance reflect a learning-based paradigm by, for example, framing teaching "effectiveness" in terms of student achievement of published learning outcomes. The Southern Association of Colleges and Schools (2011) offers a good example in a statement, originally crafted around 2001, suggesting that, for employment decisions, faculty "competence" be gauged not only in terms of "undergraduate and graduate degrees [and] related work experiences," but "demonstrated competencies and achievements that contribute to effective teaching and student learning outcomes" (principles 3.7.1).

However, it appears that accreditors are starting to recognize the importance of helping colleges and universities connect assessment of student learning with assessment of instruction—if for no other reason than to prevent a higher-ed version of the K–12 "accountability" debacle, in which learning, teaching, and the connections between these activities became oversimplified to the point that parents, politicians, and pundits began promoting standardized test scores as the sole determinant of good teaching. For example, the new edition of the popular institutional-assessment guide *Assessing Student Learning* includes a section on using assessment results to improve both learning *and* teaching. In it, author Linda Suskie (2009), a long-time accreditor and former vice president of the Middle States Association of Colleges and Schools, suggests that instructors may need to "take a hard look" at the "content and requirements" of their courses and "reconsider [their] teaching methods" if student achievement appears "disappointing" (303–5). Beyond clarifying the role that faculty should play in student achievement of learning outcomes, some accrediting agencies appear to be considering how their principles for assessing student achievement might inform faculty evaluation processes. In its recent higher-ed accreditation redesign, for instance, WASC (Western Association of Schools and Colleges 2012) not only reaffirmed the link between teaching and learning but also aligned recommendations for faculty "performance appraisal" with criteria for assessing student learning. While their previous (Western Association of Schools and Colleges 2008) accreditation handbook recommended "peer and student evaluation of instruction" as sources of "evidence of teaching effectiveness" (3.3), the new handbook explains that faculty evaluation should be "consistent with best practices in performance appraisal, including multisource feedback" (Western Association of Schools and Colleges 2012, 3.2).

Still, until accreditors are both explicit and unified in their perspectives on how teaching influences learning—and how that influence can be evaluated—administrators will not be inspired to make that link themselves. Those in a position to help influence faculty evaluation discussions can, and should, take steps to help administrators see the intersections between the two assessment activities before accreditors feel pressured to specify the intersections for us. In fact, because many of us know what meaningful educational assessment looks like, having participated in student learning assessments for decades, we are in an ideal position to assist with campus-wide rethinking of faculty evaluation practices. One strategy I've used involves discussing faculty evaluation *as* assessment, making the point that, from an accreditation perspective, all assessments—whether of learning outcomes or other institutional outcomes (regarding, e.g., planning, administration, and/or community engagement)—should involve collecting "examples of evidence that could substantiate achievement" of those outcomes (Middle States Commission on Higher Education 2011, v). Most administrators will accept that within an outcomes-based framework the assessment of faculty performance would require evidence of the outcomes of instructional behaviors—and that the priority outcome would be learning. Further, they will typically agree that the relationship between such behaviors and student learning cannot easily be assessed through the student surveys and peer observation protocols commonly used to evaluate instruction. Such recognitions can be a first step toward a willingness to entertain alternative evaluation practices.

Another good strategy is to introduce into the larger faculty evaluation system smaller-scale approaches that are aligned with current accreditation standards and principles. My university's former composition director, for example, spearheaded efforts in the writing department to improve the usefulness (and, thus, the validity) of both the student evaluation and peer observation processes using a learning outcomes-based assessment approach. To complement the standardized, university-sanctioned student course survey focused on teaching behaviors (e.g., instructor enthusiasm, organization, clarity of presentation), she helped the department develop a form focused on learning, with questions based on our learning outcomes (e.g., "Did you learn how to support a point? Respond to the work of peers? Evaluate sources?"). Similarly, she designed an outcomes-based peer observation process that now requires instructors to articulate what they will be doing in a given class and how the activities support course or program outcomes—and asks that observers focus on those connections. As a way to influence conversations about faculty evaluation beyond the department, my colleague and I use information collected through these methods in the reports of faculty we mentor and/or supervise, even though our dean typically only requests results of the university student surveys, especially for non-tenure-line faculty. In addition, though our reviews of faculty teaching usually begin with a discussion of the student survey responses, which are then supported, or not, with discussion of other "methods," I started to do the reverse when I was department chair—to begin with a discussion of other evidence and *then* explain how the student evaluations confirmed or complicated that information.

Such strategies work best if they reflect a basic knowledge of both accreditation criteria (aka "standards" or "characteristics") and the educational assessment concepts that inform those criteria. It's a good idea, then, for anyone hoping to persuade reluctant administrators to accept a different faculty evaluation model to become conversant with the criteria and "guiding principles" of various regional and disciplinary accrediting bodies, which are readily available on their websites.

When discussing faculty evaluation with administrators and colleagues outside of my department, I have found it helpful to reference accrediting agencies whose standards include phrases like student "achievement" of "learning outcomes" in sections devoted to both learning and teaching and emphasize the importance of collecting both indirect and direct evidence from different sources (students, faculty, administrators, and support staff). I have also found that administrators outside of the humanities seem particularly persuaded by references to the standards of disciplinary agencies that accredit programs in business, science, and education. It is worth noting, for example, that agencies such as ABET (Accreditation Board for Engineering and Technology), AACSB (American Association of Colleges and Schools of Business), and APA (American Psychological Association) all offer guidelines for evaluating teaching that assume a complex relationship between teaching practices and successful student learning.

CONCLUSION

Of course, a multiple-methods approach will not solve all of the problems associated with faculty evaluation. Any evidence, indirect or direct, quantitative or qualitative, can be used incorrectly or irresponsibly. Anson and Dannels (2002) argue, for instance, that the most well-informed evaluation process can be undermined by uninformed evaluators—i.e., those who are unfamiliar with the literature on teaching and learning, and thus unacquainted with the variety of acceptable classroom approaches and methods (98–99). In fact, even teaching portfolios, offered throughout this chapter as a model for sound evaluation, can be misused by evaluators who don't understand—or don't support—the approach.

Also, as the literature on teaching portfolios makes clear, resistance to a multiple-methods evaluation approach doesn't just come from administrator-evaluators; it comes from faculty as well. Like administrators, faculty often express concerns about the time it takes to collect, collate, and reflect on various kinds of evidence of teaching success, even when they agree with the basic tenets of the approach (Seldin, Miller, and Seldin 2010, 54–57). Faculty concerns are exacerbated when the time spent demonstrating teaching effectiveness in various ways appears not to be valued as much as the time spent researching and writing for publication (see, e.g., Seldin 1990, 13–14).

Finally, though it makes good sense to link assessment of teaching with assessment of learning, administrators and faculty may resist if the effort is framed in terms of "accountability." Though the decades-long "accountability movement" has centered around K–12 education, it has gradually expanded to implicate postsecondary education in the decline of national economic health, a trend well-illustrated by the US Department of Education's (2006) call for "higher education institutions" to not only "measure student learning using quality assessment data," but also make results "available in a consumer-friendly form" to "students, policymakers, and the public" (24). Though accrediting agencies have historically resisted imposing outcomes or assessment methods on member schools, they are now facing enormous pressure to do so, as illustrated by WASC's recently revised accreditation handbook—which aligns new "core competencies" with graduation "expectations and proficiencies" (Western Association of Schools and Colleges 2012)—and outlined in the controversial Degree Qualification Profile (DQP) developed by Lumina, a private foundation overseen by a collection of CEOs and top-level college administrators (Lumina Foundation for Education 2011). Though the DQP is based in sound educational research and theory, what has alarmed some educators is that curricular standards are presented as "a point of departure for agreement on more detailed and specific expectations regarding the *development of programs, courses, assignments, and assessments*" (2; emphasis added). Given both the role instructors play in development of courses, assignments, and assessments, as well as the growing public mistrust of a professoriate perceived to do little more than write papers "for each other on abstruse topics" and discourage "dissident ideas" (Jaschik 2013), it is not hard to imagine that "agreement" on how faculty might be evaluated across colleges would soon be on the agenda of Lumina and other organizations in the business of saving higher education. It is also not difficult to imagine how attractive a one-dimensional, readily-quantifiable evaluation method might be to uninformed or unfriendly external parties looking for a fast, inexpensive way to see if faculty are doing their jobs. In this light, Ed White's early advice about student learning assessment seems relevant to efforts to challenge common faculty evaluation practices: "Institutions at risk of such well-motivated intrusion should know that a responsible assessment program in place is the surest defense against pressure for inappropriate testing" (White 1990, 196).

References

Anson, Chris M., and Deanna P. Dannels. 2002. "The Medium and the Message: Developing Responsible Methods for Assessing Teaching Portfolios." In *Composition,*

Pedagogy, and the Scholarship of Teaching, ed. Deborah Minter and Amy M. Goodburn. 89–100. Portsmouth, NH: Heinemann, Boynton/Cook.

Arreola, Raoul A. 2007. *Developing a Comprehensive Faculty Evaluation System: A Guide to Designing, Building, and Operating Large-Scale Faculty Evaluation Systems*, 3rd ed. San Francisco: Anker.

Bain, Ken. 2004. *What the Best College Teachers Do.* Cambridge, MA: Harvard University Press.

Baldwin, Tamara, and Nancy Blattner. 2003. "Guarding against Potential Bias in Student Evaluations: What Every Faculty Member Needs to Know." *College Teaching* 51 (1): 27–32. http://dx.doi.org/10.1080/87567550309596407.

Barr, Robert B., and John Tagg. 1995. "From Teaching to Learning: A New Paradigm for Undergraduate Education." *Change* 27 (Nov/Dec): 13–25.

Braskamp, Larry A., and David C. Braskamp. 1998. "The Pendulum Swing of Standards and Evidence." *CHEA Chronicle* 1 (5). http://www.chea.org/Chronicle/vol1/no5 /index.html.

Elbow, Peter. 1994. "Making Better Use of Student Evaluations of Teachers." In *Evaluating Teachers of Writing*, ed. Christine A. Hult, 97–107. Urbana, IL: NCTE.

Fite, David. 2006. "Using Evaluation Data for Personnel Decisions." In *Evaluating Faculty Performance: A Practical Guide to Assessing Teaching, Research, and Service*, ed. Peter Seldin and Associates, 181–200. Bolton, MA: Anker.

Halonen, Jane S., and George B. Ellenberg. 2006. "Teaching Evaluation Follies: Misperception and Misbehavior in Student Evaluations of Teachers." In *Evaluating Faculty Performance: A Practical Guide to Assessing Teaching, Research, and Service*, ed. Peter Seldin and Associates, 150–65. Bolton, MA: Anker.

Harris, Michael, and Roxanne Cullen. 2012. *Leading the Learner-Centered Campus: An Administrator's Framework for Improving Student Learning Outcomes.* San Francisco: Jossey-Bass.

Haswell, Richard H., and Susan McLeod. 2001. "Working with Administrators: A Dialogue on Dialogue." In *Beyond Outcomes: Assessment and Instruction within a University Writing Program*, ed. Richard H. Haswell, 169–85. Westport, CT: Ablex.

Higher Learning Commission of the North Central Association of Colleges and Schools. 2007. *Criteria for Accreditation.* http://www.policy.hlcommission.org/Policies/appendix -a.html.

IDEA Center. n.d. "Research and Papers: Value and Limitations of Student Ratings." http://www.theideacenter.org.

Jaschik, Scott. 2013. "New Purdue President Outlines Critiques of Higher Education." *Inside Higher Ed*, January 21. https://www.insidehighered.com/news/2013/01/21/new -purdue-president-outlines-critiques-higher-education.

Kinkead, Joyce, and Jeanne Simpson. 2002. "The Administrative Audience: A Rhetorical Problem." In *The Allyn & Bacon Sourcebook for Writing Program Administrators*, ed. Irene Ward and William J. Carpenter, 68–77. New York: Longman.

Kulik, James A. 2001. "Student Ratings: Validity, Utility, and Controversy." *New Directions for Institutional Research* 2001 (109): 9–25. http://dx.doi.org/10.1002/ir.1.

Lumina Foundation for Education. 2011. *The Degree Qualifications Profile.*

Merritt, Deborah J. 2007. "Bias, the Brain, and Student Evaluations of Teaching." *St. John's Law Review* 82: 235–87.

Millis, Barbara J. 2006. "Peer Observations as a Catalyst for Faculty Development." In *Evaluating Faculty Performance: A Practical Guide to Assessing Teaching, Research, and Service*, ed. Peter Seldin and Associates, 82–95. Bolton, MA: Anker.

Middle States Commission on Higher Education. 2011. *Characteristics of Excellence in Higher Education: Requirements of Affiliation and Standards for Accreditation.*

Minter, Deborah, and Amy Goodburn. 2002. "Introduction: Why Document Postsecondary Teaching?" In *Composition Pedagogy and the Scholarship of Teaching*, ed. Deborah Minter and Amy M. Goodburn, xv–xix. Portsmouth, NH: Heinemann, Boynton/Cook.

Mirtz, Ruth. 2002. "Teaching Statements and Teaching Selves." In *Composition Pedagogy and the Scholarship of Teaching*, ed. Deborah Minter and Amy M. Goodburn, 43–53. Portsmouth, NH: Heinemann, Boynton/Cook.

New England Association of Schools and Colleges. 2011. *Standards for Accreditation.* Commission on Institutions of Higher Education. http://cihe.neasc.org/standards -policies/standards/standards-html-version.

Northwest Commission on Colleges and Universities. 2010. *Standards for Accreditation.* http://www.nwccu.org.

O'Neill, Peggy, Cindy Moore, and Brian Huot. 2009. *A Guide to College Writing Assessment.* Logan: Utah State University Press.

Seldin, Peter. 1990. "Academic Environments and Teaching Effectiveness." In *How Administrators Can Improve Teaching: Moving from Talk to Action in Higher Education*, ed. Peter Seldin and Associates. San Francisco: Jossey-Bass.

Seldin, Peter. 1984. *Changing Practices in Faculty Evaluation: A Critical Assessment and Recommendations for Improvement.* San Francisco: Jossey-Bass.

Seldin, Peter and Associates. 1990. *How Administrators Can Improve Teaching.* San Francisco: Jossey-Bass.

Seldin, Peter, J. Elizabeth Miller, and Clement A. Seldin. 2010. *The Teaching Portfolio: A Practical Guide to Improved Performance and Promotion/Tenure Decisions.* San Francisco: Jossey-Bass.

Southern Association of Colleges and Schools. 2011. *The Principles of Accreditation: Foundations for Quality Enhancement.* http://sacscoc.org.

Suskie, Linda. 2009. *Assessing Student Learning: A Common Sense Guide*, 2nd ed. San Francisco: Jossey-Bass.

Turner, Caroline Sotello Viernes, and Samuel L. Myers, Jr. 2000. *Faculty of Color in Academe: Bittersweet Success.* Boston: Allyn and Bacon.

US Department of Education. 2006. *A Test of Leadership: Charting the Future of US Higher Education: A Report of the Commission Appointed by Secretary of Education Margaret Spellings.* http://www2.ed.gov/about/bdscomm/list/hiedfuture/reports/final-report .pdf.

Wachtel, Howard K. 1998. "Student Evaluation of College Teaching Effectiveness: A Brief Review." *Assessment and Evaluation in Higher Education* 23 (2): 191–211. http://dx.doi .org/10.1080/0260293980230207.

Western Association of Schools and Colleges. 2008. *Handbook of Accreditation.* http://www .wacsenior.org.

Western Association of Schools and Colleges. 2012. *Handbook of Accreditation.* http://www .wascsenior.org.

White, Edward M. 1989. *Developing Successful College Writing Programs.* San Francisco: Jossey-Bass.

White, Edward M. 1990. "Language and Reality in Writing Assessment." *College Composition and Communication* 41 (2): 187–200. http://dx.doi.org/10.2307/358159.

10

TEACHER EVALUATION IN THE AGE OF WEB 2.0
What Every College Instructor Should Know and Every WPA Should Consider

Amy C. Kimme Hea

A college composition graduate teaching assistant who doesn't often use technology discovers that he has a few "bad" ratings on RateMyProfessors .com. What recourse does he have? What does this mean for his future job search?

A writing program administrator (WPA) is hiring adjuncts to teach first-year composition, and through a Google search of one candidate, the WPA is led to the adjunct's Academia.u status report that expresses her exhaustion with grading composition papers. What does this mean for her hiring status?

In his life outside of the academy, an untenured faculty member sits on the advisory board of a non-profit invested in the humane treatment of animals. His contributions to this organization are not conducted during his work hours or with work resources, yet a member of his tenure review committee searches for the faculty's webpage as part of his tenure review and stumbles upon meeting minutes from the non-profit's advisory board. How is the faculty member's tenure case affected by information related to his political interests?

These scenarios and the ethical concerns they raise about online teacher presence are not easy to contend with.[1] In fact, for some of us these fictional scenarios are all too similar to our own lived experiences as composition teachers, faculty members, community advocates, and WPAs. As social networking has become a mainstay of our academic lives, it has become nearly impossible to separate our online teacher and administrative presence from other dimensions of our personal and political realities. While feminist and critical scholars have

DOI: 10.7330/9780874219661.c010

long argued that the political is personal and that a false binary exists between them, today the digital dissolution of such boundaries leads to important considerations of the ways teachers are evaluated with or without their knowledge, and sometimes even without an option to explain, respond, or resist.

Some academics may argue that teachers willingly trade their privacy rights by opting to represent themselves through technologies such as social networking sites, blogs, and other social media. At present, however, we are not just *writing* the web but are being *written by* the web. Even the most recalcitrant faculty member who opts not to use a computer for her work can likely be located through a simple name and faculty affiliation search. From here, electronic copies of her publications, reviews of that research, and results of her teaching evaluations, not to mention other non-work-related information, can likely be located. The web's search capabilities and its archiving functions are not new, but fundamental changes have occurred in both the public's growing awareness of Google's—and other search engines'—data storage practices and our own increasing reliance on social media such as Facebook, LinkedIn, and Academia.u, where we and our "friends" offer detailed pieces of personal information about ourselves and others. Rather than merely wrangling with the way the web delivers information, we as teachers and administrators must contend with its ability to trace, archive, and even claim ownership to data about us (see Kimme Hea 2007; Johnson-Eilola 2010).

For my part, I am invested in better understanding teacher and administrator online presence as it relates to evaluation practices. Rather than adding my voice to the heated debate over the validity and reliability of evaluation data, I want to examine the ways in which we must contend with the rise in online evaluation—valid or not, reliable or not—that stands to impact all teachers and administrators (see Coladarci and Kornfield 2007; Felton, Mitchell, and Stinson 2004; Otto, Sanford, and Ross 2008). In this essay, I argue that teachers and WPAs have a shared responsibility to develop a critical understanding of teacher evaluation, and that such an understanding must take into account previous teacher evaluation practices, local institutional contexts, and the discourses and practices of Web 2.0 technologies and social media platforms. To this end, I offer a brief historical trace of teacher evaluation and its turn toward technological concerns. Considering this historical work, I situate my own discussion of teacher evaluation in the age of Web 2.0 through the figuration of three contemporary news stories—data mining, Manti Te'o, and Edward Snowden. It is my contention that these figurations—partial, situated stories that offer important insights into larger narratives about online life—articulate key concerns about privacy, context, information accuracy, and dissemination (Haraway 1992, 86). Arguing that online evaluation practices are more than merely technological manifestations but also cultural practices that come to inform our online presence, I suggest some starting points for teachers and WPAs to build contextualized and responsive teacher evaluation practices, ones that strive to address the complex articulations of teacher and administrator online presence in the age of Web 2.0.

HISTORY OF TEACHER EVALUATION

To be sure, teacher evaluation has never been trusted, is always under revision, and represents key political and cultural assumptions about the roles of teachers, students, and even education itself (see Stronge and Tucker 2003, 12–13). Whether summative evaluation—used for the purposes of hiring, retaining, and firing teachers—or formative evaluation—deployed to create teacher development, certification, and education programs—one fact remains: teacher evaluation cannot be separated from its historical context. Concerns about teacher evaluation in the field of rhetoric and composition can be traced to the 1956 Conference on College Composition and Communication (CCCC) workshop entitled "Professional Status of Composition/Communications Staff," where participants asserted that upper administration should not be the sole determiners of good teaching, suggesting instead that colleague classroom visits, as well as other evaluation methods, should be included as measures of teacher quality (Estrin 1958, 113).[2] In the next decades, the merits of teacher evaluation continued to appear in national debates on education and among scholarly discussions in our field. At the national level, Kenneth Eble's (1970) influential monograph based upon a two-year study of college teaching, *The Recognition and Evaluation of Teaching*,[3] emphasized student participation in teacher evaluation and advocated for "open evaluations" of teachers—published both locally to the department and even more widely to the university community (35). In the 1980s, scholars sitting on the CCCC Committee on Teaching and Its Evaluation in Composition (1982) outlined key factors in evaluating writing teachers. The committee stressed the need to consider teacher evaluation in relation to the unique demands placed on *writing* teachers. In light of the day-to-day practices of teaching writing, the committee advocated for six evaluation instruments that include input from administrators, teachers, and students. This process-driven, complex teacher evaluation model was complemented by calls at the end of this decade from assessment scholars Edward M. White (1985, 180–86; 1989, 208; 1994) and Faigley and Witte (1983, 51–56), who underscored the committee's recommendations as they advised WPAs to attend to teacher recruitment, retention, and evaluation as part of larger writing program assessments.[4]

THE TECHNOLOGICAL–ONLINE TURN

The turn to computer technology came in 1994 with Deborah Holdstein's essay "Evaluating Teachers in Computerized Classrooms," found in Christine Hult's (1994) edited collection *Evaluating Teachers of Writing*— the only edited collection in our field devoted exclusively to issues of teacher evaluation (until this one). Holdstein emphasized the need to assess writing teachers in a computer classroom in relationship to both the new demands of the technologies and the training offered to these teachers (Holdstein 1994, 168). Holdstein's essay focused on the integration of word processing, grammar, and spell checking programs, as well as different ways to incorporate computers in the service of process-based writing pedagogies. While Holdstein's essay did important historical and rhetorical work in that it voiced the belief that technology impacts our writing classrooms and thus teacher evaluation, it also conceived of the computer as a tool to support the writing process, not necessarily as a means to change the very dynamic of the classroom and writing itself. Timely in 1994, Holdstein's piece challenged the negative stance that computers should not be present in writing classrooms, but her position belied the soon-to-come arguments that suggest that networked classrooms and the World Wide Web changed both writing itself and the teaching of writing, even if members of the field cannot agree on exactly how and why.

The conflict that surrounds the changing view of writing and teaching writing with technology soon became further intertwined with the ways we evaluate computers and composition teachers and scholars. As part of the online turn in teacher evaluation, the CCCC Committee on Computers and Composition (1998) published the "CCCC Promotion and Tenure Guidelines for Work with Technology" (PTGWT) report to directly address the unique aspects of teaching and learning with technology. This professional position statement argued that evaluative practices (digital and paper course observations and portfolios) are not only about individual teachers and classrooms but also about the collective contributions of computer compositionists and techno-rhetoricians to the field of rhetoric and composition. This statement helped embolden scholars in our field to argue for changes in evaluative practices for teaching and scholarship. In 1997, Janice R. Walker examined the ways computer compositionists might represent their scholarly work in tenure and promotion reviews. In her *Kairos* web text "Fanning the Flames: Tenure and Promotion and Other Role-Playing Games," Walker (1997) described the ways in which technologies change writing itself, but she also noted that the Modern Language Association's 1998 statement on "Evaluating Computer-Related Work in the Modern Languages" seemed only to professionally legitimize computer composition research that could be translated into traditional categories.[5] Thus, while computers and composition scholars might be able to "fit" their work into such categorical systems, they still must either disregard work that could not be shaped in that way or argue for changes to the evaluation system itself (Walker 1997). This particular historical moment reveals the ways in which teacher and scholar presence come to be articulated in relation to technological shifts. As teacher and administrative presence moves online, search engines—and soon-to-come social media—allow for the access to information and resources not merely about a focused aspect of our work, either teaching or research, but about *all* aspects of our lives.

Taking up Walker's call to change evaluation criteria to account for the contribution of techno-rhetoricians, Michael Day and Sibylle Gruber, both publishing in 2000, attended to summative evaluations of computer compositionists in relation to publication and teaching. To this end, Day reminded colleagues that the surveillance aspects of the technologies that computer compositionists study and deploy in their teaching can be used against them to argue for teacher inadequacies during hiring or annual and tenure reviews (Day 2000, 33). Drawing on the PTGWT report, Day provided a set of recommendations for teachers and administrators, placing important attention on the demands of research and teaching with and about technology. Similarly concerned with summative evaluation, Gruber took a slightly different position, "offer[ing] new perspectives on how the multiple positions of computers and compositionists as chimeras—outsiders and insiders in multiple worlds—can be used to help enact change in a system that upholds largely traditional values and that often only gives lip service to innovation, diversity, and heterogeneity" (Gruber 2000, 42). Despite their difference in approach, both Day and Gruber championed the need to shift evaluation practices to account for the influence of technology.[6] Teacher evaluation thus becomes a growing concern in relation to the means by which technologies capture and store data, as well as the ways in which administrators review and evaluate contributions of computer compositionists. Technologies come to represent fundamental changes in the teaching of writing. Thus, other members of our field, not just computer compositionists, also understand that a teacher's online presence goes well beyond the direct observation of faculty through classroom visits, the completion and publication of student questionnaires, or the lines of a scholar's curriculum vitae to include archived, searchable, and publically owned data to be mined.

OUR CURRENT CONTEXT OF WEB 2.0

At present, the impact of online teacher evaluation, Web 2.0 technologies, and social media transgresses, yet again, the boundaries between scholars and teachers who deploy online technologies for their teaching and research and those who would not necessarily characterize themselves as new media scholars, computers and writing community members, or techno-rhetoricians. In her essay "E-Valuating Learning: Rate My Professors and Public Rhetorics of Pedagogy," Kelly Ritter (2008) draws attention to the ways that RateMyProfessors.com is significant not just to techno-rhetoricians but to all teachers and scholars in our field. In her adept rhetorical analysis of student discourse communities on the website, Ritter asserts that online, public evaluation websites instantiate students' participatory, "right-to-know" positions and challenge faculty members' assumptions that their teaching evaluations are not for public consumption, even if they agree that their pedagogies are already made public to their students through their scholarship (262). In other words, Ritter advances the notion that this public teacher evaluation site is worthy of our attention because, despite its limitations—which both students and teachers recognize—the site represents one way of understanding relationships among online discourses, public pedagogy, and intellectual and physical factors that inform teaching and learning (277). The idea that RateMyProfessors.com should draw scholarly attention is a position stated by researchers in many of the other studies I examined. Despite disciplinary boundaries and various research methodologies, scholars agree that sites like RateMyProfessors.com should not be easily dismissed by professors and administrators.

FIGURATIONS OF ONLINE PROPORTIONS: DATA MINING, MANTI TE'O'S FICTIONAL GIRLFRIEND, AND EDWARD SNOWDEN

My own position is one that aligns with my colleagues—that we must pay attention to online teacher evaluation sites—but my scope is a bit broader than one specific site. I agree that such teacher evaluation sites contribute to a teacher's and an administrator's online presence, but his or her presence is also figured by narratives related to technologies other than those crafted on specific teacher evaluation sites. Here, I align myself more closely with Deleuze and Guattari's (1987) idea of assemblage, Haraway's (1991) trope of the cyborg, and Bay and Rickert's (2010) concept of dwelling.[7] Although there are philosophical differences among these three approaches, they all contend that technologies cannot be separated from our material lives, and that the consequences of the ways in which we construct and are constructed by discourses and practices of technology are profound, real, and experienced personally, corporeally, intellectually, and at the level of becoming.

For me, online presence can be understood through the figuration of three coterminous news stories: data mining, Manti Te'o's fictional social media girlfriend, and Edward Snowden's claims about the National Security Agency (NSA). All of these stories represent larger cultural and political contexts of Web 2.0 technologies and the subject of evaluation. In the age of social media, these news stories represent contemporary views that can be applied to teacher evaluation: it is not private, it may happen in decontextualized ways, it may not be accurate, and it can be published, disseminated, and made open at any time—for good or ill. These stories—and others like them[8]—also raise ever-present issues about power, privilege, class, race, and gender that remain integral to our conversations about technology and evaluation. Before turning to specific practices that may allow teachers and administrators to consider their own online presence, I articulate the issues that these three stories figure, drawing on the ways they are always in tension with particular contexts and lived experiences. Thus, these tensions cannot be resolved, but they must be contemplated as part of the larger cultural milieu of the web.

Data mining arguably implodes assumptions about privacy—online or offline—as our demographic data, habits, and social practices are digitally recorded through cards swiped at stores, online surfing and shopping, and even other hard copy data being translated into digital archives. In American Public Media's series on data mining, Stacey Vanek-Smith asks Andreas Weigend—former chief scientist at Amazon.com, corporate consultant, and teacher of courses on the "social data revolution" at Stanford University, UC Berkley, and Tsinghua University—about privacy. He responds: "Maybe privacy was just a blip in history . . . it ended with the Internet, when basically, there was no place to hide left" (Vanek Smith 2010). In Web 2.0, we experience ourselves and others across different articulations of space, time, and context, and this experience can often be misinterpreted, with one person's assumption of privacy being violated by someone else's assumption about information being public. This phenomenon is not new to Web 2.0 technologies—diaries, letters, chat rooms, MUDs, and MOOs have all been articulated around a private–public binary. Current discussion of private–public boundaries, however, cannot necessarily account for the ways information will be used in the future to define, represent, and construct us and our online presence as teachers and scholars.

Consider another Web 2.0 figuration: the bizarre and entangled story of Notre Dame football star Manti Te'o and his fictional social media girlfriend Lennay Kekua (Zeman 2013). This saga illuminates the ways in which Web 2.0 technologies can provide decontextualized—and even false—information, disseminating it quickly across social media platforms and even historically legitimate news outlets. After the star player devoted game performances to his late grandmother and girlfriend, who reportedly died within hours of one another, news stories abounded about the tragedy that Te'o faced. Later, a series of reports moved from the accusation that Te'o willfully tricked the media for the sake of publicity, to the investigation that finally found he was tricked into a cyber-relationship with the non-existent Kekua, and Te'o was exonerated. His life, however, was scrutinized first for his gall at the publicity stunt (when the public believed he had fabricated the story) and then for his naiveté (once it was revealed that he had been duped). Although Te'o was eventually proven innocent of trying to garner public sympathy and broad publicity to fuel his football career, his reputation suffered (irreparably) through the twists and turns in this social media drama. Despite the ultimate truth being revealed, the damage had been done. By decontextualizing the information and disseminating it widely and quickly, social media helped both to perform the act of deceit and to encourage legitimate news to move quickly to report on this breaking news fueled by the public's desire to know the latest in the case. Web 2.0 allows for fragments of information to circulate quickly and prompts the recirculation of information through retweets, sharing, tagging, and "like" features. False social media profiles, dissemination (and recirculation) of tweets and profile updates, and even viral videos and other quick-consumption practices can complicate—if not obliterate—critical thought and investigative savvy. In his apocalyptic view of technologies, Paul Virilio (1986) characterizes such effects as part of *dromology*, or the study and logic of speed (47). As information moves quickly, fragmented and dispersed, its very movement becomes the goal, and the content—although obviously forceful—is nearly overlooked in the desire to circulate the story as quickly as possible.

Other news offers the story of Edward Snowden, a former NSA contractor who accused the US government of broad surveillance of civilians at home in the United States and abroad, including listening in on phone calls, collecting data on Internet searches, and accessing other forms of electronic data. In an exclusive interview with *The Guardian*, Snowden suggests that his disclosure was motivated by NSA's abuse of the public, stating, "when NSA makes a technical mistake during an exploitation operation, critical systems crash . . . without asking for public permission, NSA is running network operations against them that affect millions of innocent people . . . No, the public needs to know the kinds of things a government does in its name, or the 'consent of the governed' is meaningless" (Greenwald 2013). Cited as irresponsible by some and lauded for sharing information that may expose government's crimes by others, this story has spawned debate about data ownership and surveillance in this country (Savage 2013; Toobin 2013). This story provides yet another important consideration about the openness and effects of data. Whether Snowden is touted as preserving citizen freedom or labeled a traitor, there is a shared assumption that such information dissemination is history making and life changing. The use of data in the time of Web 2.0 is a shifting territory that will not be easily resolved.

TEACHER ONLINE PRESENCE

As these news stories illustrate, our own online presence is constructed, contested, and ever changing. In terms of teacher evaluation, we teachers and administrators cannot turn back the historical clock to return to Estrin's day when only 50% of teachers received some form of teacher evaluation (Estrin 1958, 113), and we would not necessarily want to do so. Instead, we can start by acknowledging that the push to measure, respond, improve, and remain ever-suspect of teacher evaluation is intertwined with our field's articulation of its mission and its day-to-day work. I believe teachers must understand both our historical past and our contemporary figurations of Web 2.0 technologies in order to craft critical responses that take into account our present, complicated cultural, political, and technological milieu.

Here, I offer some considerations that must be thought of as part of a broader plan to develop more democratic teacher evaluation programs. These considerations are not meant to replace the many astute recommendations from scholars or the well-researched professional position statements in our field, nor do I suggest that these recommendations eliminate the contested and contradictory nature of the emergence of certain technological practices. Instead, I see this listing as a starting point for thinking critically about teacher evaluation in the age of social media. I also want to stress that teachers' local contexts must be taken into account when determining the best approach to evaluation at their home institutions (see chapters 1 and 7; Simon and Banchero 2011).[9]

My position on teacher online presence is not an either/or stance in terms of public versus private or social media and Internet use versus technological fasting. Neither position with use as freedom or use as submission seems beneficial (or likely even feasible). Rather, we might consider the ways that teachers and administrators can come together to understand web practices, examining both the source of the teacher information (i.e., is the teacher revealing something that he or she wants to make public?) and its contribution to a broader understanding of the teacher's professional image (i.e., How will this information affect the teacher? What is its relationship to other information about him or her? Does it provide context for his or her whole teaching record rather than one moment?). Teachers and administrators should actively assert their own teacher and administrative online presence as part of a means to create a broader, more thoughtful narrative about their teaching and their programs. In other words, teachers and administrators can respond by thinking carefully about the ways they might come to represent themselves on the web; about the policies and broad social, cultural, and political trends related to Web 2.0 technologies; and about their local situations. I believe a multilayered approach to analyzing and participating in this technological domain is key.

For teachers, you may want to:

Assess Your Online Teacher Presence.

- Even if you do not teach online, surf the web, or use a computer, there is likely personal information about you on the web. To understand the range of your own online teacher presence, you can conduct frequent and diverse Internet searches on your name and university affiliation to see what information exists about you. Keep in mind that websites such as spokeo.com can "aggregate publicly available information from phone books, social networks, marketing surveys, real estate listings, business websites, and other public sources," and this information is presented to users of the site (www.spokeo.com/privacy).

- You cannot rely on website privacy settings to prevent archiving and disseminating information about you. While nearly all companies with

required accounts for login and use have privacy policies, those policies are limited in their scope. Read and understand their limits.

- Consider that any technologies you may deploy to monitor others can
likely be used to monitor you as well. In other words, online teachers
may have access to student login frequency and times, but the site
administrators also have access to your own login habits. Some learning management systems also gather information about grading practices from their teacher users. All of these data are potentially becoming part of a student-offered database.

Thus, certain information may even be available to students from
the university or through learning management systems (LMS). For
example, the University of Arizona just adopted Gmail for all students, and graduate teaching assistants in the writing program quickly
reported that students in their courses were "impromptu" chatting
with them. While the feature can be turned off, the default—just as
with Facebook—is to make other users aware when you are logged
into the site. Another recent example was a request from ASUA
(Arizona State and University of Arizona)—a student organization—to
have the university administration "pull" syllabi from faculty course
management sites and make those documents publically available so
that students could "shop" for courses. This idea was discussed at a
university-wide council meeting, but the involuntary pulling of course
data via the course management system was abandoned after some
discussion of faculty rights.

- Be aware of free and for-profit technologies that may be tapping into
your publically available or official teacher data records. MyEdu and
other local websites publish teacher evaluation data online, and there
are company sites marketing themselves to students as a means to
"Plan your class schedule semester-by-semester to raise your GPA by
managing time, balancing hard classes with easy classes and taking the
best professors" (www.myedu.com/class-schedule/).

And, depending on your home institution's LMS (for example,
Desire2Learn), there are companies promising students similar
options to ease the college experience by claiming that its new product (Degree Compass) "delivers an interactive and intuitive application that helps students identify the courses in which they will be
academically successful *before they even register*. Powered by a predictive
algorithm that taps into the success of thousands of students who have
taken the same degree path, Degree Compass presents a collection of
courses that are necessary for the student to graduate, core to the student's major, and in which the student is expected to be academically
successful" (D2L n.d.; emphasis original).

You should also be aware of the way your campus may be
supporting such services (often because of demands from student
organizations) and should be involved in discussions about their
implications for teaching and learning. One means of maintaining
an active role in creating campus technology policies is to volunteer

for university-, college-, and department-wide technology committees. Also, your campus student newspaper (if you have one) is another means to learn about technological issues.

Actively Create and Disseminate Your Own Online Teacher Presence.

- You can use data mining tools—such as Google Analytics (www .google.com/analytics/)—to monitor your own website. Such tools allow you to monitor IP addresses and other data about visitors to your website.

- You also can use other online resources like Privacy Fix (www .PrivacyFix.org) and Ghostery (www.Ghostery.com) to "opt out" of data tracking services.

- If you are reluctant to make your course materials widely available on the web, you can post your course materials and other resources on websites that are "by invitation only"—Ning, Group.com, and other social networking site services—but keep in mind that the use of these sites does not guarantee your materials will be archived or disseminated in ways you can control.

- In relationship to your teaching and scholarship, you must provide your own narrative to help colleagues and administrative reviewers understand the value of your work. You will not be able to prevent others from searching the Internet for information about you, but you can offer your own interpretation of data about yourself. If you want to know when someone searches for you on the web, you can join Academia.u and receive alerts when someone searches your name.

     Additionally, think about the ways your teacher presence need not be focused on summative or institutional evaluations; rather, teachers can provide insights into their values while always keeping in mind the ways different persons might read such information (see chapter 7 for a discussion of public, formative teacher evaluation and see Hyland 2012 for a discussion of academic identity and homepages).

- Sites such as RateMyProfessors.com now offer teachers the opportunity to respond to student comments. As Chris Anson notes in chapter 7, "Professors Strike Back" (RateMyProfessors.com) is one such option. Depending on your inclination, you can elect to respond to student comments, but keep in mind that these video comments too are archived and searchable. It may be preferable to discuss the rating on your own site instead.

Create Positive, Contextualized Change in Teacher Evaluation at Your Home Institution.

- You can start your own local—or national—discussion of teacher evaluation practices and urge colleagues to set forth specific guidelines for the ways that teacher evaluation data will be gathered, archived, disseminated, and used in personnel reviews. These conversations must address issues of power and presence in relation to evaluation practices. You can also call for more formative, not just summative, evaluation practices and ask for support of teaching in your program and department.

Understand Emerging Technologies and the Ways They May Impact Teacher Evaluation.

- New technologies will impact teacher evaluation and all of our assumptions about privacy and ownership. For example, continued growth in online teaching and learning, social media and networking, mobile applications, and cloud computing are all poised to change our assumptions about data ownership and distribution (consider MOOCs, online tools such as D2L's Degree Compass, and even those technologies we might not yet imagine). As Selfe (1999) so aptly noted, all teachers and scholars in our field need to pay attention to the ways that new technologies emerge and circulate in our culture.

  In addition to our field's discussions of technology, you should engage with other media outlets that offer valuable insights into technology trends, stay attuned to technology policy discussions at the legislative level, and pay attention to corporations that attempt to sell certain Web 2.0 technologies to educational venues. In all cases, these same sources of information may target students, parents, and upper-level administrators directly, and we teacher-scholars need to be participants in these conversations, bringing our research expertise to the dialogue about teaching, learning, and technology (see McKee's 2011 "Policy Matters Now and in the Future: Net Neutrality, Corporate Data Mining, and Government Surveillance" to understand privacy, policy, and regulation as important territories for teachers).

ADMINISTRATIVE ONLINE PRESENCE

Considerations for teachers also apply to WPAs. Assessing and creating our own presence—and even our programs' (e.g., more programs are creating their own Facebook pages)—as well as contextualizing, leading, and understanding teacher evaluation and Web 2.0 technological potentials, are all significant aspects of a WPA position in the age of Web 2.0 and social media use. WPAs have an additional obligation to ensure that all teachers are evaluated ethically, despite any "findings" about them. To this end, I want to add three more obligations to a WPAs' listing of responsibilities and practices (including those posted above):

With Teacher Input, Create a Program Policy about Online Teacher Evaluation and Online Teacher Presence.

- The WPA can initiate important discussions and even create a working group to articulate a program policy about online teacher evaluation data and online teacher presence.
- WPAs cannot necessarily prevent students, faculty, or other administrators from searching for teachers in our programs, but WPAs can establish guidelines about the applicability of such data. Teachers must be involved in crafting such a policy to ensure that it represents all teachers across the program and reflects knowledge of local and national discussions about evaluation practices and technology.

Understand Teacher Evaluation—In Any Form—As Related to Issues of Power.

- As noted in many of the historical moments in teacher evaluation, power is central to the ways in which evaluation is created, maintained, disseminated, and applied. Social inequities in our culture are not erased—and some scholars would say are exacerbated—in relation to evaluation and even some Web 2.0 and social media articulations. WPAs have a responsibility to address these inequities in our policies and practices. It must be clear that teacher presence is likely connected to current—and even future—roles and statuses within the program. WPAs should be available to discuss with graduate students—who will be entering the job market—and faculty—who may be applying for tenure and promotion, or even contract renewal—their conscious choices about their self-representation in Web 2.0 venues.

Support Formative Teacher Evaluation.

- As additional support, WPAs can create opportunities for teachers to come together to talk about the formative aspects of teacher evaluation. Rightly so, WPAs and other rhetoric and composition faculty have emphasized preventing unethical summative evaluation practices, but we also must be attentive to the formative dimensions of teacher evaluation. These formative evaluations can be supported through informal events where teachers gather to discuss their teaching with one another, as well as through the creation of podcasts and social networking sites about local teaching issues. In this way, face-to-face and social media can be a means to share resources and information about teaching.

Finally, and perhaps most importantly, WPAs and teachers must understand their own local teaching and learning context. As the opening fictional stories about teacher and administrator positions in relation to online presence suggest, teachers and administrators must actively engage and work together to provide ways of telling their own stories about teaching and learning in Web 2.0 spaces. They must also understand how other stakeholders may read those stories. All teacher evaluation practices should take into account the ways in which histories, cultures, politics, and practices inform both summative and formative evaluation. From its earliest articulations, teacher evaluation comes to stand at its worst as a means to challenge a teacher's competency and at its best as a way to initiate curricular innovations and establish vital writing programs. It is my hope that in the age of Web 2.0 and social media use, we actively inform ourselves about technologies, deploy them critically, and strive for teacher evaluation that creates more thoughtful practices and humane programs for all members of our community.

Notes

1. I am using the term *presence* as opposed to *identity* or *persona*. Identity, although never fixed or stable, assumes that an individual has distinct characteristics that set her apart from others and that she actively performs in relationship to those characteristics. Persona or "assumed identity" suggests an individual is masking her "real identity" by performing as someone else. I am using "presence" to connote all the digital information that exists *about* an individual, whether that information is willingly offered *by* her, provided by others, or even gathered by the technologies she uses with or without her knowledge. In other words, "presence" attempts to account for individual and collaborative bits of data that are dispersed, archived, and not always easily controlled by any one individual or that individual's varied online personae. Presence also suggests the "supernatural" and the concept of "influence"—both of which are apt tropes for the ways in which Web 2.0 technologies come to impact individuals.

2. Following the 1956 CCCC convention's "Professional Status of Composition/Communications Staff" workshop, members of the 1957 CCCC workshop, entitled "Measuring the Quality of Teaching," wanted to understand the various methods and purposes of teacher evaluation at that time. Estrin (1958) surveyed all the 1957 workshop participants and found that only about half of them received some type of teacher evaluation, with classroom visits and student responses—statistical, essay, or teacher-created forms—being the norms (113). Estrin does not provide information about response rates, and his sample is probably skewed, but it is interesting that teacher evaluation was not fully mandated during this time.

3. Jointly sponsored by the American Association of University Professors and the Association of American Colleges, and supported by a grant from the Carnegie Foundation, "The Project to Improve College Teaching" was a collaborative research project. Kenneth Eble's (1970) monograph *The Recognition and Evaluation of Teaching* comes out of this research, and the book helped to legitimize students' voices in teacher evaluation practices.

4. The committee worked from a model of writing teacher responsibilities—the actual day-to-day practices of teaching writing—to advocate for the following six evaluation instruments: (1) departments and administrators to determine the assumptions, goals, and standards for judging writing that underlie the program or course, and that evaluators of instruction be familiar with all of these; (2) teachers to describe and to evaluate their own courses; (3) direct observation of classes in

writing; (4) series of questions that can be asked of the assignments (or invitations) for writing; (5) a set of suggestions for evaluating a teacher's responses to students' writing; and (6) a set of suggested questions from which a teacher or administrator can draw in preparing a form for student rating of a writing program, course, and teacher (Faigley and Witte 1983, 217–19).

5.   The 1990s also brought continued professional interest in assessment and teacher evaluation—reports on writing assessment with teacher evaluation as a component or teacher evaluation as an exclusive concern are published by professional associations related to language learning and the teaching of writing, a selection of which includes the Association of Departments of English Ad Hoc Committee on Assessment (Association of Departments of English 1996); the Council of WPA's "The Portland Resolution: Guidelines for Writing Program Administrator Positions" (Council of Writing Program Administrators 1992); CCCC's Committee on Teaching and Its Evaluation in Composition (Conference on College Composition and Communication Committee on Teaching and Its Evaluation in Composition 1982); MLA's Committee on Computers and Emerging Technologies in Teaching and Research (Modern Language Association 2000b); the CCCC Committee on Computers and Composition's report on promotion and tenure guidelines for work with technology (Conference on College Composition and Communication Committee on Computers and Composition 1998). I discuss these latter two committees in a later section. All of these statements indicate the professional need to make assessment and teacher evaluation integral to the work in our field.

Further, as writing assessment continues to develop in the field, many historical perspectives on writing assessment emerge, particularly Kathleen Blake Yancey's (1999) "Looking Back as We Look Forward: Historicizing Writing Assessment," Edward M. White's (2001) "The Opening of the Modern Era of Writing Assessment: A Narrative," and Brian A. Huot's (2002) *Rearticulating Writing Assessment for Teaching and Learning*. I do not review the extensive literature on writing assessment in the later decades, as most of this work is focused on the evaluation of the student and his or her writing rather than the teacher. But I believe that any of our student evaluation practices implicitly necessitate certain acceptable teacher practices in the writing classroom. For example, the rise of student portfolios requires teachers to support formative evaluation, multiple drafts, and other pedagogical practices. Rather than extend my own historical tracing in the direction of student evaluation or whole program assessment, I remain as closely connected to teacher evaluation as possible.

6.   The Modern Language Association (MLA) revised its 1998 guidelines in 2000 and reviewed them again in 2002 (Modern Language Association 2000a). This statement, now entitled "Guidelines for Evaluating Work with Digital Media in the Modern Languages," is undergoing yet another review, and was posted online in 2010 by the MLA Committee on Information Technology for member and non-member comment.

In 2004, CCCC's "Position Statement on Teaching, Learning, and Assessing Writing in Digital Environments" mentioned teacher evaluation as part of digital learning (College Composition and Communication Conference 2004), and then in 2008 NCTE published its statement entitled "21st Century Curriculum and Assessment Framework," in which teacher evaluation is discussed at more length (NCTE 2008).

7.   All of these concepts work to breakdown the separation of subject, object, and life world and instead function to create connections that are non-essentialist and anti-reductive. In particular, all of these concepts attempt to work out subject-object

connections in relationship to language, technology, and experience—considering all of these terms as multiplicities in and of themselves and across systems. I want to stress, however, that I understand the larger mission of these authors is different and as are even the degrees that they might agree (or not) on the ways the concepts work against certain systems of domination.

8. Consider the high profile cases of Shirley Sherrod, where a false story about her circulated that prompted her resignation (see O'Keefe 2010), and Julian Assange, the controversial founder of Wikileaks, who brought to the forefront issues of data collection in today's Web 2.0 world (see Barnes and Gorman 2010; Hough and Malkin 2010).

9. The State of Texas, as Anson notes, created a value algorithm to measure teacher value, claiming it important information for taxpayers. The story was covered in 2010 by the *Wall Street Journal* (see Simon and Banchero 2011).

References

Association of Departments of English. 1996. Report of the ADE Ad Hoc Committee on Assessment. Retrieved from http://www.ade.org/reports/assess_rpt.pdf.

Barnes, Julian E., and Siobhan Gorman. 2010. "Website Releases Secrets on War." *The Wall Street Journal*, July 26. http://online.wsj.com.

Bay, Jennifer, and Thomas Rickert. 2010. "Dwelling with New Media." In *RAW: (Reading and Writing) New Media*, ed. Cheryl E. Ball and James Kalmbach, 117–39. Cresskill, NJ: Hampton Press.

Conference on College Composition and Communication Committee on Computers and Composition. 1998. "Promotion and Tenure Guidelines for Work with Technology." NCTE. http://www.ncte.org/cccc/resources/positions/promotio nandtenure.

Conference on College Composition and Communication Committee on Teaching and Its Evaluation in Composition. 1982. "Evaluating Instruction in Writing: Approaches and Instruments." *College Composition and Communication* 33 (2): 213–29. http://dx.doi.org/10.2307/357630.

College Composition and Communication Conference. 2004. "CCCC Position Statement on Teaching, Learning, and Assessing Writing in Digital Environments." http://www.ncte.org/cccc/resources/positions/digitalenvironments.

Coladarci, Theodore, and Irv Kornfield. 2007. "RateMyProfessors.com Versus Formal In-class Student Evaluations of Teaching." *Practical Assessment, Research & Evaluation* 12 (6): 1–13.

Council of Writing Program Administrators. 1992. "The Portland Resolution: Guidelines for Writing Program Administrator Positions." http://wpacouncil.org/positions /portlandres.html.

D2L. n.d. Degree Compass Feature Overview. http://www.brightspace.com/products /degree-compass/.

Day, Michael. 2000. "Teachers at the Crossroads: Evaluating Teaching in Electronic Environments." *Computers and Composition* 17 (1): 31–40. http://dx.doi.org/10.1016 /S8755-4615(99)00028-6.

Deleuze, Gilles, and Felix Guattari. 1987. *A Thousand Plateaus: Capitalism and Schizophrenia*. Trans. Brian Massumi. Minneapolis: University of Minnesota Press.

Eble, Kenneth. 1970. *The Recognition and Evaluation of Teaching*. Project to Improve College Teaching, Salt Lake City, UT. Washington, DC: American Association of University Professors.

Estrin, Herman A. 1958. "Measuring the Quality of the Teaching of English." *College Composition and Communication* 9 (2): 111–13. http://dx.doi.org/10.2307/355336.

Faigley, Lester, and Stephan Paul Witte. 1983. *Evaluating College Writing Programs.* Carbondale: Southern Illinois University Press.

Felton, James, John Mitchell, and Michael Stinson. 2004. "Web-Based Students Evaluations of Professors: The Relations between Perceived Quality, Easiness, and Sexiness." *Assessment & Evaluation in Higher Education* 29 (1): 91–108. http://dx.doi .org/10.1080/0260293032000158180.

Greenwald, Glen. 2013. "Edward Snowden: NSA Whistleblower Answers Reader Questions." *The Guardian,* June 17. http://www.guardian.com/world/2013/jun/17 /edward-snowden-nsa-files-whistleblower.

Gruber, Sibylle. 2000. "Technology and Tenure: Creating Oppositional Discourse in an Offline and Online World." *Computers and Composition* 17 (1): 41–55. http://dx.doi .org/10.1016/S8755-4615(99)00029-8.

Haraway, Donna J. 1992. "Ecce Homo, Ain't (Ar'n't) I a Woman, and Inappropriate/d Others: The Human in a Post-Humanist Landscape." In *Feminists Theorize the Political,* ed. Joan W. Scott and Judith Butler, 87–101. New York: Routledge.

Haraway, Donna J. 1991. *Simians, Cyborgs and Women: The Reinvention of Nature.* New York: Routledge.

Holdstein, Deborah H. 1994. "Evaluating Teachers in Computerizing Classrooms." In *Evaluating Teachers of Writing,* ed. Christine A. Hult, 167–78. Urbana, IL: NCTE.

Hough, Andrew, and Bonnie Malkin. 2010. "Julian Assange: Is 'Wikileaker' on a Crusade or an Ego Trip?" *The Telegraph,* July 31. http://www.telegraph.co.uk/news/worldnews /asia/afghanistan/7919688/Julian-Assange-is-Wikileaker-a-crusade-or-ego-trip.html.

Huot, Brian. 2002. *(Re)Articulating Writing Assessment.* Logan: Utah State University Press.

Hult, Christine A. 1994. *Evaluating Teachers of Writing.* Urbana, IL: NCTE.

Hyland, Ken. 2012. "Individuality or Conformity? Identity in Personal and University Academic Homepages." *Computers and Composition* 29 (4): 309–22. http://dx.doi.org /10.1016/j.compcom.2012.10.002.

Johnson-Eilola, Johndan. 2010. "Among Texts." In *Rhetorics and Technologies: New Directions in Writing and Communication,* ed. Stuart A. Selber, 33–55. Columbia: University of South Carolina Press.

Kimme Hea, Amy C. 2007. "Riding the Wave: Articulating a Critical Methodology for Web Research Practices." In *Digital Writing Research: Technologies, Methodologies, and Ethical Issues,* ed. Heidi A. McKee, and Dánielle DeVoss, 269–86. Cresskill, NJ: Hampton Press.

McKee, Heidi. 2011. "Policy Matters Now and in the Future: Net Neutrality, Corporate Data Mining, and Government Surveillance." *Computers and Composition* 28 (4): 276– 91. http://dx.doi.org/10.1016/j.compcom.2011.09.001.

Modern Language Association. 2000a. "Guidelines for Evaluating Work with Digital Media in the Modern Languages (archived)." http://www.mla.org/resources/documents /rep_it/cit_guidelines_2000.

Modern Language Association. 2000b. "MLA Committee on Computers and Emerging Technologies in Teaching and Research." http://www.mla.org/reports/ccet/ccet_ index.htm.

NCTE. 2008. "NCTE Framework for 21st Century Curriculum and Assessment." http:// www.ncte.org/positions/statements/21stcentframework.

O'Keefe, Ed. 2010. "NAACP, White House Responds to Ouster of USDA Worker Shirley Sherrod." *The Washington Post,* July 20. http://voices.washingtonpost.com/federal- eye/2010/07/usda_worker_quits_over_racism.html.

Otto, James, Douglas A. Sanford, Jr., and Douglas N. Ross. 2008. "Does RateMyProfessor .com Really Rate My Professor?" *Assessment & Evaluation in Higher Education* 33 (4): 355–68. http://dx.doi.org/10.1080/02602930701293405.

Ritter, Kelly. 2008. "E-Valuating Learning: *Rate My Professors* and Public Rhetorics of Pedagogy." *Rhetoric Review* 27 (3): 259–80. http://dx.doi.org/10.1080/073501908 02126177.

Savage, Charlie. 2013. "A.C.L.U. Files Lawsuit Seeking to Stop the Collection of Domestic Phone Logs." *The New York Times*, June 11. http://www.nytimes.com/2013/06/12/us/aclu-files-suit-over-phone-surveillance-program.html?ref=us.

Selfe, Cynthia L. 1999. *Technology and Literacy in the Twenty-First Century: The Importance of Paying Attention*. Carbondale: Southern Illinois University Press.

Simon, Stephanie, and Stephanie Banchero. 2011. "Putting a Price on Professors A Battle in Texas over Whether Academic Value Can Be Measured in Dollars and Cents." *Wall Street Journal*, October 22. http://online.wsj.com/article/SB10001424052748703735804575536322093520994.html.

Stronge, James H., and Pamela Tucker. 2003. *Handbook on Teacher Evaluation: Assessing and Improving Performance*. Larchmont, NY: Eye on Education, Inc.

Toobin, Jeffrey. 2013. "Edward Snowden Is No Hero." *The New Yorker*, June 10. http://www.newyorker.com/news/daily-comment/edward-snowden-is-no-hero.

Vanek Smith, Stacey. 2010. "Data Mining Pushes Marketing to a New Level." *Marketplace*. American Public Media. July 26.

Virilio, Paul. 1986. *Speed and Politics: An Essay on Dromology*. Trans. Mark Polizzotti. New York: Semiotext(e).

Walker, Janice R. 1997. "Fanning the Flames: Tenure and Promotion and Other Role-Playing Games." *Kairos* 2 (1). http://english.ttu.edu/kairos/2.1/coverweb/walker/intro.html.

White, Edward M. 1985. *Teaching and Assessing Writing*. San Francisco: Jossey-Bass.

White, Edward M. 1989. *Developing Successful College Writing Programs*. San Francisco: Jossey-Bass.

White, Edward M. 1994. "The Devil is in the Details: A Cautionary Tale." In *Evaluating Teachers of Writing*, ed. Christine A. Hult, 49–54. Urbana, IL: NCTE.

White, Edward M. 2001. "The Opening of the Modern Era of Writing Assessment: A Narrative." *College English* 63 (3): 306–20. http://dx.doi.org/10.2307/378995.

Yancey, Kathleen Blake. 1999. "Looking Back as We Look Forward: Historicizing Writing Assessment." *College Composition and Communication* 50 (3): 483–503. http://dx.doi.org/10.2307/358862.

Zeman, Ned. 2013. "The Boy Who Cried Dead Girlfriend." *Vanity Fair*, June. http://www.vanityfair.com/culture/2013/06/manti-teo-girlfriend-nfl-draft.

11

USING NATIONAL SURVEY OF STUDENT ENGAGEMENT DATA AND METHODS TO ASSESS TEACHING IN FIRST-YEAR COMPOSITION AND WRITING ACROSS THE CURRICULUM

Charles Paine, Chris M. Anson,
Robert M. Gonyea, and Paul Anderson

The Consortium for the Study of Writing in College (CSWC)—a collaboration between the Council of Writing Program Administrators (CWPA) and the National Survey of Student Engagement (NSSE)—has developed a 27-question survey focusing on writing instruction that, since 2008, has been administered (along with NSSE's "core" survey) 247 times (at 202 different institutions) to over 57,000 first-year students and over 85,000 seniors.

Considering the context of this collection (focusing on teacher and course assessment), it's important to understand that both the NSSE and the CSWC surveys were designed to assess engagement and general educational effectiveness at the inter-institutional and institutional levels. As members of these organizations, we aimed primarily to test the widespread belief (among writing specialists and others) that instructors can use writing assignments and activities to enhance students' learning, engagement, and attainment (Anderson et al. 2009; Kinzie, Gonyea, and Paine 2009). We also aimed to create an instrument that would complement the NSSE core survey and help individual institutions assess and improve the quality of undergraduate experiences at their schools. Because of these aims, the items in both surveys primarily ask students how often they engage in certain "good practices" for *all* courses and "during the current school year." In short, the CSWC survey was designed for assessment at the national, inter-institutional, and institutional levels, not at more local levels, such as for program and course assessment. However, despite these initial intentions, these surveys and

DOI: 10.7330/9780874219661.c011

this general approach (with some reworking) can be used to assess programs, courses, and teachers.

In this chapter, we provide an overview of both surveys, including ideas and cautions for using this general method as a novel approach to program and teacher assessment.

- Background
  We describe the origins, aims, and general structure of the NSSE (student engagement) and the CSWC (writing-instruction) survey.
- The CSWC survey and national findings
  We describe how the CSWC was developed and offered, and provide a brief overview of major findings of the national study.
- Program and teacher assessment
  We describe how WPAs can adopt and adapt both the CSWC questions and the general approach to local needs.
- Some benefits, cautions, and general principles for sharing results
  We describe some best practices (what to do and what to avoid) for using this approach, and we provide a few ideas for sharing results and making improvements.

BACKGROUND OF NSSE: ORIGINS AND AIMS

The National Survey of Student Engagement was conceived in the late 1990s to, first and foremost, help institutions assess the quality of undergraduate education by providing "actionable" data that schools could use to understand and improve their students' undergraduate experience; second, to "discover more about and document effective educational practice in postsecondary settings" (Kuh 2009); and, third, to "advocate for public acceptance and use of empirically derived conceptions of collegiate quality" (10).

NSSE's developers aimed to help fill a gap in 1990s assessment practices. Institutions, accrediting agencies, government, and other stakeholders relied on assessment tools (such as media rankings) that focused very little on undergraduates' experience. Rather, these tools primarily measured inputs (student selectivity, resources, faculty reputation) and outcomes highly influenced by inputs (retention, graduation rates, percentage of alumni who enter graduate school or become donors). Because institutions, faculty, and staff can do little to influence these inputs, such assessments do not yield data that are "actionable"— i.e., that do not, as Banta, Jones, and Black (2009) put it, "yield meaningful results that faculty and staff can use to identify necessary changes" (21). In order to influence and improve teaching and learning, faculty need to have and understand "high-quality, behaviorally oriented data about aspects of the student experience that are related to student success" (Kuh 2009, 14; see Kuh for a more detailed account of NSSE's origins, purpose, and processes).

To help fill this gap, NSSE created a survey (piloted in 1999 and first administered nationally in 2000) that focused on student engagement. As the survey's website explains, "student engagement" represents two critical features of collegiate quality. The first is the amount of time and effort students put into their studies and other educationally purposeful activities. The second is how the institution deploys its resources and organizes the curriculum and other learning opportunities to get students to participate in activities that decades of research studies show are linked to student learning (NSSE n.d.a).

NSSE's survey instrument asks three kinds of questions about (1) students' level of participation in educationally purposeful activities (e.g., amount of time devoted to studying and co-curricular activities); (2) institutional requirements (for reading and writing, types of projects and exams); and (3) perceptions about the college environment (support, quality of interactions with faculty, peers, and staff). The survey instrument has been revised (and is currently being revised again), but the basic structure has not changed significantly (see Kuh 2009, 11–12; surveys from 2000 to the present are available at NSSE, n.d.d).

CSWC: ORIGINS AND AIMS

NSSE's core survey asks six questions related to students' writing (see appendix 11.1), but it was developed without input from writing instruction experts. Two of the questions ask about the writing process (e.g., integrating sources and writing multiple drafts), three ask about how many papers of different lengths were written, and one question asks students to self-report on how much their writing has improved. Most important, those six questions do not capture what writing experts believe to be the best practices for writing instruction, whether that instruction occurs in FYC (first-year composition) or WAC/WID (writing across the curriculum/writing in the disciplines) contexts.

This was the assessment gap targeted by CSWC efforts. Our primary aim was to develop a rigorous multisite research tool that might yield data demonstrating the value of high-quality writing instruction and that in turn would help WPAs across the country advocate for their FYC and WAC/WID programs in this time of constantly diminishing resources.

While the scholarship of teaching and learning has offered us widespread support of writing to learn, the movement hasn't been nearly as well supported in the research. Hundreds of studies have been published on all sorts of investigations of the relationship of writing and learning, but, as several meta-analyses or syntheses of this research have shown, overall results demonstrate a relationship between these teaching practices and student outcomes that are weak at best. In a meta-analysis of thirty-five research studies, Ackerman (1993) points out that "The high number of published accounts of successful classroom practices based on writing as a mode of learning suggests that such practices offer the potential to transform classroom environments" (343; see also Bangert-Drowns, Hurley, and Wilkinson 2004). Yet, Ackerman's review shows generally weak and mixed results.

For this reason, it's been difficult to generalize that empirical research supports the relationship of writing and learning. First, the great majority of studies have been local, conducted in a particular class at a particular institution and subject to the vagaries of context. It's obviously much more difficult to conduct a study across different institutions, which has meant that the existing research studies are small scale. It's also difficult to compare studies because they have widely different operational definitions of "learning" as well as methods for assessing it: Is it the recall of factual information? The ability to abstract from particulars, to engage in self-critique, or to synthesize alternative views on an issue? In addition, what actually *happens* with the writing? Under what conditions is it assigned and supported? What instructional interventions accompany it? How is it woven into the fabric of instruction?

We set out to create an instrument and conduct a study of the relationships of writing and learning that would be: (1) large scale (many four-year institutions representing a cross-section of higher education in the United States and including thousands of students); (2) based not on specific, individual cases but on a large aggregate of practices; (3) located not in specific disciplines but across the entire range of students' experience as freshmen and seniors; (4) located temporally not across a single assignment sequence or single course but across an entire year or longer; and (5) focused on the nature of practices used for writing and the relationship of these practices to other measures of student learning and development.

THE CSWC SURVEY AND NATIONAL FINDINGS

With these goals in mind, in the summer of 2007, some of the Council of Writing Program Administration members first contacted Bob Gonyea, associate director at the Indiana University Center for Postsecondary

Research, where the national survey is housed. The twenty-seven-item survey (appendix 11.2) was developed in consultation with NSSE's experts in higher education research and over eighty members of the CWPA, all acknowledged experts in the teaching of writing and in FYC and WAC/WID program administration. Like the developers of the NSSE core survey, we aimed to develop survey items that represented "good practices in undergraduate education," focusing almost entirely on students' writing behaviors and teachers' specific practices and avoiding evaluation or satisfaction type questions. There are good reasons to believe the CSWC survey is well designed, benefits from good validity, and makes a useful tool in the WPA's assessment toolbox:[1]

- In close collaboration with NSSE's experts on survey development and research, the questions were developed by experts in the field, an indication of good content validity.
- The survey is easy to complete, well understood, and accessible to students, as we have inferred from exceptionally low "did not complete" rates.
- The CSWC survey—administered 247 times, at 202 different institutions, with over 140,000 respondents—has yielded data that demonstrate the writing survey items are associated with deep approaches to learning and with general gains in higher education, an indication of empirical validity.
- A corresponding set of writing questions appended to the Faculty Survey of Student Engagement (FSSE) has been developed and administered at 46 institutions, with 2,995 faculty respondents who assign writing in their classes; WPAs can use this to gauge faculty attitudes and values about writing instruction and compare them with students' reported experiences.

In short, we can be confident that the CSWC survey provides a valid and powerful instrument for assessing students' writing behaviors. Perhaps even more important for program and course assessment, the survey provides an empirically proven foundation that WPAs can adopt and adapt to their local situations.

The CSWC writing scales can be combined into three reliable scales representing different forms of good practice in writing instruction: (a) encouraging interactive writing activities, (b) assigning meaningful writing tasks, and (c) explaining writing expectations clearly. Our research shows that these three scales had significant and substantial effects on deep approaches to learning in students' coursework, as well as on students' self-reports of learning and development in general education, personal and social development, and practical competencies (Anderson et al. 2009). What's more, these positive relationships existed regardless of students' individual characteristics, majors, and the *amount that they wrote*. Thus, it's clear that students who experienced these good practices in using writing to learn were more likely to also engage in deep learning and report greater gains in learning and development, regardless of the amount they were expected to write.

USING THE NSSE/CSWC APPROACH FOR PROGRAM AND TEACHER ASSESSMENT

Many WPAs and others have used the NSSE and CSWC survey's "off the shelf," by which we mean having NSSE administer the survey at the institutional level. When administered by NSSE, which is obligated to make results across institutions commensurable, the surveys cannot be reworked to fit the local conditions and needs. A growing number of WPAs are using the CSWC survey to assess and improve FYC and WAC/WID programs. We describe some of these efforts in the final section.

However, driving data down to the *course* level with "off the shelf" surveys has not been attempted (to our knowledge) because, simply, there would not be enough respondents per class for meaningful interpretation[2] (on the concept of "driving data down," see McCormick and BrckaLorenz 2009). Further, NSSE does not frame its questions in ways that would lead students to describe their experiences for any specific class. For instance, here are some of the "stem questions" from the NSSE core survey:

> "In your experience at your institution during the school year, about how often have you done each of the following?"

> "To what extent does your institution emphasize the following?"

And from the CSWC survey:

> "During the current school year, for how many of your writing assignments have you done each of the following?"

> "During the current school year, for how many of your writing assignments has your instructor done each of the following?"

Nonetheless, such program-level assessments can be quite relevant for course-/teacher-level assessment if they are combined and triangulated with different kinds of methods and data (like those described below).

ADAPTING THE CSWC SURVEY FOR SPECIFIC WRITING PROGRAMS AND INDIVIDUAL CLASSROOMS

Here we describe how programs can rework the CSWC survey, tailoring their custom surveys or their end-of-semester student evaluations of instruction (SEIs) to local concerns and administering the survey to only a selected group of courses. Such custom instruments would benefit from the empirical validation of the national, inter-institutional results, but they could also investigate additional issues or describe their students' behavior and teachers' practices using familiar local terminologies that would be understandable and useful to their students and faculty. But because the CSWC survey has proven accessible to a broad range of students, we recommend that the basic shape of the survey and the form of the questions be adhered to whenever possible. More specifically, certain terms might be changed to the terms used locally, and questions might be deleted or added, but the general structure should be left intact.

There are good reasons for tailoring the CSWC survey to local programs. First, as we were crafting the language for the survey questions, we kept in mind that these twenty-seven questions had to be instantly understandable to a very diverse set of respondents, from first-year students to final-semester seniors across the United States. Therefore, the questions themselves were intentionally generic in character, avoiding technical or local terms. For instance, question 1F (see appendix 11.2) asks how often students have "Visited a campus-based writing or tutoring center to get help with your writing assignment before turning it in." Although it's impossible to tell from the final product, this question went through numerous drafts, was evaluated by survey experts, and was focus-grouped with students before we settled on this language, which proved most clear to a diverse, naïve, nontechnical audience. For example, the term "writing center" was confusing for many. However, if this question were reworked for a single school that has a well-known writing center, it might be rendered into more direct and simple language.

The more important reason for creating a local survey involves a widely agreed upon principle in current writing assessment theory and practice: (1) writing assessment (or any assessment) yields the most meaningful results when multiple methods and multiple sources of information are used and (2) the direction, shape, and goals of writing assessment should be determined by concerns that are "site-based," "locally controlled," "context-sensitive," and accessible (O'Neill, Moore, and Huot 2009, 57; see also Adler-Kassner and O'Neill 2010; Broad 2009; Huot 1996, 2002). Clearly, the NSSE and CSWC surveys provide just one source of data and can hardly be considered site-based, locally controlled, etc. (a point NSSE stresses in its publications and other communications). Therefore, we describe two methods for such local administrations: (1) using NSSE's Classroom Survey of Student Engagement

(CLASSE) (National Survey of Student Engagement n.d.b) or (2) adopting and adapting the CSWC survey and administering it locally.

USING NSSE'S CLASSE FACULTY AND CLASSE STUDENT

CLASSE was developed in cooperation with NSSE by Robert Smallwood and Judy Ouimet. Schools that are administering both the NSSE's and the CSWC's surveys in a given year can also administer CLASSE. (Note: CLASSE is not currently administered by NSSE; it requires a local administration. For details about CLASSE, see Smallwood n.d., 2010)

CLASSE addresses a concern about faculty survey data that is common among instructors, who often argue that NSSE (and CSWC) results are of little use to them because "These less-engaged students are not *my* students" (Smallwood and Ouimet 2009, 194). In fact, as we've noted, it would be highly problematic to "drive down" the institutional data from both surveys to the course level (see McCormick and BrckaLorenz 2009). CLASSE aims to remedy that disconnect by adapting the NSSE core survey to the class level and administering it locally.

As Smallwood explains, CLASSE can disaggregate a school's NSSE data more precisely, "captur[ing] relevant student engagement results at the course level" (Smallwood n.d.). CLASSE not only localizes levels of engagement but also builds faculty buy-in because it gathers data from both students and faculty. Further, CLASSE can be adapted to address the local concerns of faculty and administrators—but only to a limited extent. Specifically, although none of the CLASSE questions can be changed, up to eight course-specific items can be added.

CLASSE improves faculty buy-in by adopting a strategy that is similar to the one used by NSSE's Faculty Survey of Student Engagement (FSSE). CLASSE actually comprises a pair of surveys, CLASSE Student and CLASSE Faculty: "The *CLASSE Faculty* assesses which engagement practices faculty particularly value and perceive as important for student success within a designated class. The *CLASSE Student* assesses how frequently students report these practices occurring in that class" (Nelson Laird et al. 2009, 76). As Smallwood and Ouimet (2009) explain, because the responses to CLASSE Faculty and CLASSE Student can be compared, the results are particularly useful for fostering rich and useful conversations among faculty about improving their teaching along the lines deemed most important to them. For example, if a faculty member believes that a certain practice is important but her students report engaging in that practice less often than other students in similar classes, she can reasonably infer a disconnect that needs further investigation, followed, possibly, by changes in her teaching practices.

ADOPTING AND ADAPTING THE CSWC SURVEY

To our knowledge, a locally administered and reworked version of the CSWC survey has not been administered programmatically as an SEI. Because others have developed SEIs that address local concerns and that supplement or supplant existing evaluations (e.g., O'Neill, Moore, and Huot 2009, 145–47; Weiser 1994, 141–43), and because the CSWC survey provides a proven foundation for such custom SEIs, we offer this strategy here as potentially useful for assessing and improving programs and/or teacher effectiveness. Like the CLASSE survey, such an SEI would need to be administered by the program (several SEI products may be available through a school's assessment office or are available for purchase). This SEI would be customized to address those practices most important within a given FYC or WAC/WID program, as described by O'Neill, Moore, and Huot (2009, 144–47). Specific items could be added, dropped, or altered, but (as explained previously) the basic shape of the original CSWC survey and the characteristics of its items would be largely retained. In addition, space could be made available for explanatory comments about individual items or groups of items.

For example, a FYC program may consider peer evaluation as a central concern and defining practice for all courses and may have adopted a student learning outcome similar to "Students should learn to critique their own and others' work" (Council of Writing Program Administrators 2008). The WPA of this program might choose to expand upon or alter items 1C and 1E from the CSWC survey (appendix 11.2). Other defining characteristics or good practices for writing courses— e.g., small-group or individual conferences, revision and repurposing, use of writing centers, genre awareness, civic writing—could be emphasized, rephrased to match the program's lexicon of terms, or dropped altogether. All of these are "covered" in the CSWC, but the SEI should be reworked to match the program's overall goals and meet the most urgent assessment questions.

Tailored SEIs could be used in numerous ways and in numerous combinations with other sources derived from other methods. They could be used for formative, mid-semester assessment, or for more summative, end-of-semester assessment. Standards of comparison across teachers (similar to NSSE's "Engagement Indicators") could be defined, or progress across semesters could be assessed (see NSSE n.d.e). Finally, the results from these SEIs—which are indirect measures of teaching effectiveness and student learning—could be compared with direct measures (e.g., evaluating student samples) to determine whether the program's supposed "good practices" really are associated with better student performance. As the final section explains, this kind of SEI could yield results that are meaningful for internal constituencies (e.g., WPAs and the teachers themselves), but they might be difficult for external constituencies to understand if they weren't interpreted and framed responsibly.

SOME BENEFITS, CAUTIONS, AND GENERAL PRINCIPLES FOR SHARING RESULTS

It's important to understand that neither the NSSE instrument nor the CSWC survey provides direct measures of student learning and achievement. Rather, as Kuh (2009) explains, "student engagement data are 'process indicators,' or proxies, for learning outcomes" (9). While these process indicators "point to areas that schools can do something about to improve student and institutional learning" (9), they provide only a part of the assessment puzzle and should be linked to other data sources, such as conversations (or more formal focus groups) among faculty, staff, and students; direct measures of achievement (such as portfolio scoring and standardized tests); other surveys; and so forth. Like all assessment—including, perhaps especially, teacher assessment—NSSE results need to be contextualized for a variety of audiences and purposes.

There are benefits and cautions associated with this approach. The NSSE and CSWC surveys ask about specific students' *behaviors* and teachers' *practices* rather than global evaluations and about what students and teachers *have done,* not how students feel or how they would evaluate the class and teacher overall. Therefore, these approaches could mitigate the effect of the many "background characteristics," which may unfairly skew SEI results and over which teachers have little or no control—for example, class size; expected grade; meeting time; teacher's personality, gender, appearance, etc. (Wachtel 1998; see also O'Neill, Moore, and Huot 2009, 144–47). As Algozzine et al. (2004) have noted, despite plentiful research, we do not yet sufficiently understand how such factors influence SEIs, but prevalent "mythologies" about SEIs appear to attribute far more influence to background characteristics than is warranted by the research. They suggest involving faculty more closely in the process, a strategy advocated here (and also by Nelson Laird et al.

2009; Smallwood and Ouimet 2009). The behavior- and site-specific SEIs we describe here might prove highly useful for communicating with audiences that Shupe (2008) calls "internal" (teachers, WPAs, other writing experts) when they focus primarily on teaching and program improvement. However—and here's the caution—for Shupe's "external constituencies," behavior-oriented data would need to be framed and shared carefully. These external audiences (institutional leaders, faculty outside the field, and the public) may too quickly collapse results into single scores when they focus primarily on proving effectiveness and accountability. When reporting results to institutions, NSSE foregrounds its Engagement Indicators (formerly called Benchmarks of Effective Educational Practice) such as "Level of Academic Challenge" and "Student-Faculty interaction," which are statistical composites of results from individual questions; this presentational strategy can head off score-collapsing by stakeholders (Chen et al. 2009; Kuh 2003). Even so, we believe these approaches could provide novel methods and data sources that can be used for a variety of constituencies, from institutional leaders to WPAs to individual faculty members.

Even for their internal uses of assessment results, WPAs should carefully consider how they will use behavior-oriented survey results. First, consider how you want to maintain the always-precarious balance between (a) control and coherence and (b) freedom, discovery, and individual responsibility (see Dively [2010] for an illuminating narrative of one program's efforts to achieve a prudent and stable balance). As Martin and Paine (2002) describe, as WPAs consider the often-conflicting values of various stakeholders (students, teachers, the institution, faculty across disciplines, and the public):

> On the one hand, we want to give these teachers—experienced as well as new ones—as much free rein as possible to discover and practice what works best for them and their students. . . . On the other hand, we have our own beliefs about what constitutes good writing and good writing instruction, we want to articulate and practice a relatively coherent and stable philosophy of writing, and we are obliged to ensure a degree of consistency across all sections of first-year English. (222)

SEIs that focus on students' behaviors and teachers' practices might tempt a WPA to tip in the direction of mere surveillance, uniformity, and accountability. After all, teachers with outlying scores can be identified, rewards and penalties could be distributed, and the WPA becomes (or is perceived to have become) the "program cop." Rather, we suggest you remember best practices for assessment—transparency, involving all faculty in the process, developing clear and reasonable standards of performance, and stressing improvement and professional responsibility over accountability.

Most important, behavior-oriented survey data (like all assessment data), should be used primarily to facilitate—not to supplant or to poison—rich faculty discussions about teaching and learning. This is especially important when doing the sensitive work of teacher assessment. Rather than announcing what the data show or asking the data to speak for themselves, invite participants to look for patterns or contrasts between

- the program's survey findings and other findings;
- the program's survey findings and its mission, strengths, and challenges;
- the survey questions and the training they have received about writing instruction;
- the class' survey responses and the responses of students in the program generally; and/or
- the responses of a fictitious teacher's students and the responses of students in the program generally.[3]

We could not possibly articulate every possible method or purpose for using such data, but it's essential that you take the time to help teachers and others understand the roles, possibilities, and limitations of survey data. Some may mistrust such data entirely, while others may accept it too uncritically. Everyone must understand that such data—as one element in a balanced, multifaceted approach—can yield helpful insights for improving programs or improving the effectiveness of individual teachers.

APPENDIX 11.1
Writing-Related Items on the NSSE Core Survey

In your experience at your institution during the current school year, about how often have you done each of the following? *(Very often, Often, Sometimes, Never)*

- Prepared two or more drafts of a paper or assignment before turning it in
- Worked on a paper or project that required integrating ideas or information from various sources

During the current school year, about how much reading and writing have you done? *(None, 1–4, 5–10, 11–20, More than 20)*

- Number of written papers or reports of **20 pages or more**
- Number of written papers or reports **between 5 and 19 pages**
- Number of written papers or reports of **fewer than 5 pages**

To what extent has your experience at this institution contributed to your knowledge, skills, and personal development in the following areas? *(Very much, Quite a bit, Some, Very little)*

- Writing clearly and effectively

APPENDIX 11.2

The CSWC Survey Instrument

1. During the current school year, for how many of your writing assignments have you done each of the following? (5 = All assignments, 4 = Most assignments, 3 = Some assignments, 2 = Few assignments, 1 = No assignments.)

1A Brainstormed (listed ideas, mapped concepts, prepared an outline, etc.) to develop your ideas before you started drafting your assignment

1B Talked with your instructor to develop your ideas before you started drafting your assignment

1C Talked with a classmate, friend, or family member to develop your ideas before you started drafting your assignment

1D Received feedback from your instructor about a draft before turning in your final assignment

1E Received feedback from a classmate, friend, or family member about a draft before turning in your final assignment

1F Visited a campus-based writing or tutoring center to get help with your writing assignment before turning it in

1G Used an online tutoring service to get help with your writing assignment before turning it in

1H Proofread your final draft for errors before turning it in

2. During the current school year, in how many of your writing assignments did you (5 = All assignments, 4 = Most assignments, 3 = Some assignments, 2 = Few assignments, 1 = No assignments):

2A Narrate or describe one of your own experiences

2B Summarize something you read, such as articles, books, or online publications

2C Analyze or evaluate something you read, researched, or observed

2D Describe your methods or findings related to data you collected in lab or fieldwork, a survey project, etc.

2E Argue a position using evidence and reasoning

2F Explain in writing the meaning of numerical or statistical data

2G Write in the style and format of a specific field (engineering, history, psychology, etc.)

2H Include drawings, tables, photos, screen shots, or other visual content into your written assignment

2I Create the project with multimedia (web page, poster, slide presentation such as PowerPoint, etc.)

3. *During the current school year, for how many of your writing assignments has your instructor done each of the following? (5 = All assignments, 4 = Most assignments, 3 = Some assignments, 2 = Few assignments, 1 = No assignments)*

3A Provided clear instructions describing what he or she wanted you to do

3B Explained in advance what he or she wanted you to learn

3C Explained in advance the criteria he or she would use to grade your assignment

3D Provided a sample of a completed assignment written by the instructor or a student

3E Asked you to do short pieces of writing that he or she did not grade

3F Asked you to give feedback to a classmate about a draft or outline the classmate had written

3G Asked you to write with classmates to complete a group project

3H Asked you to address a real or imagined audience such as your classmates, a politician, non-experts, etc.

4. *Which of the following have you done or do you plan to do before you graduate from your institution? (4 = Done, 3 = Plan to do, 2 = Do not plan to do, 1 = Have not decided.)*

4A Prepare a portfolio that collects written work from more than one class

4B Submit work you wrote or co-wrote to a student or professional publication (magazine, journal, newspaper, collection of student work, etc.)

Notes

1. For more information about CSWC and its findings, see Anderson et al. (2009); Kinzie, Gonyea, and Paine (2009).
2. Until 2011, in most cases, only a random sample of 20–40% of first-year and senior students was invited to participate. However, as of 2011, NSSE no longer "samples," but instead invites *all* first-year and senior students to participate. With this 100%-sample invitation, it may be that—for some schools—response rates will be high enough to be practicable for course assessment. Higher response rates may make diving down to the course level more practical in situations where the number of respondents, not the nature of the question, is the impediment to course-level analysis.
3. For ideas on using survey results to facilitate discussions, see NSSE n.d.f, "Working with NSSE Data: A Facilitator's Guide."

References

Ackerman, John M. 1993. "The Promise of Writing to Learn." *Written Communication* 10 (3): 334–70. http://dx.doi.org/10.1177/0741088393010003002.

Adler-Kassner, Linda, and Peggy O'Neill. 2010. *Reframing Writing Assessment to Improve Teaching and Learning*. Logan: Utah State University Press.

Algozzine, Bob, John Gretes, Claudia Flowers, Lisa Howley, John Beattie, Fred Spooner, Ganesh Mohanty, and Marty Bray. 2004. "Student Evaluation of College Teaching: A Practice in Search of Principles." *College Teaching* 52 (4): 134–41. http://dx.doi.org /10.3200/CTCH.52.4.134-141.

Anderson, Paul V., Chris M. Anson, Robert M. Gonyea, and Charles Paine. 2009. "Summary: The Consortium for the Study of Writing in College." *NSSE Institute Webinar*. http://nsse.iub.edu/webinars/archives.cfm?showyear=2009&grouping=Tue sdays.

Banta, Trudy W., Elizabeth A. Jones, and Karen E. Black. 2009. *Designing Effective Assessment: Principles and Profiles of Good Practice*. San Francisco: Jossey-Bass.

Bangert-Drowns, Robert L., Marlen M. Hurley, and Barbara Wilkinson. 2004. "The Effects of School-Based Writing to Learn Interventions on Academic Achievement: A Meta-Analysis." *Review of Educational Research* 74 (1): 29–58. http://dx.doi.org/10 .3102/00346543074001029.

Broad, Bob. 2009. "Organic Matters: In Praise of Locally Grown Writing Assessment." In *Organic Writing Assessment: Dynamic Criteria Mapping in Action*, ed. Bob Broad, Linda Adler-Kassner, Barry Alford, Jane Detweiler, Heidi Estrem, Susanmarie Harrington, Maureen McBride, Eric Stalions, and Scott Weeden, 1–13. Logan: Utah State University Press.

Chen, Pu-Shih Daniel, Robert M. Gonyea, Shimon A. Sarraf, Allison BrckaLorenz, Ali Korkmaz, Amber D. Lambert, Rick Shoup, and Julie M. Williams. 2009. "Analyzing and interpreting NSSE data." In *Using NSSE in institutional research*, ed. Robert M. Gonyea and George D. Kuh, 35–54. New Directions for Institutional Research, no. 141. San Francisco: Jossey-Bass. http://dx.doi.org/10.1002/ir.285.

Council of Writing Program Administrators. 2008. "WPA Outcomes Statement for First-Year Composition." In *Council of Writing Program Administrators*, http://wpacouncil.org /positions/outcomes.html.

Dively, Ronda Leathers. 2010. "Standardizing English 101 at Southern Illinois University Carbondale: Reflections on the Promise of Improved GTA Preparation and More Effective Writing Instruction." *Composition Forum* 22. http://compositionforum.com /issue/22/siuc.php.

Huot, Brian. 1996. "Toward a New Theory of Writing Assessment." *College Composition and Communication* 47 (4): 549–66. http://dx.doi.org/10.2307/358601.

Huot, Brian. *(Re)Articulating Writing Assessment for Teaching and Learning*. 2002. Logan: Utah State University Press.

Kinzie, Jillian, Robert M. Gonyea, and Charles Paine. 2009. "Using Results from the Consortium for the Study of Writing in College." In *Webinar Archives: Using Results from the Consortium for the Study of Writing in College*.

Kuh, George D. 2003. "What We're Learning about Student Engagement from NSSE: Benchmarks for Effective Educational Practices." *Change: The Magazine of Higher Learning*, 35 (2): 24–32. http://dx.doi.org/10.1080/00091380309604090.

Kuh, George D. 2009. "The National Survey of Student Engagement: Conceptual and Empirical Foundations." In *Using NSSE Institutional Research*, ed. Robert M. Gonyea, and George D. Kuh, 5–20. New Directions for Institutional Research, no. 141. San Francisco, CA: Jossey-Bass. http://dx.doi.org/10.1002/ir.283.

Martin, Wanda, and Charles Paine. 2002. "Mentors, Models, and Agents of Change: Veteran TAs Preparing Teachers of Writing." In *Preparing College Teachers of Writing:*

Histories, Theories, Programs, Practices, ed. Betty P. Pytlik and Sarah Liggett, 222–32. New York: Oxford University Press.

McCormick, Alexander C., and Allison BrckaLorenz. 2009. "Driving Data Down: Using NSSE Results in Department, School, and Major-Level Assessment Activities." *NSSE Institute Webinars.* http://nsse.iub.edu/webinars/archives.cfm?showyear=2009 &grouping.

Nelson Laird, Thomas F., Robert Smallwood, Amanda Suniti Niskodé-Dossett, and Amy K. Garver. 2009. "Effectively Involving Faculty in the Assessment of Student Engagement." In *Using NSSE Institutional Research,* ed. Robert M. Gonyea, and George D. Kuh, 71–81. New Directions for Institutional Research, no. 141. San Francisco, CA: Jossey-Bass. http://dx.doi.org/10.1002/ir.283.

NSSE. n.d.a. "About NSSE." In *National Survey of Student Engagement.* http://nsse.iub. edu/html/about.cfm.

NSSE. n.d.b. "Classroom Survey of Student Engagement (CLASSE)." In *National Survey of Student Engagement.* http://nsse.iub.edu/_/?cid=211.

NSSE. n.d.c. "Customizing Your NSSE Institutional Report: A Guide to Selecting Your Comparison Groups." In *National Survey of Student Engagement.* http://cpr.iub.edu /uploads/Customizing%20Your%20NSSE%20Report.pdf.

NSSE. n.d.d. "NSSE Survey Instrument." In *National Survey of Student Engagement.* http:// nsse.iub.edu/html/survey_instruments_2011.cfm.

NSSE. n.d.e. "Using NSSE Data." In *National Survey of Student Engagement.* http://nsse.iub .edu/pdf/Using_NSSE_Data.pdf.

NSSE. n.d.f. "Working with NSSE Data: A Facilitator's Guide." In *National Survey of Student Engagement.* http://nsse.iub.edu/pdf/2008_Institutional_Report/Working%20 with%20NSSE%20Data-A%20Facilitators%20Guide.pdf.

O'Neill, Peggy, Cindy Moore, and Brian Huot. 2009. *A Guide to College Writing Assessment.* Logan: Utah State University Press.

Shupe, David. 2008. "Toward a Higher Standard: The Changing Organizational Context of Accountability for Educational Results." *On the Horizon* 16 (2): 72–96. http:// dx.doi.org/10.1108/10748120810874487.

Smallwood, Bob. n.d. "Overview." *CLASSE: Classroom Survey of Student Engagement.* http:// www.assessment.ua.edu/CLASSE/Overview.htm.

Smallwood, Bob. 2010. "Participation." *CLASSE: Classroom Survey of Student Engagement.* Tuscaloosa: University of Alabama.

Smallwood, Robert, and Judith Ouimet. 2009. "CLASSE: Measuring Student Engagement at the Classroom Level." In *Designing Effective Assessment,* ed. Trudy W. Banta, Elizabeth A. Jones, and Karen E. Black, 193–97. San Francisco: Jossey-Bass.

Wachtel, Howard K. 1998. "Student Evaluation of College Teaching Effectiveness: A Brief Review." *Assessment & Evaluation in Higher Education* 23 (2): 191–212. http://dx.doi .org/10.1080/0260293980230207.

Weiser, Irwin. 1994. "Teaching Assistants as Collaborators in Their Preparation and Evaluation." In *Evaluating Teachers of Writing,* ed. Christine A. Hult, 133–46. Urbana, IL: National Council of Teachers of English.

12

DOCUMENTING TEACHING IN THE AGE OF BIG DATA

Deborah Minter and Amy Goodburn

Little more than a decade ago we introduced the collection *Composition, Pedagogy, and the Scholarship of Teaching* (Minter and Goodburn 2002) by identifying organizations within higher education that had called for more structured and systematic ways of documenting teaching. Those organizations included the Carnegie Foundation for the Advancement of Scholarship in Teaching and Learning and the American Association of Higher Education Peer Review Project. In a span of roughly ten years, the accountability movement has taken hold in higher education, and the stakes for representing teaching and learning have grown even higher. Current public discourse increasingly asks whether higher education itself is of value, whether students are learning, and whether there is a "value added" to student learning from their experiences in college classrooms (Arum and Roksa 2010; Hacker and Dreifus 2010; Selingo 2013). Not surprisingly, institutions have become more proactive about developing systems to provide evidence about student learning (the Voluntary System of Accountability, the National Institute for Learning Outcomes Assessment, the Student Achievement Measure Project, etc.). Indeed, numerous states (including Ohio, Tennessee, Texas, and Louisiana) are moving to funding models based on retention and graduation rate data for postsecondary institutions (Addo 2013; Haslam 2012).

Coupled with this focus on what—and whether—students are learning within particular courses is the prioritization of the national "completion agenda": ensuring that students are completing undergraduate degree requirements in a timely and cost-effective manner. Implicit within these discussions is the notion that teachers need to be more productive in teaching students and advancing them toward graduation. For example, the *Chronicle of Higher Education* recently reported that

DOI: 10.7330/9780874219661.c012

Florida State University president Eric Barron pledged to "look at fresh-man retention and graduation rates, survey students about their uni-versity experience after graduation, test them for how much they know about a subject before and after a course, and calculate cost per student credit hour" in efforts to counter an alternative plan for sweeping revi-sions to Florida higher education (June 2011).

Alongside these calls for accountability and completion—indeed, some would say, driving them—is a rapidly changing technological land-scape that multiplies available options for capturing information about teachers and learners. New technologies have expanded what, where, who, and how we teach in exciting ways. These technologies have also expanded options for digitally representing, reflecting on, and sharing our work as teachers. That the changing technological landscape has transformed how we think about writing and the teaching of writing is evident from recent professional statements (Conference on College Composition and Communication 2013; National Council of Teachers of English 2008; Conference on College Composition and Communication 2004). As the capacity to mine enormous amounts of student data grows, campuses seek access to increasingly sophisticated ways of analyzing stu-dent achievement. In this essay, we examine the implications of these developments for our work as teachers and administrators, exploring the opportunities and concerns that emerge as advances in technology change the range of options and expectations for how teachers can doc-ument, reflect on, and share classroom practices.

TECHNOLOGICAL SHIFTS TO CONSIDER

As co-editors, we smile when we recall the arguments for and labor asso-ciated with the website that accompanied *Composition, Pedagogy, and the Scholarship of Teaching.* We had initially pitched the idea of an accompa-nying CD-ROM (remember those?) along the lines of *Coming of Age: The Advanced Writing Curriculum,* an edited collection published two years earlier that included a CD with the course materials, syllabi, etc. refer-enced in the text (Howard, Shamoon, and Jamieson 2000). The hope of this kind of apparatus is clear enough: find a cost-effective way to share teaching and assessment artifacts (such as teaching philosophy state-ments, course portfolios, peer observations, and job application mate-rials) as well as guided heuristics teachers could use to develop their own teaching documentation. Beyond showcasing "best practices," we viewed the website as an opportunity to participate in an ongoing and public conversation about "how composition pedagogy is documented, valued, and assessed across a range of institutional contexts" (Minter and Goodburn 2002, ix). We didn't anticipate that a decade later, teachers would routinely (and sometimes be required to) post their teaching materials on course management systems such as Blackboard, or that databases such as MERLOT: Multimedia Educational Resource for Learning and Online Teaching or courseportfolio.org would enable teachers to find and share peer reviewed teaching and learning materials within and across disciplinary and institutional communities.

Over the past decade, Amy has co-coordinated University of Nebraska–Lincoln's Peer Review of Teaching Project, a year-long faculty development program that supports faculty in developing electronic course portfolios (housed at www.courseportfolio.org). She has worked with over 300 UNL faculty, helping them document the intellectual work of their teaching via course portfolios.[1] Teachers, Debbie among them, have identified both formative and summative purposes for creating these portfolios, including curricular revision, program design, promotion and tenure consideration, teaching award applications, and accreditation reviews. Technologies for representing and sharing pedagogical work digitally have multiplied the possibilities for capturing and reflecting on scenes of teaching and learning in ways that weren't imaginable when we co-authored our collection.

Just as technologies for digitally capturing, reflecting on, and sharing our teaching have increased and improved both in ease of use and in platform independence, the capacity to track and manipulate large amounts of student data has become more possible (as students interact with course materials within learning management systems in greater numbers) and more affordable (as computing capacity becomes cheaper). Manyika et al. (2011) describe big data as "datasets whose size is beyond the typical database software tools to capture, store, manage, and analyze" (3). These data are analyzed via algorithms "to infer the users' knowledge, intentions, and interests and to create models for predicting future behavior" (Bienkowski, Mingyu, and Means 2012, 7). As the capacity to mine enormous amounts of student data continues to grow, campuses have greater access to sophisticated analyses of student performance and success. For instance, several institutions have developed homegrown predictive, analytic, and educational data mining programs focused on student retention, course performance, and time to degree completion. These programs can identify when a student fails to take a course within a degree program, for instance, and put registration holds on their accounts until students meet with an academic advisor. Some of these programs even remove students from highly subscribed majors altogether based on failing grades in required courses.

Related to the emergence of big data is the power of learning analytics, which "addresses the application of known methods and models to answer important questions that affect student learning and organizational learning systems" (Bienkowski, Mingyu, and Means 2012, 12). Some of the discourse surrounding the use of learning analytics posits a brave new world where all learners receive individualized education based on their needs and abilities, enabling the teacher to create optimized conditions for learning:

> What if a professor teaching algebra could look out at her students and, in the blink of an eye, see exactly what each student understands, and what they don't?
>
> It may sound like science fiction. But according to the companies that are selling increasingly sophisticated teaching tools, it is merely science.
>
> . . . Arizona State University has become ground zero for data-driven teaching in higher education. The university has rolled out an ambitious effort to turn its classrooms into laboratories for technology-abetted "adaptive learning"—a method that purports to give instructors real-time intelligence on how well each of their students is getting each concept. (Kolowich 2013)

The technologies of data mining and learning analytics are often conceptualized as working hand in hand. As Bienkowski, Mingyu, and Means (2012) describe:

> These online or adaptive learning systems will be able to exploit detailed learner activity data not only to recommend what the next learning activity for a particular student should be, but also to predict how that student will perform with future learning content, including high-stakes examinations. Data-rich systems will be able to provide informative and actionable feedback to the learner, to the instructor, and to administrators. (3)

Given the national pressure for postsecondary institutions to increase student retention and graduation rates, it's not surprising that numerous commercial products have been developed to engage in both data mining and learning analytics. Companies such as the Education Advisory Board, Starfish Solutions, and Blackboard Analytics sell commercial products that promise to employ "technology that transforms data into performance" (Blackboard Analytics 2014) and deliver "critical intelligence on student risk" (Education Advisory Board 2014). One company's website announces: "Hundreds of thousands of students at schools across the country currently use *Pearson MyLab with Knewton Adaptive Learning* titles in subjects including reading, economics, math, and writing" (Knewton 2014). Kolowich (2013) reports on this partnership, which is fueling a transformation in the teaching of basic math at Arizona State University. Kolowich explains Knewton Adaptive Learning's concept of a "'knowledge graph': a comprehensive map of how different concepts are related to one another in the context of learning." The data tagged by Knewton's software is data tracked within Pearson MyLab's educational software as students interact with it. The patterns that emerge are fed back to Knewton so the algorithms can be refined and help fine-tune the learning software. Thus, with each iteration, the educational software adapts more successfully (at least theoretically) to learners' needs (Kolowich 2013).

What makes the technological developments of data mining and learning analytics both attractive and concerning is its capacity to reach over and across a whole range of previously disconnected course experiences in the hope of identifying meaningful correlations between learning experiences and students who have grown in their capacities to think critically and write compellingly. It is exciting to think that new technologies might enable better predictions of the educational experiences necessary to best support individual students in their learning. Our concern, however, is that the role of individual teachers in student learning might become obscured in the drive for such data, and that teachers' renderings and reflections on the classroom might lose significance in relation to other forms of evidence about student learning. In short, we fear that forms of documenting teaching that have been supported in colleges and universities over the past decade or more could be undermined or displaced by big-data solutions for determining what constitutes effective teaching. In this essay, we seek to reclaim some of what the field has learned through the scholarship of teaching, and suggest how we might harness the opportunities of big data for enhancing and expanding—rather than displacing—the power of documenting our work with teaching and learning.

WHAT HAVE WE GAINED FROM INITIATIVES TO DOCUMENT TEACHING AND LEARNING?

In chapter 2, DeCosta-Smith and Roen trace the rise of the teaching portfolio as well as scholarship in composition that emerged in response to this movement. Without repeating that history here, we simply point to the research Seldin et al. (1999) provided to suggest a growing reliance on a set of genres related to the documentation of teaching. More specifically, Seldin et al. report an increase of more than 30% in the number of college deans who use systematically collected student ratings of their classroom experience in the assessment of teaching quality (88% versus 54.8% twenty years earlier). College deans who reported using some type of faculty self-evaluation of teaching effectiveness had grown to nearly 58% (up from 37% between 1978 and 1998). Among these gains in the years spanning the first calls to document teaching and the subsequent years of efforts both within and beyond composition to effectively act on such calls are common forms of teaching documentation (such as teaching portfolios, student evaluations, peer observations, teaching philosophy statements, etc.).

For example, one genre for documenting and assessing teaching that has currency within higher education is the course portfolio. A course portfolio is a reflective investigation of how course structures, teaching techniques, and assessment strategies enhance or detract from student learning. William Cerbin (1994) proposed one of the first course portfolio models for representing this intentional inquiry into student learning. His prototype has been influential for many teachers who have documented their work in publications such as *The Course Portfolio* (Hutchings 1998) and *Opening Lines* (Hutchings 2000). A course portfolio provides a window into what occurred during a *particular* course, highlighting what worked and what did not, showcasing the student learning that resulted, and outlining modifications and goals for future iterations of the course. A quick review of university teaching and learning center websites illustrates that course portfolios have become a common genre for helping faculty document teaching and learning.[2] Indeed, the extent to which these genres have taken hold institutionally is reflected in Irwin Weiser's (2012) essay, "Symposium on Peer Review," where he notes that

> as conceptions of scholarship expand, particularly as more institutions recognize that teaching and engagement activities can certainly be understood as scholarly, it becomes necessary for tenure and promotion committees to develop better understandings of how those activities can be evaluated—how teaching portfolios, text books, curriculum development, and institutional, professional, and even community service can be documented and evaluated both by internal and external peer reviewers. (669)

Our account of the movement to document teaching points not only to the emergence of shared genres and a concomitant tradition of scholarly conversation about them but also to the ways in which this movement maps onto the practice of peer review—a prominent method in higher education for assessing the significance and quality of scholarly work.

Despite these benefits, some have suggested that the movement to document teaching has sometimes sponsored forms of representation that too often *imply* student learning rather than demonstrate it. The value claimed for teacher representation is often situated in individual teacher development—with formative feedback aimed at impacting an individual teacher's classroom practice. Certainly, as WPAs we have gained insight into the FYC curriculum—and even proposed modifications to it—as a result of reviewing a group of teaching portfolios from teachers in our program. But, for the most part, teaching portfolios as they are used at our institution are designed to showcase the quality of each individual teacher's pedagogical work. Similarly, summative uses for teacher documentation (such as promotion and tenure files or annual evaluations) also tend to be localized—focused on a particular teacher. What course portfolios or other forms of teacher documentation often do not provide is aggregated evidence of learning across classrooms or even across a span of undergraduate student experience. In our view, it would in fact be difficult for a teacher or administrator to collect and make sense of data about student learning across several portfolios within a department or institution. With the over 300 portfolios on UNL's course portfolio site, for instance, one can search individual portfolios, but determining patterns, themes, or trends across them is very difficult. How can the intellectual work around teaching be collected across an institution or across several institutions to provide evidence of or insights into students' learning? These questions became all too real when a senior administrator challenged Amy to "quantitatively prove" that having faculty create course portfolios improved their teaching and their students' learning as a condition of continued funding for UNL's peer review of teaching project. Thus, for all the gains made in the documentation of teaching, the field has yet to deeply explore how new data mining or learning analytic technologies might extend our efforts to document the impact of writing instruction and writing program administration.

THE PROMISE AND PERILS OF BIG DATA

In their recent essay, "Local Assessment: Using Genre Analysis to Validate Directed Self-Placement," Gere et al. (2013) recount efforts to better understand the effectiveness of their institution's directed self-placement mechanism by comparing the rhetorical moves and linguistic features of students who self-placed into FYC with those of students who self-placed into a preparatory course. Of particular interest for the purposes of this essay is the corpus-based text analysis at the center of this project, in which more than 650 student essays were coded and mined for rhetorical moves and linguistic features. In short, Gere et al. were able to process (as data) an enormous amount of student writing and—through careful and rigorously tested analysis—validate the directed self-placement instrument at their institution.

An example of how "big data," more specifically, can impact our understanding of the work the field undertakes (or is called to undertake) is evident in a recent study of students enrolled in online courses, in which researchers used a data set of 500,000 courses taken by over 40,000 community and technical college students in Washington state. In this research, Xu and Jaggars (2013) examined correlations between student attributes such as gender, age, ethnicity, previous academic performance, and students' ability to adapt to online classes. The researchers found that, while students generally struggle in their efforts to adapt to online classes, "[m]ales, younger students, students with lower levels of academic skill, and Black students were likely to perform particularly poorly in online courses relative to their performance in face-to-face courses" (19). In addition, student adaptability *by discipline* demonstrated the greatest negative effect for persistence and course grade in English classes (20).

Writing program administrators are also beginning to harness the potential of big data to respond to demands for accountability. In their 2012 essay, "Data Mining: A Hybrid Methodology for Complex and Dynamic Research," Lang and Baehr (2012) compellingly argue that new data mining methodologies can support composition researchers and WPAs by enabling large-scale empirical studies supported by measurable data (175). Drawing on Chris Anson's principles of research methods, they argue that "data, whether it involves curriculum, individual assignments, student performance, instructor training, or any other element, must be put forward as part of any discussion of writing in order to move it from belief-based to an evidence-based conversation" (183). Celebrating several earlier landmark studies within composition, Lang and Baehr imagine how current data mining methodologies would have improved those efforts, while pointing to the promise of future research that can now be undertaken across a program or multiple institutions. (See Connors and Lunsford's 1993 examination of teachers' comments on student papers, as well as Nystrand's 1999 study of peer response.)

While their essay focuses on the value of this research for the field of composition by identifying new questions, determining the validity of taken-for granted assumptions, and enabling the replication of data-driven studies across multiple contexts, Lang and Baehr (2012) also provide examples of how WPAs might use data mining to respond to accountability pressures. Their essay includes a brief case study detailing how they used data mining in their roles as WPAs, first to identify sources of higher-than-average failure rates in some course within their writing program, and second to respond to administrators who had initially identified the problem.

The details of this scenario are familiar to many WPAs. A letter from the Office of Institutional Research to the department chair identified FYC course sections (by instructor) in which high numbers of students received Ds, Fs, or Ws. Lang and Baehr used data from their FYC database to determine why students in these particular sections were performing poorly. According to their account, they first ruled out teacher factors (course evaluations, standard assignments, etc.) and then turned to student factors (GPA, high school preparation, etc.). Their analysis revealed that missing assignments were the main culprit in the cohort's low rate of success, and they developed proactive support structures—such as student reminders and revised teacher development offerings—in response to this analysis. "Using both data and text mining," the authors write:

> . . . enabled us to more quickly rule out potential causes of the problem and move toward developing potential solutions.
>
> What is valuable here, beyond the obvious local benefits of being able to respond to the initial charge contained in the institutional research letter, is the potential for other programs to take these methods and apply them in their own contexts to answer similar questions posed on their campuses. Regardless of the answers they might discover, the methods can transfer from campus to campus, and program administrators and scholars can explain easily at what points they modify or extend the original studies. (Lang and Baehr 2012, 190)

Lang and Baehr are optimistic that some kinds of standard data mining practices could be shared through various networks (such as the Council of Writing Program Administrators). Equally important, however, is supporting writing teachers and WPAs in building the kind of fluency with these practices that allows them to argue for what big data can—and can't—do, and to advocate for methodologies that are effective and ethical. In "Critical Questions for Big Data," danah boyd and Kate Crawford make several observations about the increasing use of big data. While the examples they draw upon are largely in the domain of social media use, we find their cautionary argument relevant for our work with students. First, they remind readers that big data tools don't simply measure activity; they shape the reality they measure: "It is not enough to simply ask, as Anderson has suggested, 'what can science learn from Google?' but to ask how harvesters of Big Data might change the meaning of learning"(boyd and Crawford 2012, 666). Moreover, claims to objectivity and even accuracy—too often left implicit in data-driven decisions on campus—can be misleading. After all, "interpretation," the authors argue, "is at the center of data analysis" (668). boyd and Crawford also warn against presuming that big data is inherently somehow better: "The size of the data should fit the research question being asked; in some cases, small is best" (670).

From our perspective, one of the most important points boyd and Crawford (2012) make focuses on the ethical questions inherent in the potential of data gathering and mining. They observe that there are "significant questions of truth, control and power" (673) in the kinds of big data initiatives at the center of increasing number of institutional research projects—across all kinds of institutions (public, private, for-profit, not-for-profit, educational, and otherwise). We see at least three categories of questions involving the ethical use of data in gathering information about students' success in classrooms: privacy, intellectual property rights, and faculty governance. We acknowledge that our field has a long tradition of engaging these questions. Still, we may need to redouble our efforts as classroom data becomes big data and big business.

We can map these critical questions onto the case study that Lang and Baehr (2012) offer and expand some of the questions their case study raises. We're impressed, for example, by the researchers' reframing of the problem: while the letter from the Office of Institutional Research identifies low grades "by instructor"—pressing (it would seem) to make "teachers' work" the object of analysis—Lang and Baehr reframe the analysis to account for student performance. Still, there are important ethical questions about data in either framing. For instance: Do teachers and students understand and expressly (or implicitly) consent to have the data generated from their work in the classroom available for this kind of institutional analysis? Once the work moves from institutional analysis to publication, do the ethical questions shift? Would the questions shift again if the result of the analysis were developing or refining a learning analytics product for the market?

We might also ask what data mining makes possible in the moment Lang and Baehr represent. Could "small data"—say, bringing teachers together to ask questions about student success—have yielded this same insight? Would the institution value the results of this smaller-scaled research in the same way as the original data-driven analysis? Perhaps, the researchers are protecting the teachers' interests by not involving them: Why worry teachers (especially contingent faculty and graduate students) with institutional missives suggesting that their failure rates are not acceptable? As former WPAs, we are all too familiar with the complicated considerations that factor into decisions regarding how to respond to these sorts of institutional concerns. Still, if student learning has, at times, seemed overshadowed by representations of classroom practice, teaching seems similarly absent from too many efforts to use big data to document and understand student achievement.

LOOKING AHEAD

The rise of the scholarship of teaching movement and its attendant calls on postsecondary teachers to engage deeply and systematically with the documentation of teaching has been grounded in the desire to better understand—to inquire into—effective classroom practice. As we've suggested in this essay, our field has responded to that call in significant ways—developing a tradition of genres, scholarship, and institutional practices for seriously engaging and reflecting on the work of teaching. In our view, the rise of big data and learning analytics is located in this same inquisitive spirit and interest in better understanding how to support student learning. It will be critical for teachers to take responsibility as stakeholders—and to be viewed *as stakeholders* by the institution—as more colleges and universities move toward a greater reliance on learning analytics. Opportunities for teachers to develop fluency with this kind of large-scale data might include seeking information about the courses one regularly teaches and incorporating such information into course portfolios. WPAs might proactively seek information about patterns related to students' success in the program's courses. Equally important, though, is to continue to educate ourselves on what big data can—and can't—do. We must insist on the value of so called "small data." When faced with questions regarding the quality of work in particular classrooms by particular teachers, we (as administrators) ought to continue to advocate for the usefulness of teacher-authored representations of and reflections on their pedagogical practice, as well as the usefulness of carefully conducted peer evaluation.

In "Analytics: What We're Hearing," president and CEO of EDUCAUSE Diana Oblinger (2012) writes that "Analytics is a matter of culture—a culture of inquiry: asking questions, looking for supporting data, being honest about strengths and weaknesses that the data reveals, creating solutions, and then adapting as the results of those efforts come to fruition" (98). In this way, the move toward analytics promises to emphasize the same kinds of concerns and habits of mind that WPAs have, for decades, brought to bear on composition classrooms. These decades of experience and scholarship have focused on the opportunities and complexities of pulling educational data and setting that data beside teacher and student representations of their classroom work, and they have given the field an important kind of expertise in negotiating complicated ethical terrain. As a field, we may not have all the answers, but we have developed processes for bringing stakeholders together and for using data to foster hard conversations with a view toward creating better, more inclusive educational institutions. As boyd and Crawford suggest, limiting access to big data risks creating new kinds of digital divides—or, to frame it more positively (as Oblinger 2012 does): "When people are in control, have ownership of quality data, and can trust the data, everything changes" (99).

As former composition coordinators in our English department, and as current administrators at the University of Nebraska–Lincoln, we see some promise in how data mining might assist our goals to improve student retention and learning. We, too, have reviewed spreadsheets listing classes with high dropout/failure/withdrawal rates and examined reports that identify courses in which student withdrawals or failures are correlated with lower rates of degree completion. Nearly every day, we are involved in conversations, task forces, and initiatives designed to support students in their time to degree completion (four year plans, electronic advising, etc.). Our institution is increasingly exploring how predictive analytics might enable us to identify first-year students in need of extra support (tutoring, peer mentoring, advising, supplemental instruction, and success coaching) so that we can support and retain them. This year, UNL opened an electronic early warning system that invites instructors to raise flags and referrals if students are not attending or not meeting academic expectations for performance.

Coupled with this enthusiasm, though, is a tempered concern about the presence of teachers in these discussions and a strong commitment to ensuring that teachers continue to be actively present as the nature of decision making in postsecondary institutions shifts toward centralized data mining and learning analytics. We look forward to what the field helps to build both in terms of increasing access and student success, and in terms of building increasingly sophisticated understandings of writing pedagogy through representing and reflecting on the practice of teaching writing.

Notes

1. For more information about this work, see *Making Teaching and Learning Visible: Course Portfolios and the Peer Review of Teaching* (Bernstein et al. 2006) and *Inquiry Into the College Classroom: A Journey toward Scholarly Teaching* (Savory, Burnett, and Goodburn 2007).
2. For example, see the University of Michigan's Center for Research on Learning and Teaching http://www.crlt.umich.edu/tstrategies/tstpcp; The Ohio State University's Center for the Advancement of Teaching http://ucat.osu.edu/read/teaching-portfolio; and the University of Pittsburgh's Center for Instructional Development and Distance Education www2.cidde.pitt.edu/teaching-portfolios.

References

Addo, Koran. 2013. "Legislators Propose Linking State Higher Education Funding to Graduation Rates." *The Advocate*, March 13. http://theadvocate.com.

Arum, Richard, and Josipa Roksa. 2010. *Academically Adrift: Learning on College Campuses*. Chicago: University of Chicago Press. http://dx.doi.org/10.7208/chicago/9780226028576.001.0001.

Bernstein, Daniel, Amy Nelson Burnett, Amy Goodburn, and Paul Savory. 2006. *Making Teaching and Learning Visible: Course Portfolios and the Peer Review of Teaching*. Bolton, MA: Anker.

Bienkowski, Marie, Feng Mingyu, and Barbara Means. 2012. *Enhancing Teaching and Learning through Educational Data Mining and Learning Analytics: An Issue Brief*. Washington, DC: US Department of Education, Office of Educational Technology.

Blackboard Analytics. 2014. www.blackboard.com/Platforms/Analytics/Overview.aspx.

boyd, danah, and Kate Crawford. 2012. "Critical Questions for Big Data: Provocators for a Cultural, Technology, and Scholarly Phenomenon." *Information Communication and Society* 15 (b): 662–79. http://dx.doi.org/10.1080/1369118X.2012.678878.

Cerbin, William. 1994. "The Course Portfolio as a Tool for Continuous Improvement of Teaching and Learning." *Journal on Excellence in College Teaching* 5: 95–105.

Conference on College Composition and Communication. 2004. "Position Statement on Teaching, Learning and Assessing Writing in Digital Environments."

Conference on College Composition and Communication. 2013. "A Position Statement of Principles and Example Effective Practices for Online Writing Instruction (OWI)."

Connors, Robert, and Andrea Lunsford. 1993. "Teachers' Rhetorical Comments on Student Papers." *College Composition and Communication* 44 (2): 200–23. http://dx.doi.org/10.2307/358839.

Education Advisory Board. 2014. www.eab.com/Technology/student-success-collaborative/About-the-student-success-collaborative.

Gere, Anne Ruggles, Laura Aull, Damián Perales Escudero Moisés, Zak Lancaster, and Elizabeth Vaner Lei. 2013. "Local Assessment: Using Genre Analysis to Validate Directed Self-Placement." *College Composition and Communication* 64: 605–33.

Hacker, Andrew, and Claudia Dreifus. 2010. *Higher Education?: How Colleges Are Wasting Our Money and Failing Our Kids—and What We Can Do About It*. New York: Times Books.

Haslam, Bill. 2012. "Tie Funding to Graduation Rates." *Time*, October 17.

Howard, Rebecca, Linda K. Shamoon, and Sandra Jamieson. 2000. *Coming of Age: The Advanced Writing Curriculum*. Portsmouth: Heinemann.

Hutchings, Pat, ed. 2000. *Opening Lines: Approaches to the Scholarship of Teaching and Learning*. Menlo Park, CA: Carnegie Foundation for the Advancement of Teaching.

Hutchings, Pat, ed. 1998. *The Course Portfolio: How Faculty Can Examine Their Teaching to Advance Practice and Improve Student Learning.* Washington, DC: American Association for Higher Education.

June, Audrey Williams. 2011. "Florida May Be Next Battleground Over Faculty Productivity" *The Chronicle of Higher Education.* Chronicle.com.

Knewton. 2014. http://www.knewton.com/partners/#pearson.

Kolowich, Steve. 2013. "The New Intelligence." *Inside Higher Ed.* insidehighered.com.

Lang, Susan, and Craig Baehr. 2012. "Data Mining: A Hybrid Methodology for Complex and Dynamic Research." *College Composition and Communication* 64: 172–94.

Manyika, James, Michael Chui, Brad Brown, Jacques Bughin, Richard Dobbs, Charles Roxburgh, and Angela Hung Byers. 2011. *Big Data: The Next Frontier for Innovation, Competition, and Productivity.* New York: McKinsey & Company.

Minter, Deborah, and Amy Goodburn. 2002. *Composition, Pedagogy, and the Scholarship of Teaching.* Portsmouth: Heinemann.

National Council of Teachers of English. 2008. "The NCTE Definition of 21st Century Literacies." *NCTE Executive Committee.*

Nystrand, Martin. 1999. "Dialogic Discourse Analysis of Revision in Response Groups." In *Discourse Studies in Composition,* ed. Ellen Barton and Gail Stygall.

Oblinger, Diana G. 2012. *Analytics: What We're Hearing.* Educause.

Savory, Paul, Amy Nelson Burnett, and Amy Goodburn. 2007. *Inquiry into the College Classroom: A Journey toward Scholarly Teaching.* Bolton, MA: Anker.

Seldin, P., et al. 1999. *Changing Practices in Evaluating Teaching: A Practical Guide to Improved Faculty Performance and Promotion/Tenure Decisions.* Bolton, MA: Anker.

Selingo, Jeffrey J. 2013. *College Unbound: The Future of Higher Education and What It Means for Students.* New York: Houghton Mifflin Harcourt.

Weiser, Irwin. 2012. "Peer Review in the Tenure and Promotion Process." *College Composition and Communication* 63: 645–72.

Xu, Di, and Shanna Smith Jaggars. 2013. "Adaptability to Online Learning: Differences across Types of Students and Academic Subject Areas." CCRC Working Paper No. 54. Community College Research Center.

ABOUT THE AUTHORS

PAUL ANDERSON is the director of Writing Across the University and a professor of English at Elon University. His research interests include assessment, the relationship between writing and learning, writing in the disciplines, ethical issues in person-based research, and technical and scientific communication.

CHRIS M. ANSON is a distinguished university professor and director of the Campus Writing and Speaking Program at North Carolina State University, where he teaches graduate and undergraduate courses in language, composition, and literacy and works with faculty across the disciplines to reform undergraduate education in the areas of writing and speaking. He has published fifteen books and over one hundred articles and book chapters relating to writing and has spoken widely across the United States and in twenty-eight other countries. He is currently the immediate past chair of the Conference on College Composition and Communication. His full curriculum vitae is at www.ansonica.net.

NICHOLE BENNETT is the dean of liberal arts at Burlington County College in Pemberton, New Jersey. She has worked with faculty, staff, and administrators in academic support capacities at Marquette University, Rider University, SUNY College at Plattsburg, and Northampton Community College. She is the president for the College Reading & Learning Association and a reviewer for the International Tutor Training Program. She is a member of the National Association for Developmental Education and has served as managing editor for *The Learning Assistance Review*. She recently received an "Outstanding Professional Service Award" from New York College Learning Skills Association. She also writes the Bits & Bytes technology column for *Research and Teaching in Developmental Education*.

KARA MAE BROWN is an English lecturer and the director of first-year writing at Northeastern University. Her work on curriculum development has appeared in the *Journal of College Writing*. Her works of short fiction and narrative nonfiction have been published in *Bluestem Review, Flint Hills Review, Summerset Review,* and *Word Riot.*

AMY E. DAYTON is an associate professor of English at University of Alabama. She has published essays in *Rhetoric Review, MELUS: The Journal of Multi-Ethnic Literature of the United States, College English, Enculturation,* and *English Journal.* She served as a faculty-in-residence for the University of Alabama's residential college program, and has worked with the university's writing program to develop and implement its teacher-training program. Her current research focuses on composition pedagogy, assessment, and multilingual histories of community literacy. She teaches advanced writing and graduate seminars on literacy and composition theory.

MEREDITH DECOSTA is an English instructor and manager of full-time English faculty at Grand Canyon University in Phoenix, Arizona. Her recent publications and research studies have focused on embedding real world writing into classrooms, evaluating online writing instructors, and exploring the literacy practices of ethnically and linguistically diverse students. Meredith co-authored a Teachers College Press book titled *Real World Writing for Secondary Students: Teaching the College Admission Essay and Other Gate-Openers for Higher Education.*

KIM FREEMAN is the author of *Love American Style: Divorce and the American Novel* and various articles on literature and composition in journals such as *a/b: Autobiography Studies* and *American Literary Realism.* She has also published fiction in various journals, such as *Meeting House* and *Prick of the Spindle.* She earned a PhD in English from the University of Connecticut, she has taught at Northeastern University in Boston, and she currently teaches writing at UC Berkeley.

CHRIS W. GALLAGHER is a professor of English and the associate dean of teaching, learning, and experiential education at Northeastern University in Boston. He is the author of four books, most recently *Our Better Judgment: Teacher Leadership for Writing Assessment* (with Eric Turley). He has also published on writing pedagogy, writing assessment, and educational policy in numerous journals in rhetoric and composition as well as in education.

ROBERT M. GONYEA is associate director of the Indiana University Center for Postsecondary Research. He coordinates research and reporting for the National Survey of Student Engagement and associated projects. His current research interests include the assessment of college and university quality, writing as a form of engagement in learning, high-impact practices for undergraduate learners, and survey design. Bob's work has appeared in *Research in Higher Education, Journal of Higher Education, Journal of College Student Development, Liberal Education, New Directions for Institutional Research,* and other higher education publications.

AMY GOODBURN is the associate vice chancellor of academic affairs and a professor of English at the University of Nebraska–Lincoln. Her research interests include teacher research and documenting and assessing teaching and learning in postsecondary classrooms. Her recent publications include *Making Teaching and Learning Visible, Inquiry into the College Classroom,* and *Rewriting Success in Rhetoric and Composition Careers.* Her teaching contributions have been recognized with a College Distinguished Teaching Award, the UNL Scholarly Teaching Award, and induction into UNL's Academy of Distinguished Teachers.

BRIAN JACKSON is coordinator of university writing at Brigham Young University. His book *Trained Capacities* (co-authored by Greg Clark) compiles reflections on what we can learn about rhetoric and democratic practice from American pragmatist John Dewey. Though he writes on religious and political rhetoric, he tells strangers at parties that he's a writing teacher and a trainer of writing teachers. He lives in Provo, Utah, at the foot of the Rockies, with his wife Amy and four kids.

AMY C. KIMME HEA is a writing program director and an associate professor of rhetoric, composition, and the teaching of English at the University of Arizona and author of *Going Wireless: A Critical Exploration of Wireless and Mobile Technologies for Composition Teachers and Researchers.* She recently completed a special issue of *Technical Communication Quarterly* on social media, and her scholarly interests include computers and composition, writing program administration, and technical communication.

DEBORAH MINTER is an associate professor of English and associate dean of University of Nebraska–Lincoln's College of Arts and Sciences, with responsibility for academic programs. She teaches undergraduate rhetoric and composition courses and graduate courses focused on pedagogy and writing instruction. She co-edited *Composition, Pedagogy, and the Scholarship of Teaching* with Amy Goodburn. Her work has also appeared in several edited collections and such journals as *College Composition and Communication, Pedagogy,* and *College English.*

CINDY MOORE is an associate professor of writing at Loyola University, Maryland, where she currently serves as associate dean of arts and sciences. Her publications include books and articles on writing, writing instruction, professional development, and assessment. Most of her scholarship, including the chapter in this collection, reflects her many years of administration at various levels and at four different universities.

GERALD NELMS is the academic director for developmental writing and a faculty member in English at Wright State University. From 2010 through 2012, he was a visiting instructional consultant at the University Center for the Advancement of Teaching at The Ohio State University, and for twenty years before that he was a faculty member at Southern Illinois University Carbondale. There, he directed its Communication Across the Curriculum and Writing Studies programs. Jerry's scholarly work has focused on writing across the curriculum; composition history, theory, and teaching; teaching writing mechanics and stylistics; plagiarism; knowledge transfer; instructional consultation; and how people learn.

CHARLES PAINE is a professor at the University of New Mexico, where he directs the Rhetoric and Writing and Core Writing programs. He is an enthusiastic member of the Council of Writing Program Administrators, currently chairing the Research Grants Committee and formerly serving on the executive board. With Bob Gonyea, Paul Anderson, and Chris Anson, he started the Consortium for the Study of Writing in College, a collaboration between the National Survey of Student Engagement and the CWPA. His most important work is teaching courses across the rhetoric and composition curriculum, including FYC, rhetoric/composition history and theory, teaching writing practica, and others.

DUANE ROEN is a professor of English at Arizona State University, where he also serves as head of interdisciplinary and liberal studies and as assistant vice provost for University Academic Success Programs. His recent publications have focused on public service, mentoring, the framework for success in postsecondary writing, faculty as public intellectuals, assessing teaching and learning, and the WPA Outcomes Statement for First-Year Composition. His most recent books are *The WPA Outcomes Statement: A Decade Later* and the third edition of *The McGraw-Hill Guide: Writing for College, Writing for Life.*

EDWARD M. WHITE is a visiting scholar in English at the University of Arizona. He directed WPA's consultant-evaluator service for fifteen years, and in 1993 he was elected to a second term on the executive committee of CCCC. He is the author or editor of fifteen books and more than one hundred articles and book chapters on literature and the teaching of writing. His work has been recognized by the publication *Writing Assessment in the 21st Century: Essays in Honor of Edward M. White* and by the 2011 CCCC Exemplar Award. His book on the assessment of writing programs, *Very Like a Whale* (co-authored with Norbert Elliot and Irvin Peckham), was published in 2015 by Utah State University Press.

INDEX

Page numbers in italics indicate illustrations.